RADIO

The Book

Fourth Edition

Steve Warren

ELSEVIER

AMSTERDAM • BOSTON • HEIDELBERG • LONDON
NEW YORK • OXFORD • PARIS • SAN DIEGO
SAN FRANCISCO • SINGAPORE • SYDNEY • TOKYO
Focal Press is an imprint of Elsevier

Focal Press

Elsevier Focal Press
200 Wheeler Road, 6th Floor, Burlington, MA 01803, USA
525 B Street, Suite 1900, San Diego, California 92101-4495, USA
84 Theobald's Road, London WC1X 8RR, UK

 This book is printed on acid-free paper.

Library of Congress Cataloguing in Publication Data

Warren, Steve, 1945-
    Radio : the book / Steve Warren.– 4th ed.
        p. cm.
    Includes index.
    ISBN 0-240-80696-4 (alk. paper)
    1. Radio broadcasting. I. Title.
    PN1991.5.W37 2004
    384.54–dc22

                                                                    2004020548

British Library Cataloguing in Publication Data
A catalogue record for this book is available from the British Library

ISBN: 0-240-80696-4

04 05 06 07 08 09 9 8 7 6 5 4 3 2 1

Printed in the United States of America

Dedication

It would take another book to list all the people, places, and influences that have shaped my career and given me the building blocks to create fun, compelling, and rewarding radio programming. I'd particularly like to thank all the people along the way who allowed me the latitude to try something new and those who broke with tradition and did not fear to zig while everyone else zagged.

Clearly, I pay homage to my many program directors, managers, and fellow announcers from whom I acquired multiple viewpoints when making decisions.

My hobby, passion, and personal interest has always centered around two things—food and radio. On Friday, August 13, 2004, Hurricane Charley swept through Punta Gorda, Florida, a town appearing early-on in my radio resume (WCCF). Hurricane survivors credit local radio with keeping them informed during the aftermath of the storm. When living there back in 1964, I watched my favorite media icon and gourmet role model, Julia Child, as the fledgling French Chef on black & white TV. Coincidentally, on exactly the same day as Hurricane Charley hit, Julia Child passed on to that great kitchen in the sky.

I visited Punta Gorda a few days after the storm, and both Punta Gorda and Julia, as well as the lessons learned from each, were very strong in my thoughts.

Preparing great radio is like preparing great food. Have fun, make it interesting, but be prepared for crisis.

I dedicate this work to the multiple and varied influences on our lives, even though we may not recognize them at the time.

CONTENTS

PREFACE

This will be the fourth time I have tackled the project of writing about radio. In earlier editions I asked myself, "Why write a book about radio in the first place?" but early in the 1970s when I was working at my first New York City radio job (WPAT), I had lots of time to think about where I was and how I got there. It seemed like a quantum leap from a high school station in New Albany, Indiana (WNAS), to being on the air in the top radio market in the world. At that time I thought I would put pen to paper and document how I made the journey. It took about a year of inconsistent effort to gather what finally amounted to a collection of anecdotes and stories I'd accumulated in ten years. I called the collection *Floaters, Drifters, and Prima Donnas* after the somewhat less than respectful opinion held by some radio station owners referring to announcers. Although I shared the stories with my family and friends and printed a few dozen copies of the book, I saw that it was not yet time for writing memoirs.

It's all perspective. When I thought that finally getting a job on the air in New York was the zenith of my career, I soon discovered that it was not the end of an upward professional climb, but the beginning of another series of goals and achievements. The years on the air in New York and then my program director jobs taught me many lessons about major-market thinking and politics. I also became more acutely aware of the enormous stakes at risk in major-market radio and the incredibly talented people who participated at that level, both on the air and in management. I have regularly expressed concern over the ability of many of today's consultants to operate with little or no relationship to the listener, just to data, statistics, and philosophy. It's not that those aren't crucial elements, but they take on new meaning when applied to a real group of people instead of a disembodied number. I've always known that you learn best by doing and that anyone purporting to be in the communications industry should strive to *communicate* with the end users of the product. For these reasons, I've always continued to stay closely involved with actual on-air broadcasting, including doing occasional weekend shifts at area stations or hosting my weekly syndicated show.

In 1980, following the collapse of the WKHK-FM attempt to be New York's country music station, I grew a little weary of being a pawn in the game plan known to only a few corporate officers. I also felt that as long as I stayed on the air full-time, I was pigeonholing myself as air talent, doomed to following the direction of others and finding little audience for my own thoughts and opinions. By this time I had worked for a radio network, been in Country Music, News-Talk, Top 40, MOR, Classical, Adult Contemporary, Urban, Easy Listening, and several dozen other broadcasting circumstances that defied format identification altogether. When I accepted my first major-market program director job at WPTR in Albany right after leaving WKHK, I really turned the corner professionally in terms of fulfillment. WPTR started a string of programming success stories that have continued to this day and have been the most gratifying experiences of any in my career.

I also noted the stickers on my luggage and which states and cities I had called home for greater or lesser periods of time (depending upon the level of accomplishment). I was delighted to have conquered several legendary stations, including some of the big 50,000 watt AM giants heard across America. The cities and stations include the following:

State	City	Station
Kentucky	Louisville	WKLO, WTMT, WLRS, WLKY-TV
Indiana	Indianapolis	WIRE, WGEE, WAIV, WIFE, WISH/TV, WTLC
Indiana	Corydon	WPDF
Indiana	New Albany	WNAS, WOWI
Indiana	Elwood	WBMP
Delaware	Wilmington	WAMS
New Jersey	Millville/Vineland	WMVB
New Jersey	Paterson	WPAT AM-FM
New Jersey	Camden	WCAM
New Jersey	Newark	WNJR
New York	New York	WHN, WNBC, WRFM, WKHK, WNWS, CBS,
	(3 times)	WNEW, WYNY, WNCN, WAXQ
New York	Poughkeepsie	WKIP
	(2 times)	
New York	Albany (2 times)	WPTR-AM
		WPTR-FM
New York	White Plains	WFAS AM-FM
New York	Long Island	WHLI
California	Los Angeles (twice)	Unistar Network
California	Long Beach	KFOX
California	San Francisco	KNBR, KNAI
Florida	Punta Gorda	WCCF;
Florida	Sarasota (twice)	WSPB;
Florida	Tampa	WFLA, WDAE
Florida	Port Charlotte	WEEJ
Pennsylvania	Philadelphia	WPEN, WSNI, KYW;
Pennsylvania	Chester	WEEZ
Texas	San Antonio (twice)	KKYX, KTSA
Illinois	Chicago	WCLR
Ohio	Dayton	WING

In most cases I became a resident of the city in which I was working. In others, I worked only temporarily but spent enough time in the market to make friends and get to know the town. Concurrently with regular jobs, I did call-letter collecting, whereby I knew friends or acquaintances at other stations where I was permitted one courtesy shift or guest appearance. In one form or another (live or syndicated), I've been on over 200 stations.

With the experiences I've shared over the years, radio has become a hobby as well as a career. When I turned toward programming full time, I felt like I opened a door to far greater opportunity than ever before, able to call upon unused portions of my background to apply to new and challenging situations. I discovered that working through others was a far better expression of my ability than exclusively working through my own talents. As I stepped from being on the air to being part of management, I felt that finally my opinions could matter and that ideas and concepts that had fallen on deaf ears for years would see the light of day (how's that for a mixed metaphor?). It also was gratifying to work with younger, less experienced announcers and share with them the knowledge and tricks necessary to move their careers ahead. Sitting on the other side of the desk also gave me far greater insight into the management viewpoint of station operations.

The overriding theme of how I choose to program a radio station is a combination of sharing and avoidance therapy. I never at any time in my announcing career was convinced that program management fully shared information with me that made me feel a part of the team. With the notable exceptions of Ruth Meyer during my years at WHN and Edd Neilson at WGEE and again at WKIP, I felt it was a them-versus-us atmosphere in many stations. Ruth had just completed one of America's biggest success stories as program director for the legendary WMCA Good Guys, so she had a very good handle on working with talent and experimenting with new ways to do things. Edd had previously been with WJRZ, just across the Hudson River (in New Jersey) from New York City, where the country format was really first heard in the greater New York market, if not officially on a New York station. Edd was huge into personality and extreme fun. Otherwise, at just about every other station, I was predictably expected to perform in a certain way and respond in an established manner but rarely told why. It was like there were deep, dark programming secrets that only program directors knew, and radio would cease should those secrets escape to the air talent. It was like Harry Potter meets Marconi.

Many program directors had become possessive about their programming treasures and were unwilling to share them. These secrets ranged from how Arbitron worked to exactly what were the station goals we were trying to achieve. Conversely, as I began my programming career, I found quite the opposite to be true. The more information and knowledge I shared with my staff, the smarter they were and the greater the assets. They even became a new resource in devising new strategies and better understanding the direction of the station. They were a viable part of the body of knowledge necessary to make it happen, rather than beasts of burden. I also found that by training and sharing duties, responsibilities, and strategic information with other staff members, I could move into more creative areas within the station, no longer having to do everything myself. It's gratifying to watch people learn, then add their own touch to the task. What about the philosophy behind avoidance therapy? I'd really like to say that absolutely everyone in radio is a magnificent person. As we know, people in radio reflect the same cross-section of sizes and shapes as does the rest of society. I mean there's good management and there's bad management. I'd have to admit that among the zillions of wonderful things I have been able to see and do, and among the many talented, gracious people in radio, I have regrettably also encountered some unbelievably stupid, uncaring, selfish, and wasteful behavior by a tiny handful. I'm not making a big deal over this, because I was fortunate enough to know the good from the bad and move on. But there were some really wonderful people who might have made a contribution to radio who became discouraged by their experience. If you take away anything from this book, it is my hope that you'll appreciate that it takes good people to make good radio. Good radio people know and care about their audience. Although there's probably a small pulp novel to be written about some of the things I've seen or experienced, there's really no place for them in this publication. Radio remains a viable business enterprise and, as such, needs to be accountable to owners and shareholders, which in times of weak economy and increased competition may result in seeing an apparently more ruthless style of management. This is not uncommon in any commercial industry. There are necessarily unpleasant things that one must do in management-employee relationships, but there are also choices as to how these situations can be handled. Seeing a few good people hurt *has* influenced me and my career, so I put this information right before you. Being successful in radio will be hard work and a demanding test of your professional and personal relationship skill set.

Regarding the contents of this book, the sheer volume of information I've learned, picked up, or stolen is just too great to keep bottled up. Now that I've invested a few decades consulting a variety of stations, formats, and people, I can pull from an even greater range of my past experiences to identify with my clients' needs. During my years of programming Country, my knowledge of Top 40 or MOR music went unused. With Oldies, I had little use for the News-Talk experiences I had acquired. It's as though I have a file drawer open to every format, available for sharing with other broadcasters. Welcome to my file cabinet.

One of the truths I've learned is that no real radio professional is format specific. Most of us enter the business with some ideals about sounding like our favorite radio personalities and playing our favorite songs. Soon after getting on the inside of the business, that goes away, and the need to learn and grow kicks in. Because we play the same songs over and over again, our love affair with the music soon goes away as well. Early on, we tend to look at what we do more as a job, then later, as a career. Accordingly, the decisions about changing jobs, accepting new offers, and going to new markets become more about our personal and professional goals than about the music we play and the market we're working in. During the boom days of Rock 'n' Roll radio of the 1960s, just about every Top 40 deejay started his career playing the standards of the day—bands, pop vocals, orchestras. Many worked at network-driven stations taking programming from New York, L.A., or Chicago. When Top 40 started to happen, those willing to change and try something very new made the transition to the new format.

A decade later, when modern Country started to be a huge format, some of the best Top 40 deejays popped over to the Country stations and rode the wave of their successes. Just about every major talk host or news anchor at today's leading news-talk stations started by being a deejay, playing some music format, somewhere. Good radio people perceive that the music, jingles, commercials, and other programming elements are just tools. Utilization of those tools to acquire and keep listeners is the full-time job, regardless of format, music, or market size. Be really good at the basics and you can work in any format. Beware of the carpenter who blames shoddy work on his tools.

Personally, I enjoy formats that best allow me to communicate with the listener. I like to say fun things and make people feel good. My personal version of a day far away from Paradise is reading liner cards and playing 10-in-a-row. Sure, there are music-intensive formats, but there are fun, entertaining ways to do that, too. In the United States, we're going through a second generation of programmers and announcers whose skills and versatility may have been hampered by their being mandated to rely on predictable presentation, few station-audience relationships, and minimal on-air presence of their own personality. The spoken word is a beautiful thing. Assembling words to express, inform, delight, enlighten, amuse, alert, and entertain is not a bad thing. When I hear music stations boast of less talk, I usually punch on over to the next station, because I'm not going to hear someone stepping out and trying something clever and new. I got into radio because of the *people* I heard on the air and the things they said, not to be an anonymous voice, enumerating a relentless sequence of similar sounding songs. Music formats are made for radio, but the presentation of the music can make the difference between a successful station and an unsuccessful one. Reducing the responsibility of the radio personality probably contributed more to the success of automation, the satellite-delivered programming, than any other factor. Personally, over the years, as stations I was working for started to head in the direction of highly structured, minimally spontaneous presentation, I started heading in the opposite direction, usually to another company.

So now, here we all are a few decades later, and there's no more tucking away years of experience, but constantly using the information, refining it, and adapting it to new situations. In the interest of sharing and in being consistent with my overall programming philosophy, it's time to put into a usable, easy-to-understand formula the methods and systems that work for me. Each station and company has its own set of guidelines and rules to follow. I don't expect the material in this book to address every circumstance and fit every station, format, or opportunity. It might best be utilized as a fall-back point, a list of basics, an idea book, or an encyclopedia for thought-starters. In the first edition of this book, some of the chapters were narratives on thinking and philosophy; others were lists of ideas, quotations, and proverbs. In the second edition I expanded many of those philosophies to include additional thoughts as suggested by readers of the first edition and some new material covering issues more prominent now than just a few years ago. I hope that all of these ideas make the thought processes begin to work toward solving your programming situation.

It is my intention that this current edition will become part of your arsenal to stay fresh, creative, and competitive in your market and your career. While negotiating with the NAB to publish the first edition of this book, we were collectively struck by the dearth of guidance-driven material on radio programming. Both within the professional sector and on bookshelves of private booksellers, there's virtually nothing instructive for anyone seeking a career in radio or seeking to improve himself or herself within the radio industry. There are dozens (in some cases hundreds) of books about other performance careers, including acting, singing, film-making, television, journalism, puppetry (no connection intended), and art. No radio. Knowledge is, at its lowest denominator, a collection of experiences. To enumerate those experiences and to arrange them in an instructional manner is the only discipline required to turn a drawer full of notes and memorandums into a book. OK? Tag, I'm it.

This is not a history of radio. Many books have been written about the Golden Age of radio and the history of the medium. More recently, there have been several books written about the Second Golden Age of radio, specifically the Rock 'n' Roll Era and the popular deejays and artists of that time. I'll leave the biographical and chronological stuff to the archivists and historians.

The purpose of this book is to address some issues that concern the operation of a radio station. Here's another weapon in your arsenal to defeat your competitors. Whether owner, manager, air talent, or program director, you are in varying degrees responsible for the success of the radio station. In the recent decade of over-researched music, over-asked listeners, boilerplate promotions, so-called safe music, and card reader ten-in-a-row mentality, there needs to be some way to break the cycle. Hit songs don't start out that way. They earn their chart position. Outstanding contests evolve from good contests which evolve from bad ones. Before listener reaction can be measured, it has to be evoked. Rather than spend page after page telling you about the kind of radio that tests well, I'd like to open a few doors to the kind of radio that is fun and that can be developed from original ideas.

If you accomplish nothing else by reading this book, use it as a springboard for a kind of thinking that frees you long enough from mediocrity to try something on your own. I've tried to give some answers here to some typically asked questions. But I've also raised some new questions for you to ponder and solve. This book should be used as a catalyst for activating new and original ideas. It is a chronicle of how one person sought answers and applied them. So if there is a real shortage of training material and opportunities for radio programmers, then let's write some. If that lack of material is partly due to the lack of sharing as previously mentioned, then let's share some. If the reason for lack of programming instruction is partly because of the ever-changing nature of the business itself, then let's isolate the unchanging and universal truths that always work. Finally, if there's been no prior radio programming book because most programmers are just too busy programming to focus on a time-consuming literary project, then let's make some time as part of a career to assemble such information. Were it not for avid note-keeping, this work would not have been possible. The editions of this book almost wrote themselves over the past decade. The programmers of tomorrow will come from somewhere. It is my hope they will evolve from their own creativity and ability, tempered by the knowledge shared with them by some of us who've been there.

ACKNOWLEDGMENTS

In assembling the materials for this latest edition, I would like to thank the following personal and professional friends and institutions for their assistance:

James D. Williams   Jim has been a long and trusted friend going back to my days in New Albany. When I was completing high school, Jim came to New Albany as an elementary school teacher. His classroom had one of those FM radios in the window sill I wrote about. A few years later we taught elementary school 6th grade classes across the hall from each other in Indianapolis. I was also a DJ at WTLC working nights, but taught during the day. Jim was able to monitor my radio career for many years. He is not only a skilled instructor, but has a vast command of English and has worked valiantly translating radio-speak to common usage. Growing up in Kentucky and listening to the radio offerings of the 1940s and 1950s, Jim has also been a valuable resource in radio and media history. Known by his students as Conan the Grammarian, he has made a valiant effort to make this book not only informative but, I hope, easy to understand and to enjoy.

The Arbitron Company   I must thank the many employees of Arbitron who have worked tirelessly on their product from year to year and have never failed to provide explanations and a depth of understanding for their products and services. Brad Bedford, Bob Michaels, Pierre Bouvard, and many other employees at Arbitron have taught and informed me, although not directly or officially, about their product for many years.

Al Skop   Al and I originally worked together in Albany when I was program director at WPTR-FM. I hired him for our afternoon drive shift and as assistant program director. In that position he was directly in the line of fire for many of the ideas and philosophies expressed herein. Later, joining me at Sirius in a similar capacity, he was a valuable sounding board for ideas and an excellent administrator for our formats and programming projects. As administrator of The Country Oldies Show web site for several years, he has assisted greatly in opening up some time in my schedule to work on this project.

Edd Neilson   Edd is the G.M and P.D. with whom I worked in Indianapolis (WGEE) and Poughkeepsie (WKIP). He taught me that funny was good, that humor was paramount, that goofy was cool, that clever was welcome, and that real radio must remain engaging and creative to remain viable. He taught me to break rules.

David V. Leonard   My G.M. in Albany (WPTR-AM) and later at Dayton (WING) came from the station rep (Chrystal) sales side of the radio business. As his first general manager job, Dave inherited me as his program director. and we learned his/my side of the business from each other. He taught me, above all, to write things down. This book is a direct product of that advice.

Ruth A. Meyer   As my program director at WHN in New York, Ruth brought along a world of experience as the former program director at the legendary WMCA Good Guys. She taught that teams work more effectively than individuals and that diversity and talent are part of the texture of great radio. Although we worked together for only two years (1973-1975), we have remained loyal personal friends. As a world traveler, Ruth was able to orchestrate many of my early European trips as well as provide insight into international broadcasting. Many, many hours of discourse on radio have poured from fine dinners together and French wine.

The Listener   Finally, I thank any listener, anywhere, who might have called or written or remembered anything I may have done on the air or behind the scenes that gave me the response and the feedback to assure me that someone was listening and that I made a small difference in his or her day.

ABOUT THE AUTHOR

Steve Warren has been a professional radio broadcaster/personality for over 40 years, starting at the age of 16 as the son of a Louisville, KY, radio announcer. He worked across the United States as an on-air personality, then came to New York City, America's #1 Radio market, where he survived the intense competition with successful positions on WHN, WNBC, WKHK, WYNY, WNCN, and the CBS Radio Network. As a program director, he enjoyed success in diverse markets and formats including work at WGEE, Indianapolis, IN (AC); WAMS, Wilmington, DE (Top 40); WPTR, Albany, NY (Country); WING, Dayton, OH (Oldies); KKYX, San Antonio, TX (Country); and KTSA, San Antonio, TX (MOR). He is sought after as a teacher and international instructor on radio programming and is an adjunct faculty member for the International Academy of Broadcasting in Montreux, Switzerland. His expert knowledge and love of the radio industry has secured him a respected position as a radio authority for broadcasting trade seminars and publications. Not only a fun, entertaining radio personality, but a gifted actor on stage, TV, and film, he has been MC and host to events at Radio City Music Hall, Lincoln Center, and Carnegie Hall. Steve is topical, engaging, and informative, speaking with authority on the contemporary media and entertainment scene. Since 1994, he has been heard every week across the United States and in several foreign countries on his syndicated *The Country Oldies Show*. From 1999 to 2003, Steve developed and implemented the country channels for Sirius Satellite Radio and was the first voice ever broadcast on Sirius. Before that, he was radio editor of Radio Ink Magazine and prolific interviewer of radio group owners and industry leaders. He continues to be involved in program consulting via MOR Media International, Inc. and has embarked on a pet project, The Radio-Studio Network to distribute creative and unique independently produced radio programs. His pleasures include softball, domestic and European travel, great restaurants, theatre, and cooking. You might even find him serving up a Swiss fondue as a guest chef in a popular restaurant. He lives two blocks from Times Square in Manhattan with a good friend and a bad cat.

Ruth A. Meyer

THE LISTENERS

IN TOUCH WITH THEM

Every ratings service, research company, and individual radio station has endeavored to accurately identify the specific person it may call a listener. When I teach a class about radio programming in the United States or Europe (where commercial radio is in the developmental stages in many countries), I always write in the corner of the chalkboard this phrase: "It's all about the listeners." It may not be a bad idea to make several signs with this phrase on them and post them prominently in your studio and other key offices around the radio station.

In my classroom, at every opportunity, whether the session includes discussions about technology, sales, programming, music, promotions, style, management, or any other aspect of radio broadcasting, I can safely and confidently point to the chalkboard any- where in the discussion to return the thought process to the indisputable fact that it's all about the listeners. Without the successful cultivation of some measurable and proactive listenership, radio fails. This simple phrase drives every department of the radio station and is pivotal in any decisions we make as broadcasters. Sometimes, it makes good sense to remind our air talent that they are talking to real people. It's not a bad idea for program directors to also remind themselves that their programming is designed for people. Although some of the disciplines of radio are scientific and there are formulae to deter- mine music list length and rotation patterns, a program director who spends all day star- ing at his or her computer might be missing something important about the lives and tastes of the real people on the other end of the radio signal. When driving, it's good to keep an eye on the control panel, but more important to watch the road.

No matter how much we may get caught up in our own participation in the radio indus- try and how much knowledge we acquire as day-to-day broadcasters, the listener remains the crucial individual in the success of any radio station. Without the listeners there is no success, no revenue, no ratings, no jobs, no anything. Regardless of station format, accu- rately identifying and serving listeners is paramount. While the characteristics of listeners vary from format to format and market to market, there are several general listener qual- ities that are often overlooked, including the fact that they have consciously decided to lis- ten to the radio and have selected a specific station. In addition, most people have a history with radio listening and radio stations, so they possess a basic understanding of how it works.

LISTENERS AS A RESOURCE

Listeners are a resource. They can be helpful in locating obscure music selections and can possibly provide expert commentary for news or public affairs material. Don't be afraid to invite listeners to provide information or services to the station directly. Since our com- pany has worked primarily with adult formats over the years, we've constantly been searching for hard-to-find music. Just a few words on the air have resulted in our access to thousands of selections from personal record collections that would have cost a fortune to purchase. A thank you on the air or a gesture of a station promotional item is apprecia- tion enough. Actually, these collector-contributors feel good about being a part of the station. Next time they hear one of their songs on the radio, they'll reach over, turn up the radio, and tell everyone in the room that you're playing *their* song. When programming Adult Standards (MOR) at KTSA in San Antonio in 1988, I mentioned on the air that I was looking for a few difficult-to-find records. I got a call from a retired Air Force guy (there are lots of Air Force retirees living in San Antonio) who had the songs I wanted. He invited me to his home where he allowed me full access to his superb, perfectly catalogued record collection. As it turns out he flew hundreds of missions as a B-29 pilot in World War II. As a kid, my bedroom was full of model B-29 airplanes, so what began as using a listener for a music resource became a personal resource for hearing firsthand about what it was like to fly the Super-fortress.

SO HERE'S WHAT I'M GETTING AT

Throughout this book, there will be many references to the radio listeners. It's also important to keep in mind that every aspect of radio broadcasting evolves from and revolves around its listeners. As the aging of America marches forward, new demographics reflecting the tastes and needs of older listeners will be more important. Similarly, but on the opposite end of the age spectrum, children are beginning to adopt some radio listening habits. For the first time, people under the age of 12 are being included in ratings reports. The development and success of Radio Disney in many markets have proven that radio can attract and retain preteen audiences and on AM radio stations, in most cases. As we spend our careers inside a radio studio, handling the day-to-day chores that fill up our shifts, on the other side of the radio signal are people listening, handling theirs. Saying just the right thing at just the right time, playing just the right song at just the right moment can alter a listener's day. Each incident may be small, but collectively may amount to a significant influence over time. Scattered throughout this book are anecdotes and tales from my personal experiences in radio. Some of them are as a professional broadcaster, others as a casual listener.

Take a few minutes before diving into the following chapters and do the following: Go find a radio somewhere in your house or office. Turn it on and flip to the AM dial low end (540 is the lowest actual AM frequency), then slowly move up the dial stopping briefly at every station you can hear. Stop long enough to actually hear what's being said or to identify the music, format, or topic. Keep going all the way up to the top of the AM dial (up to 1700), stopping at each station. Now flip over to the FM dial and do the same thing, moving from bottom to top (88-108) and spend a few moments with each station.

If you are like most people, you have your favorite station or two (or three), but did you actually know about all those others? We regularly jump among our favorites and seldom stop to check what else is out there. It's much like ordering the same thing off the menu every time we go to the same restaurant. Although most of those other stations don't mean much to you, each one means something to someone else in your community or it wouldn't be there. The collective influence of all those stations has shaped and molded the position in the market of the stations you actually do listen to. They collectively compose and define the radio market and each one of them is there, day in and day out, every day, doing what they do. Each station has a staff of people responsible for its programming, technical operation, sales, and business affairs. Some of these stations may be co-owned by the same company and may be in the next room, just feet away from your favorite station. When you go to sleep at night, those stations are still there, as they are when you are listening to your favorite CD, when you're watching TV, or even when you are out of town.

Our airwaves are full, actually crammed to the brink, with radio stations. There are more independent radio stations in the United States than in any other country. Radio began and remains a private enterprise in the United States. An individual may own a radio station just like he or she may own a pizza shop or plumbing business. Unlike most countries in the world, the U.S. government has never been in the business of owning radio stations. From the inception of commercial radio in the United States, private enterprise has held title to the stations. The marketplace has determined their success and failure by how we, the listeners, react and respond to what they do.

We were somewhere near the 11,000-radio station mark as this book went to press. That number may fluctuate very slightly, usually upward, with new licenses being granted all the time and with the creation of new, low-power FM facilities added to the pile.

Radio is a local enterprise and the local marketplace has prevailed at cultivating an industry that is informative, entertaining, and pervasive. Each of these stations exerts its influence on each of its listeners in an ongoing ebb and flow of tuning in and tuning out, channel changing, and chasing the clock.

We, as broadcasters, may never know if the song we just played was the last song someone would ever hear, just like we may never know that the same song was playing in the background while a new life was being created.

Listeners. It really *is* all about them.

Listeners.
It really *is* all
about them.

BASIC RADIO REALITIES

GETTING STARTED

The focus of this book primarily is programming. That is the product we sell and where the creative process is called upon to generate profit-making ideas. It's also the part of the industry where I have spent my entire career. It is important to remember that programming interfaces with every other department in the radio station, usually on a daily basis. Therefore, it is as important to view those other departments from a programming perspective. Knowledge of each of the interdependent departments of a radio station is very important, but having actually to hold a position within those departments is not required. As we mentioned in the beginning of the book, so little has been written about programming that the information is almost conspicuous by its absence. Programming is the key element in broadcasting, but you'd never know it by browsing the radio-TV section of a bookstore. Since programming is limited only by lack of creativity, it would be presumptuous to outline ironclad rules and regulations about what works.

If programming were merely a formula, then we could dispense with this whole book and put the formula on a single handout sheet. In reality, because programming is so wide open from station to station, the best I can hope for is to stimulate the creative process and hope that many of these ideas I have found to be successful can be adapted to someone else's needs and situation.

Industry organizations such as the Radio Advertising Bureau, National Association of Broadcasters, and various State Broadcasting Associations can provide considerable quantities of valuable information regarding radio sales. In fact, the selling of radio advertising, though unique, does call on basic selling strategies from other businesses and acquires a considerable number of personnel from retail and other sales-related occupations. Over the past 10 years or so, radio sales executives have moved more toward *marketing* and away from *selling*. Although the exchange of money is still a critical issue, the development of a comprehensive marketing strategy for advertisers has become a more successful and lucrative approach than the hard sell and close. It is important for program directors to understand the role of sales. However, being an independent advocate for the programming of the station is a *more* important function and sales should never use its revenue-making position to compromise or dictate programming decisions.

The relationship between programming and other departments will reappear throughout the book where appropriate, and although we'll revisit these areas, I thought a few comments about the two most significant departments with which programming will need strong understanding and alliances would be appropriate, sales and technical/engineering.

SALES

It is often said that the *real* money in radio is in sales. This is probably true for people who enjoy selling. However, I don't think many people enter the business initially without some interest in a specific job. I really don't think anyone enters radio primarily for the money, in any department. It's a special business, combining an assortment of people in the development of a uniquely personal product. Announcers, air talent, or whatever term is selected, are actually salespeople, too. They sell the radio station's benefits to the listener.

They sell themselves at personal appearances, and they sell their ability to perform for management on an ongoing basis. The account executives representing the sales department operate in a more structured environment and work with ratings, budgets, costs, and contracts. They also operate as an adjunct to other businesses wanting to get the word out about their products and services.

In many cases, there are announcers who are looking for more stability in their lives, enjoy their community, have families, and want to stay where they are. There comes a time when the salary for announcers just can't go any higher. The more-money aspect of sales is not the salary itself, but the option to make commission. Therefore, within sales, the earning power has no set limits. There always seems to be a small percentage of radio account executives who have come through the ranks of programming. Their decisions to do so are largely personal and usually the result of a conscious career move. Programming can be a springboard to sales and management, but it is not designed to be so, nor is it subordinate professionally to those areas. The occasional adversarial relationship between sales and programming often results from misunderstanding and working at cross-purposes.

From the sales point of view, calling on clients, making promises, asking for the order, and being in and out of a car all day are all part of the difficult and underappreciated job. Salespeople often think announcers have it quite easy, doing a 4-hour shift in a studio, especially for a guaranteed salary, often rumored to be greater than their own.

From the perspective of programming, salespeople are responsible for station income, directly affecting studio equipment purchases or salaries. Salespeople may occasionally be accused of giving away the station too cheaply and making unrealistic, short-notice demands on announcers and production people in developing commercials. They also want the program director to put material on the air (like promotions and air-cluttering, low-value contests) for the sake of making a sale. Just like brothers and sisters who occasionally fight, sales and programming people frequently find themselves in spats, but they ultimately need each other. That truth usually mitigates any problems between the two departments and prevents disputes from becoming too serious. It should be the goal of a good general manager to have frequent meetings between these two important departments. The manager should continue to restate the goals of the station within proper limits and with guidelines for expected performance. There should be effective systems or operational procedures for handling interdepartmental affairs. The income-producing objective of the sales department should never be used to leverage programming decisions that may compromise the overall value of the station.

TECHNOLOGY

The minute I start writing about anything technical, the shelf life of this book is reduced by 75%. Radio technologies are reinventing themselves by geometric progressions. In the field of music reproduction alone, we've gone from vinyl records to tape cartridges to compact disc to hard disc to CD-ROM to iPod to heaven knows what next in just a decade. We are knocking on the door of new distribution technologies that still include FM, AM, (AM Stereo and AMAX), digital (DAB), direct satellite (SDARS), and beyond. I see things at broadcasting conventions these days that I have never dreamed of—but I *don't see* some of the things I saw last year, because they are already outdated.

The ease and convenience of a new technology always come at a price. An easy example is the basic telephone. In the late 1800s the telephone came into common usage and greatly improved personal and business information exchanges. But the price paid was a loss of privacy. When we put in a telephone line we give everyone permission to call us and interrupt whatever we're doing at any hour of the day or night and for any reason. How many times have you heard someone say that the telephone is driving them crazy? In the same way, consolidation of ownership and the leap to virtual programming have come at a cost—and it's about the highest cost that radio can pay.

The cost has been the loss of a valuable local service for local listeners, one that may be very different from basically the same service in another location. People depend on the personal touch that comes only from air talent that lives in the community, from air talent that many people know or have seen at a local event, and from a station that can be viewed as a constant and helpful neighbor.

An experiment in England some time ago confirms this. A whole village was wired for cable TV and was provided the service for free, with all the different kinds of programming that were available at the time. Tucked away in the offering was a little local station that concentrated on local news and community events. When the ratings for all the channels were reviewed, guess what? The little local station far outstripped any of the others. The most popular program on this station was an informal chat show broadcast at breakfast time from a pub that doubled as a restaurant. In that experiment, the medium was TV, but the same principles undoubtedly apply to radio. Another example comes to mind. In the 1950s, there was a trend toward broadcasting for an hour every day from someone's living room. Someone well known in the town would entertain, interview, and advertise right from home. These shows were very popular. They usually beat out the slicker network offerings in the same time slots. The talent might not have been at the most professional level, and the production values were certainly primitive, but people liked the person broadcasting and liked the show. What's even more important, they tuned in. The upside of the rush toward virtual programming is that it may, at ratings time, show that it doesn't pay to slight the listener—that the listener is what it's all about—and that no technical advances can ever replace the personal touch. We hope that all this may prompt a swing back toward what radio does best: act as a voice for the community right outside its front door.

People don't listen to the radio because of its technology. In many cases people listen in spite of its technology. After the first couple of decades of being fascinated by radio waves coming out of the sky, striking an antenna or crystal, and being heard on a headset, the technologies of radio remain part of the backstage of the industry. We massively overestimate the technical knowledge and/or concern our listeners have for what goes on backstage at a radio station. Radio listeners have endured a lot of problems over the years, straining to hear out-of-town stations, inferior signals, low power, interference, and scratchy records; yet they remain loyal and generally uncomplaining. After all, it's free. The all-important radio morning show including all the expense required to build it is usually most listened to on a 3-inch clock-radio speaker.

If we have something technical that really matters to a listener, we should promote it (such as higher power, greater coverage, AM stereo, digital, etc.), give demonstrations, get radio dealers involved, make something out of it, but don't expect the average radio consumer to make many radio purchases based exclusively on technology. More people buy a new radio because the old one broke than for any other reason. Most people buy boom boxes and portable devices for their ability to play cassettes and CDs rather than for radio listening. The technical aspect of radio is probably the most widely published information. Each week/month/year, there are piles of technical journals, newsletters, and magazines to keep the engineering department current with emerging technologies. Technology is a part of the economy. Equipment is bought and sold. Manufacturers' fortunes rise and fall with the stock market.

Technology represents hardware, patents, performance, legal issues, and investments. It's the usual supply and demand. Companies that manufacture radio equipment also manufacture other components for everything from national defense to telephones, transmitters to kitchen appliances. Technology is big business. Big business gets a lot of press. Technology is hardware, manufacturing, moving parts, and inventory. With nearly 11,000 commercial radio stations in the United States, each in a varying state of technical operation, we can safely assume that just about every generation of technology exists within American radio.

Whether your audio sources are digital cart machines or hard-drive audio storage, Internet downloads, CD players, or old fashioned reel-to-reel, cassette, or tape carts, what matters most is how effective you are in attracting and retaining listeners. For simplicity, I decided to take the low-tech approach in describing techniques and examples. If your radio station is more toward the high-tech end of the spectrum, great! Just adapt the ideas to your situation. There is one note on my decision to take the low-tech approach. I've been greatly honored to have previous editions of this book purchased and used in many foreign countries. In some cases, these countries are developing their independent radio industry for the first time. Although underfunded, with little formal training, and often using borrowed, donated, or second-hand equipment, they move forward with diligent enthusiasm. I don't want to leave anyone out. This book is written without regard to the available technologies of its readers, but rather as a guide to best implementation of developing a relationship with listeners.

A radio station's technology is the tool to accomplish the goals. The secret is not in the sharpness of the tool, but rather in the ability of the craftsman. Regardless of the prevailing technology of radio, at the delivery end there is still programming. We have to create something worthwhile and profitable to deliver by whatever means. The technical aspects of broadcasting are merely the tools we are given to do our work. Many truly great radio stations have become legends and made millions of dollars with the most basic of tools. For decades, radio was ruled by monaural AM stations playing vinyl records through an analog mixing board and broadcast by tube-driven transmitters. The music was scheduled (if at all) with file cards, while the program log and commercial copy were written by typewriter. As you smile at this visualization, remember that this is a description still accurately defining hundreds of small-market stations. Let's take the tools we are given in any situation and use them as best we can, but let's never find ourselves in a position to blame our tools for our own lack of imagination.

Technology is also the most mystical department of the radio station, since few people from other departments possess the skills and training necessary to be an effective broadcast engineer. For this reason, some engineers have absolute control over matters of selecting equipment, installation, and significant budget allocations. Most good engineers are team players and enjoy the same sense of job fulfillment as other members of the staff. It is usual, however, for many engineering decisions to go unquestioned by management and other department heads. Since most stations have only one full-time engineer, I strongly suggest using an independent outside engineering consultant once or twice a year, just the same as a programming or sales consultant. Broadcast engineering is an occupation that depends extensively on personal preference for types of equipment, manufacturers, installation procedures, etc. Bringing in other choices by employing the services of an engineering consultant (who sees a lot of other radio stations and has a more inclusive knowledge of available technology) may save the company time and expense, and may prove to be well worth the fee. Many engineers build a network of relationships within the radio-technical community. Through these relationships, they also develop preferences toward certain kinds of equipment and brand names. When stations employ a series of engineers or lack consistency in their engineering personnel, there can be frequent duplication of purchasing and expenses as successive engineers want to re-equip with the apparatus they like. Now that radio consolidation is a reality, engineers may have to deal with a half-dozen radio stations under one roof, but with transmitter sites spread over a wide geographical area. To the degree that there are fewer moving parts in new, digital, computer-driven equipment, the technology has gotten simpler and more modular. However, the depth of knowledge and the necessity to keep up with current advances are dizzying.

Finally, in dealing with the engineering and sales departments, the smart programmer will know how each operates and how each makes its unique contribution to the overall success of the operation. I suggest that a regular and open line of communication be established between these departments so that common goals and expectations can be met and appreciated. A good general manager, whose job is to oversee those departments, will develop a relationship as a facilitator rather than as a referee.

RADIO IS A SECONDARY MEDIUM

Radio is a secondary medium.

When radio stations first went on the air in most major American cities during the early 1920s, few people had radio receivers. Listening to the radio became almost a community event, with neighbors, family, and friends all converging on the homes of those fortunate enough to possess a radio receiver. Then, all would gather around the radio and listen, or literally stare at it, while the programs were on. At first the listening was limited by the number of headsets available, but with the advent of the *loudspeaker*, any number could join in. The radio set commanded the same focus of attention that today's TV sets do. Since radio was still a scientific and technical wonder, the commercial and money-making benefits remained largely unexplored in the early days. The way to make money then was to sell radios. This explains why some of the early pioneer broadcasting companies were actually primarily in the electronic radio manufacturing business. Companies like Westinghouse, General Electric, RCA, Crosley, and others built and operated radio stations for the sole purpose of selling more radios.

Radio was a *primary* medium in those days. There was no television, and radio was a collection of individual short-form programs. Some daily features were only 5, 10, or 15 minutes long. Weekly features were most often 30 or 60 minutes long. The time dedicated to listening depended on which programs were preferred and when they were on, so that people planned other activities around listening to their favorites. Work schedules, family chores, school homework, even civic activities or meetings were rearranged to permit time for listening to favorite radio programs. Mealtimes were changed in order to listen to popular shows like *One Man's Family*. That particular daily show ruled the schedule at my grandparents' house. Nobody ate, nobody moved, nobody uttered a sound until *One Man's Family* had concluded its daily episode. Bedtimes were compromised so the kids could hear radio personalities like Jack Benny or Fibber McGee and Molly. There were not that many radio stations on the air, so the station programming schedule demanded listeners to make the personal scheduling adjustments to listen. Today our radio stations are mostly format-on-demand, whereby each station provides a virtual steady diet of the same format and programming. To hear different programming, all we have to do is change to another station. In the early days of radio, it was necessary to observe scheduled program times to listen. Listen was the word, too. The radio comedies and dramas demanded attention. News broadcasts with up-to-the-minute information from around the world deserved and received uninterrupted attention, not passive indifference.

Radio, and TV in its early stages, set the stage for a national currency of talk. At home and at work, people would talk about what was on the night before because almost everyone would have listened (or watched). If Franklin Roosevelt gave one of his Fireside Chats, it would be discussed everywhere the next day because everyone would have been tuned in. Thus, while radio seriously cut into the sense of neighborhood and community by curtailing neighborhood strolling and chatting from front porches in the evenings, it replaced it with a larger, national community. Some people preferred Fred Allen to Jack Benny, and vice versa, but *everyone* was familiar with both of them. Radio, by limiting choices and availability, made listening more important, and people listened closely. Today, radio and television have marginalized themselves in people's lives to a greater and greater extent by oversaturation of the market and diversification to the last tiny niche. Programming has become more and more like the mountains in the backgrounds of their lives, and less and less like the central figures out in front. (Advertisers, take heed!)

Motion pictures were also a primary medium, requiring actual attendance at the theater, a financial investment, and time budgeted around the movie schedule. When television started to bud in the late 1940s and then blossom in the 1950s, the movies came into the living room, and many of the radio programs got faces. Gradually, radio personalities and motion picture stars defected to opportunities in television, leaving radio stations across America with diminishing audiences and a scramble for ideas. The idea that saved the medium of radio (at that time in history) was the implementation of the format concept.

In the early days of radio, newspapers, with their wire services, had already begun the work of creating a national American community. Radio, because it was universally understood and universally available, finished the work and became an extremely influential agent for building a sense of national identity. It did not, as some thought, lead to the creation of a national culture. Various social, ethnic, racial, and other cultural groups simply included it into their cultures to a greater or lesser extent. For example, the newscasters established a national standard for American speech, but very few Americans actually use this language themselves, although they understand it readily enough. Today local radio and network TV remain important influences but are no longer the only guests at the party. They are no longer seated as guests of honor as an automatic tribute to the gifts they bring. This is the reality that programmers are facing today.

I told you that I'm skipping over a lot of radio history here, since this is not a history book and because any library will have a variety of books on the history of radio. Let's just say that radio evolved from a program medium into a format medium. Sure, a program focus is a type of format, but let's not get too technical. Radio established itself as an outlet for playing various types of music around the clock and/or providing supplemental programming to that offered on TV. As radio stations adopted music formats, the way people listened to radio also changed. Now it was possible to listen to the radio at any time of the day or night without having to give it undivided attention. Radio became more of a companion than an entertainment. In undergoing this metamorphosis, radio became what we refer to as a *secondary* medium. This is not a bad thing. In fact, it saved the industry. Today's radio has become almost completely redefined as a secondary medium. By secondary medium, I mean that at the moment listening takes place, in a majority of cases, the listener is engaged in some other primary activity. I'm not relegating radio to second-class status. The term is *secondary*. To acknowledge the fact that the listener is performing some other priority function while listening admits to the ease with which radio can become a part of our lives. This becomes very important in programming radio stations.

To clarify the definition of secondary medium, here are examples:

Driving the car: Driving is the primary; listening to the radio is secondary.

In the kitchen: Preparing food is the primary; listening to the radio is secondary.

At the office: Doing work is the primary; listening to the radio is secondary.

The bathroom: Shower, shave, or whatever is the primary; radio listening is secondary.

Clear enough? It seems that whenever a radio is being played, listeners are doing something else that requires primary attention. Knowing what listeners do and when they do it for their primary activity can be very valuable in programming toward them. It also helps us understand why radio stations need to exercise considerable effort in getting their messages or identities across, since the impact on the listener is reduced by the importance of their primary activity. Realizing that radio is a secondary medium has led to the theories of reach and frequency schedules, repetition of spot announcements, overselling station image lines and contest rules, music rotation patterns, announcer scheduling, and commercial rates. Radio has also been the ally of other advertising media in playing a supporting role developing multimedia approaches to successful advertising campaigns by reinforcing images promoted via TV, billboards, cable, newspapers, etc.

Although there has been an onslaught of new entertainment technologies, including the VCR, DVD, cable, satellite TV and radio, CDs, cassettes, Internet, and video games, radio has maintained one distinct advantage. It is still the only medium that can be adapted to fit nonintrusively into other activities. Its portability and lack of being tethered to an outlet or requiring concentrated visual attention have been the primary selling points of radio for many years. Radio programmers *must* remember this. Failure to capitalize on radio's uniqueness and to exploit its inherent benefits should be considered unacceptable in today's media-competitive marketplace.

I am reminded that we often look too closely at some things to the exclusion of the bigger picture, like the man who gets eaten by the dog while looking for its fleas. Before becoming immersed in establishing some grand, in-depth definition of our listeners, let's step back and take a better look. We personally like to feel that we are important to the success of radio, but let's acknowledge a few truths first.

1. Listeners don't care about radio as much as we do. We are inside the industry and, therefore, surround ourselves with similar people. The rest of society's contact with radio is rarely personal, but rather, electronic and distant. How much of our day is devoted to thinking about our socks? A few minutes every morning and again every night? Someone who works at the sock factory thinks about socks all day. His or her whole life is centered around the manufacture, marketing, and sale of socks. Conversely, listeners think about radio only a few minutes a day, while we think it's our whole world.

2. Listeners are slower to accept what we do on the air and slower to forget what we have done. Music, contests, promotions, or announcer recognition all take five or ten times longer than we usually allow. When we get tired of it, we think they get tired of it, too. Similarly, listeners often cling to impressions of our radio station created months (if not years) earlier. Have you ever seen your call letters on a bumper sticker promoting a format you dropped 5 years ago?

3. Personal attention cannot be replaced. Answer all listener mail. Even something as simple as some preprinted note cards, bearing the station logo, can be welcome. Just a few lines of personal acknowledgment will probably set you apart from most other radio stations that rarely answer listener mail. Today, with e-mail, a reply can be quick and simple. If you get an e-mail, then send an e-mail. If you get a letter, write a letter. Get a fax, send a fax. Your listener has communicated with you with a method of choice, so respond in the same way.

4. The percentage of people who *will* write a letter does *not* automatically represent a collective group of people with the same opinion. There is a myth that one letter represents some phantom number of other persons with the same comment or opinion. There is no evidence of any correlated number and we often are misled by believing there is. Those who write may be expressing only an individual specific opinion not shared by anyone else. To overreact to this correspondence may be damaging.

5. This one is similar to number 4, but refers to telephone callers. Obviously, be courteous on the phone. Understand that generally phone callers want a favor, a song, a request, a dedication, or something. You might turn the call into a more valuable experience by asking questions about the caller's listening habits, why he or she likes certain music, and a description of the listening environment. In this case, the listener is doing you a favor.

6. At station-sponsored events, visit, sit, eat, and drink with listeners, not other staff members. The more we can learn about the listeners' lives, their families, their jobs, their concerns, and their interests, the better we'll be able to visualize them realistically when we design our programming and when we select what we say when we speak to them via the radio. Eating is fun. Making new friends and learning about their lives (while they're learning more about you) is a mutually positive exercise.

7. Don't be afraid to use your radio station to communicate. Radio, after years of paying the newspapers for classified advertising, has finally started advertising on its own broadcasts for employment opportunities. In fact, on-air recruitment advertising has gotten to be a popular and effective method to invite applications for sales, secretarial, and administrative radio station positions. Personally, I can't believe why this practice was so late to catch on and how it is still not used as effectively as it could be.

When the first edition of *Radio: The Book* came out in 1992, we indicated that radio was, to our way of thinking, a secondary medium. And to recant, radio was much like the television set, where people sat down at an appointed time and listened to a program. More recently, radio has gotten into the 24-hour format mode whereby you can count on a radio station much like you count on an appliance, like the electricity or the water. You turn it on and you expect something to be there. You expect it to be something that's the same every time. So a rock station will be rock 24 hours a day. Because the radio is a secondary medium, we generally are doing something else while the radio provides companionship. While we are driving a car, our focus is on our driving, or should be, and radio is the secondary medium. If we are doing work around the house, for example, working in the kitchen, working on a project in the garage or in the basement, and we have the radio on as background entertainment, it too is secondary to our primary focus. In terms of at-work listening, people are concentrating on their work, their computer, their telephone calls, their paperwork, and the radio is on as secondary companionship. With the increase in the other types of influences on people, for example, cell phones carried on people's belts and in people's pockets and purses pretty much on a 24-hour basis; with more and more hours being spent at the computer; and with the increase in opportunities to get music from other means, from watching television, from satellite radio, from downloading MP3 files, from Internet sites, from purchasing massive amounts of music on iPod devices and other audio devices, radio is being pushed even further into the background and remains a secondary, or perhaps tertiary, medium. But it still exists as a medium.

At any given moment, radio broadcasting must be ready to do the one thing that it can do best—provide an over-the-air, untethered contact with listeners. In times of emergency or national disaster, this need becomes all too clear. You don't have to have a wire to connect to an AM or FM radio station. You don't have to pay a monthly subscription fee. You don't have to buy a special device, because everybody already owns at least one AM/FM radio. That constant, free, over-the-air link between radio station and listener is ongoing.

There are nearly 11,000 commercial broadcasting licenses in the United States, and they are being bought and sold at a frenzied pace. There is always a buyer for every seller, and in most cases, the seller makes a profit when he or she sells the radio station. We know that the business of radio is an ongoing business; there are a finite number of radio stations that can be licensed in the United States because of technical limitations, and radio stations will always be a prime commodity. How we choose to use that commodity will determine the future in radio.

RADIO AS A CAREER

CAN RADIO REALLY BE A CAREER?

Radio is a career all by itself. It is not intended to be part of a career in another field. Career radio broadcasters wouldn't even think of seeking another type of occupation. It is regrettable that often, particularly at the college level, radio is lumped into a curriculum called Mass Communication or even Television and Radio. Radio usually shares a very small part of those course studies. In the case of Mass Communication, radio gets pushed aside in favor of heavier emphasis on publishing, television, journalism, the Internet, and so on. To those who are sincerely dedicated exclusively to their work in radio, radio can become an exciting, challenging opportunity. But first, there must be commitment. It takes no less commitment to succeed at radio than it does to be a great dancer, actor, musician, artist, or any other accomplished artist. Over the past several decades, countless individuals have tried their hand at radio and failed. It's an attractive field. After all, it's clean, indoor work with no heavy lifting, lots of fun, and free CDs and concert tickets; and it provides some ego benefits. Too often, persons have given up on radio because they were unable to land a job that met their needs and standards. Being on the radio often projects a far more glamorous image to the public than the behind-the-scenes work actually is. As in any performance, excellence in radio comes from arduous repetition of fundamentals. There are a few rules to follow when becoming a part of the radio community as a career:

Be Flexible

The truth is that radio requires the sort of devotion and determination that demand you go where the jobs are and accept the positions available, rather than wait for them to come to you. Too often, young radio-aspiring individuals get comfortable in their communities, accept obligations—both financial and personal—and then depend heavily on their radio station positions to maintain that status. When the radio job vanishes because of any one of a variety of reasons, so does the security. So, solidly entrenched in personal and financial commitments, you may find that it becomes impossible to relocate to another geographical area because, for example, a spouse has a career or the family bought a home, a car, or personal items. All of a sudden . . . trapped! A person's unhappiness in any career is unwittingly projected onto others, and the quality of the work or performance will suffer.

Be flexible.

Have a Passion for Radio

Following is a personal account of how my career began. I offer it as an example of what I think is typical of the way people begin their careers in radio. I've noticed that people who are successful at what they do usually begin early with their life's work and then continue as they had begun. I know of many people in radio who took a precocious interest in radio (the same is true in other fields), who built and even transmitted neighborhood broadcasts on homemade equipment, and who knew—just somehow knew—that this was what they wanted to do. This is especially true in the performance arts. Many of today's actors began as small children in TV commercials, for instance, and are now big stars. My opinion is that the strongest radio personalities are those who have made an

Have a passion for radio.

early and lifelong commitment to radio. A Johnny-come-lately who chooses a radio career because something else wasn't working out will rarely find that radio works out either.

When I was growing up in the 1950s, I developed an interest in radio. This is my earliest recollection of such an interest. I remember that we had two large radios in our home, one floor model and one table model, both with wooden cabinets. Our home didn't get our first television until midway through the decade, so listening to radio programs was the only home entertainment. As TV is today, Saturday mornings were scheduled with children's programs, the news was on at dinnertime, and comedy or drama shows were on at night.

As the 1960s rolled around, stations playing mostly network programs started to give way to music formats, so that a single music format was available all day.

Parallel to my elementary school years, my father had several jobs in radio stations in the Louisville market as an announcer. Later he had positions with record companies promoting music and artists, so being near the entertainment industry was natural. In fact, my actual radio performing debut was as a third-grader on Louisville radio station WGRC, singing *White Christmas* to an organ accompaniment. The GRC in WGRC stood for George Rogers Clark, a famous historical soldier and frontiersman of the region. Years later, the call letters were changed to WAKY (i.e., whacky) as a clear message to the audience that the station was adopting a new format of fun, entertaining, noisy, contemporary music and DJs rather than the previous historical identification, thus soon becoming a legendary Top 40 station for the Louisville market. So much for honoring history.

As I entered high school, my interests centered around some form of performing. I had appeared in just about every production through elementary and junior high school and upon arrival at high school, I auditioned for (and got into) the coveted student theater program, one of the few freshmen ever to get into the program. The New Albany High School Student Theatre had long been highly regarded in the community for its excellent productions under the guidance of director Tom Weatherston. However, only seniors were allowed to be on the WNAS staff, so even though I was fulfilling my performance angst with acting, singing, and dancing in musical comedies several times a year, my sights were set on making the WNAS staff when I became a senior. Had I not done so, I'd be writing this book about biology, the only academic subject I ever really liked.

I was graduated from New Albany High School in New Albany, Indiana, in 1963. New Albany is in extreme southern Indiana, part of the Louisville, Kentucky radio market. The school holds the distinction of having the first high school radio station in the United States, WNAS-FM, which signed on in 1948. Since educational radio was in its infancy, WNAS-FM provided only a limited broadcast schedule, created and presented by the high school students mostly during school hours. Among the programs were spelling shows, storytelling, community news, science, and coverage of high school sports events. To support the station, the school system provided an FM radio for every classroom in every elementary school. Therefore, during a part of almost every day during my elementary school experience, the class listened to a radio program in the classroom. By the time I attended high school, there was a WNAS staff audition for students interested in becoming part of the station and related curriculum. Getting a spot on the WNAS staff was as sought after as a position on one of our sports teams (except basketball; after all, it was Indiana).

By sharing the personal indulgences of my childhood, I'm showing you that my experiences are not uncommon to people looking for radio careers. Early signs of some interest in performance, comedy, music, or theater may herald the appropriate disposition toward radio. Perhaps because of WNAS-FM, New Albany High School has produced an ongoing crop of radio broadcasters. An informal poll of my professional friends over the years of studying, writing about, and performing in radio, regardless of where they attended school, has clearly revealed a higher than normal interest in performance activities.

During my early high school years, I met a junior high student in New Albany named J. L. (James Lewis) Embrey. His older sister was the playground supervisor one summer at the park near my house and J. L. tagged along while she was supervising park activities. J. L. (and sister, Barbara) were both magicians, and I had seen J. L. perform at an elementary school talent show. I had an interest in magic, so we became friends. J. L. was also extremely interested in radio and we did that radio "thing-of-all-things": We built a radio station in the basement closet of his house with turntables, tape recorders, and microphones. Of course, it wasn't a real radio station. There was no transmitter, but that notwithstanding, after school, we took turns being make-believe DJs. We also continued to use our magic skills at local social events and annual Halloween "spook rooms," where kids and adults would pay a quarter for J. L. and me to scare the hell out of them for a 30-minute show before moving on to the hot cider and candy apples. In those days, every year a professional company would rent the local movie theater (the historic Grand Theatre) and sell tickets for an entire evening of magic, spooky costumed characters running up and down the aisles, and a double feature of classic horror films. Corny? Yes. But such was our life.

As a senior, I made the WNAS staff; J.L., as an underclassman, also made it into the student theater. We were both huge fans of Johnny Carson and greatly appreciated that he was both a magician and a radio announcer before making it big on TV and "The Tonight Show." Clearly, we needed some TV on our résumé, so that same year, we pitched a Louisville TV station (WLKY-TV 32) to let us apply our magic and special effects wizardry to add some fun to the Saturday night "Shock Theatre" program of old horror movies, hosted by a local radio newsman from WAKY Top 40, "The Mighty 790" named Tom Perry. Every Saturday night the TV station provided a car to pick us up, with our magic equipment, and took us to and from the station. We provided the cobwebs, coffins, and spiders while dressed as werewolves and vampires in the background while Mr. Perry did the live commercial breaks. WLKY-TV 32 was the first commercial UHF station in the Louisville market and was an ABC network affiliate, itself a fledgling network for TV programming at the time. The station was aggressively marketing to Louisville TV viewers, telling them that the programming was unique enough to warrant the investment in the UHF adapter box required to receive the station on a conventional TV set that could receive only channels 2-13. Our TV appearances were fun and created just the right amount of envy among our school peers, but we had bigger fish to fry over on the radio dial.

As we plotted our course to hang with local radio guys, we made several individual acquaintances at local stations. This was ultimately the Trojan Horse theory at work. Get on the inside. Among J. L.'s friends at his favorite station, WAKY, was a popular nighttime DJ, named Jumpin' Jack Sanders, for whom he wrote jokes and learned bad habits. Jumpin' Jack was excused from WAKY and Louisville after being involved in some impropriety along with another WAKY employee. Jack Sanders (Jim Spence) moved to Nashville and went to work for Audrey Williams (Hank Williams' widow). He died in the 1970s.

Get on the inside.

Following graduation from high school, while attending college locally at a regional campus of Indiana University, I garnered part-time work at a few Louisville radio stations. My first job was for MY favorite station, WKLO, the other Top 40 powerhouse in Louisville. In those days almost every market had two Top 40 stations. The competition was intense and the promotions and marketing were extraordinary. If anyone ever believed that competition made the product better, they'd have textbook cases just by studying Top 40 radio in the 1960s. My WKLO experience wasn't on the air, however, much to my regret. The station designed a Summer Fun Festival to run throughout the summer of 1963 with lots of hourly prizes for the whole summer. Contestants won packages of hot dogs and buns, picnic baskets, cases of soda, etc. Summer stuff. To embellish the contest, WKLO rented a storefront on Louisville's main drag (Fourth Street) and required the contest winners to pick up the prizes there at the Summer Fun Festival Prize Center. I was hired as the proprietor of the store, so my day was spent handing out goodies to contest winners. But I did have access to the studios, got to drive the WKLO car to remotes and events, and knew all the WKLO announcers, so life was good.

Following the summer at WKLO, I got to try some real radio at WTMT (Country 620) and later at WLRS-FM (Easy Listening) as a part-time announcer. My time at WKLO had allowed me to use the production studio to record some auditions, which paid off.

Because I was still living at home, I was still hanging out with J. L., who thereafter also became a member of the WNAS-FM staff as a senior. I finally decided to leave New Albany for a semester off from I.U. to attend a radio school in Florida that offered a First Class FCC license. Before leaving, I arranged for J. L. to take over my part-time shift at WLRS-FM, and thus I handed him his first paying radio job.

Upon high school graduation in New Albany, J. L. attended Northwestern University in Chicago for a year before taking a radio job at KEWI, Topeka. Then he moved on to nights in Albany, NY, at powerhouse 50,000 watt AM station, WPTR as "The Wild Child," and ultimately winding up in Baltimore at WFBR as "Johnny Walker." He remained there as one of the market's top-rated and most talked about and controversial radio personalities for many years. J. L. Embrey (a.k.a. Johnny Walker) passed away in early 2004 at a Baltimore hospital following several years of advancing health issues. He was only 56 years old. Although we were not regularly in contact before his death, we did see each other once in a while. When we did meet, we never talked about our careers, just about New Albany, WAKY, WKLO, magic, and the radio station in his basement when we knew—we both knew.

With my First Class FCC license in hand, I returned to Indiana from Florida. This time, it was to Indianapolis, where I continued my college work at the I.U. campus. I also chose Indianapolis because I had submitted a résumé and air check while in Florida to several Indianapolis radio stations in order to secure some part-time work while in school. I got offers from both WIRE and WGEE and managed to work part-time at both stations, knocking down about 25 hours back and forth between them from Friday to Sunday every weekend, then back to school Monday through Friday. I carefully crafted my class schedule to accommodate working.

One of my jobs at WIRE was to be available some weekdays to do news interviews and drive the station news department mobile unit (a hot Dodge Dart). I was regularly assigned to get the "soft" interviews from celebrities or entertainment events, so I was immediately tagged as the entertainment interviewer for the station. Cast members of touring Broadway shows, TV personalities, authors, and comedians were all part of my beat at WIRE.

One such event was an annual magicians' convention at a venue near the WIRE studios. Magic? Radio? Gotta go. While there, I met several local performers from the Indianapolis area, and I also made the acquaintance of a young magician named Marc Berkowitz, who was just starting high school, but who was a huge fan of Johnny Carson and radio. (Magic, Carson, radio, see a trend developing, here?) , so I offered to let him sit in on some of my interviews. Marc tagged along on some of my interviews and hung out at the station while I was on the air, feeding his interest in and passion for broadcasting. Eventually, Johnny Carson actually came to Indianapolis, and I got the nod to do the interview for WIRE. Certainly, Marc *had* to come along for that interview. As it turned out, Marc asked most of the questions. I still have the recording. A few years later, I did some work designing and building a studio for WBMP, a small FM station in Elwood, Indiana. Marc came along and actually started doing some on-air work for WBMP, and thus got his first broadcasting job—before he got his driver's license. Marc was replaced at WBMP by another Indianapolis native who's gone on to bigger things—David Letterman.

I eventually moved on to New York from Indiana and Marc Berkowitz headed for college in Boston. Although he learned that radio was not his best venue, he did begin an outstanding career as a TV stand-up reporter and eventually show host and producer. Today, we know him as Marc Summers, who from 1986 through 1993 was host of Nickelodeon's legendary kid-TV hit *Double Dare*, still seen in syndication since 1988. More recently we've enjoyed Marc Summers as host of Food TV's top-rated *Unwrapped* series.

Having known two high-profile broadcasters since their junior high years was no accident. Even at that age and that many years ago, there were clear clues of the aptitude to become a success in radio or broadcasting. Over the years, as I have moved from air-talent positions into being a program director or consultant, when interviewing candidates for radio programming positions, I am rarely disappointed when I discover some indications of early interest in being a performer in some capacity, either on a résumé or in an interview.

In 99% of cases, a successful career in radio begins with an early determination not to obligate oneself too deeply; to remain flexible and open to change; to resist the temptation to get too comfortable in one spot; and foremost to be absolutely driven by the desire to succeed exclusively in radio. Use every opportunity as a learning experience and develop a professional goal horizon of at least 3 to 5 years from today's job. This means that you will accept no substitutes, and no other career opportunities can seriously be considered, no matter how lucrative or tempting. Getting into radio isn't quite like going into a monastery, but you kind of have to think that way going in. It may be more fun later when they let you ring the bells. Radio probably needs fewer people with greater talent than more people with lesser talent. As I said before, if you're not passionate about it, get out, now! I have frequently been reminded of the sad failure of some talented people to be successful radio people when I review a résumé that looks like this:

Station A for a year,

   then a trial period as an exterminator;

Station B for a year,

   then on to working for a hardware store chain for 2 years;

Station C for six months,

   then to school for a semester while working part time at

Station D followed by

   two more years selling office equipment

   . . . all in the same state!

This person is *not* a dedicated radio broadcaster. A true radio junkie will always work. Only radio. Any station. Anywhere. Anytime. To be employed out of radio is death.

Drop-Ins

The glut of occasional broadcasters or drop-ins (as I prefer to call them) helps to create a shortage of jobs for the real professional. They tie up available positions and deny them to someone who really cares. They ultimately find some way to lose the job. They generally are malcontents in the first place and talk about radio as if it's out to get them and there is some divine plan to exclude them from stardom and wealth. According to them, it's never their fault, and rarely do they have any kind words about anything or anybody in the radio work environment. I'm pleased to say that the consolidation of radio has probably reduced the drop-in rate, since stations now need better-trained, more versatile people. The number of jobs (especially in programming) is diminishing, so each remaining person accounts for a bigger share of the overall programming responsibility. Technology has also played a part in reducing the number of on-air staff, since quality people can now be used at multiple stations and even multiple markets. The exception may be in sales, since the greater effort being placed on developing revenue has created an outreach from radio sales to other sales-oriented business. Sales-oriented individuals may, therefore, decide to drop in to a radio sales occupation for a trial period.

Career Part-Timers

Not to be confused with the radio drop-in is another valuable type of radio broadcaster: the career part-timer, who makes no real effort to pursue a permanent, full-time radio career. These people often have other business interests that occupy their primary career goals. They are talented and are valuable to a station because they are available for vacations, fill-ins, weekends, or whatever. They make terrific employees because they will not likely be leaving for a better radio job, nor will they seek advancement at their present station. This is the same kind of individual who participates in a community theater but would never seriously run off to New York to seek an acting career. Again, with technology playing a bigger role in reducing the demand for air talent, the really good part-timer has become an even greater asset to radio, since the radio station gets the benefit of his/her experience and professionalism at a minimum of salary, with virtually no other company benefits or obligations to provide.

Radio Schools

Many aspects of radio broadcasting can be taught, especially the technical aspect. Talent cannot be taught. It can only be developed from what is naturally there. When viewing radio broadcasting from the outside, it appears that the buttons, knobs, meters, dials, tape machines, transmitters, etc. are incredibly complex and must be very difficult to learn. The talking part, actually saying things on the radio, now *that* looks so easy. The truth is, it's just the reverse. The basic radio operations equipment used by someone on the air can be learned in a few days (maybe hours, with little prior experience at all). But the part about *talking* . . . now that becomes a lifetime quest for perfection. The great air talents, the guys making the big bucks in radio, aren't pulling down those six-figure salaries because they change transmitter power, operate the touch-screen automation system, or get the newsroom on the air on time.

Talent and perseverance are the keys to success in radio, tempered with ingenuity and some good business sense. To seduce someone into broadcasting who is not equipped with these basics is wrong and ultimately very disappointing to the radio school student. Very often, this sort of school preys upon the young and those who may be down on their luck. These so-called schools sell them the dream of becoming a famous radio personality and persuade them to commit to thousands of dollars, worth of borrowed money (often government-subsidized loans), which the student is obliged to pay back after graduation. By the end of the course, you can be sure the typical graduate is far from ready for any meaningful job in the industry. The last thing the student needs is another disappointment, but students are often left with unfulfilled dreams of career success. Frankly, broadcasting doesn't need more people fighting for the few jobs. It needs fewer.

To pretend that there is some school-prepared certification for getting an announcer or newsperson job is simply false. Many career professionals resent the attitude that all it takes to become what they are is 6 weeks and a few thousand dollars in tuition fees. Radio realistically resembles the old European guild or apprentice way of doing things. One learns by following closely behind those who are already in the business. You learn by asking questions, hanging around stations, getting to know broadcasters personally, and listening to the radio, relentlessly—listening and listening and listening.

Although this book is frequently used as a textbook at radio schools, I must offer a word of advice. Many proprietary radio schools claim they can teach becoming a radio broadcaster, proclaiming that you'll be on the way to an exciting, challenging career field. You've seen those TV ads that make becoming a radio personality and getting a job in radio seem as likely as becoming a truck driver, dental assistant, home-repair expert, or legal aide. Always remember that these institutions are most often private businesses and, therefore, their students are actually customers. Although there's never any guarantee of job placement, someone going into a radio career from a radio school has no better opportunity or training than someone coming from any other discipline. Most such schools are staffed by local current (or former) radio people. If nothing else, contact with these people may assist in the networking process that always accompanies successful job hunting. Some hands-on experience with radio school facilities may help to familiarize a newcomer with the technical operation of a station; but classes, degrees, certification, or diplomas have never been required for entry into radio or being successful at it.

College

Most colleges now have a radio facility of some sort. It can be a good way to learn the basic technical skills, but it's not real radio. The real reason high school or college radio is not real radio is that there's *no money* at stake—no sales, no revenue vs expense picture, salaries, promotional budget, or cash flow. At the entry level, there may be occasional opportunities for students in a regular college or high school curriculum to become an apprentice in a radio station. This is probably the best entry opportunity for a radio beginner, since many apprentices go on to become part-time and then occasionally full-time employees, school obligations permitting. Beyond this, there are few chances for entering the industry and certainly even fewer for persons in their adult years looking for a career-change approach to entry into the business.

Remember the old adage, "Those who can do, those who can't teach"? This was never truer than in radio. Like every subject, radio can be studied academically. But the study of radio by an outside, third party is far different from being there day after day. The real reason that an academician is less well qualified than a practicing professional is that the academician's commitment is to teaching and the broadcast professional's commitment is to broadcasting. Yes, I teach radio classes, but I do so as a working, active broadcaster and can readily relate an experience from within days, not years, of the class. Many radio professors do have a valuable contribution to make in the overall experience of a radio student's learning process. But having just done a radio show or attended a station event the week before brings radio from then to now. The proof is in the pudding. As mentioned early in this book, I'm not writing about radio history. That's where the academic approach works. The organizing, researching, documenting, interviewing, and preparation of radio history can be a valuable tool in seeing the path the industry has followed, but it has little relevance to what we need to do *today* to get the job done. It may be a mistake to suggest that a radio historian or college instructor from an academic background (and who may personally feel very intimate toward radio) can be the best source of instruction about the immediate state of the art.

College radio always seems to take one of two paths. The college station is used as a playpen for students in mass communication, music, journalism, marketing, or other course studies. These students come in and play their favorite music for an hour or so each week. It's largely a self-entertaining exercise, and no instruction really takes place. The other path is for radio career-track students. The college station in this case has a structured set of programs, an instructor who is on the faculty to teach radio classes, and a facility designed for multiple radio broadcast and production functions. When I attended college at Indiana University and even at my high school's WNAS, being part of the radio station staff was on a tryout and audition basis. Getting on the radio staff was as competitive and demanding as landing a spot on the basketball or football team. I guess even then, the necessary passion for being a part of radio was being recognized as a prerequisite to entering the industry.

Within the college environment, the best and most flexible broadcasters seem to be the ones who pursued a liberal arts curriculum. Truly talented people from a liberal arts background understand and appreciate something substantial about a variety of subjects. After all, a radio personality is talking to listeners, not himself/herself. The more he/she knows about the subjects of concern to his/her listeners, the more he/she can identify with them. Being locked in a tiny studio and knowing everything there is to know about radio does not make you interesting to someone on the outside. Knowing something about *the listener's* way of life, politics, beliefs, values, tastes, and corner of the world does. One discipline of debate is that you can always win if you know the opponent's argument better than he or she does. A similar application of this rule works with winning listeners from competitors. My advice to new or experienced radio broadcasters has always been, It's all about the listeners. If you know them best, and act accordingly, you win!

SO YOU WANT A JOB IN RADIO? SHOW ME WHAT YOU'VE GOT

Now, supposing that you've decided you have the dedication and commitment to take on radio as your personal career, how do you get a job? First you have to prepare a set of tools—an air check, a résumé, and so on (described next)—before you can even begin to find a job. And once you've got a nibble, that's only the beginning. You must know how to negotiate and how to include what you want in the deal and leave out what you don't want.

THE AIR CHECK

An air check is not the same thing as a demo. The air check represents the on-air experience and sound. By contrast, a demo is usually prepared in a recording studio and is produced especially for a specific job-seeking purpose. Demos are usually assembled when the job applicant is not actually working for a station or not in a desired format. Demos also are produced to demonstrate alternative styles and presentations other than what their current format occupation will permit. On the other hand, an air check is recorded directly off the air during an actual broadcast, then edited later or skimmed while recording to eliminate music, commercials, or nonessential elements. Previously a skimmer was a

cassette recorder while? hooked up to the microphone on/off switch in the studio, allowing for recording of just the announcer breaks. Today, with digital recording, it's easy to record a whole shift and quickly edit out the music and commercials. For distribution and for best quality a CD is still considered the standard for air check/demo applications. Program directors will be listening for voice quality, naturalness, realistic conversational delivery, authority, humor, and content. The CD will also be accompanied by a résumé. The résumé synthesizes career achievements in writing while the demo CD does the same in audio.

Always Have a Current Air Check

The air check should be less than a month old. If you are presently employed, you should be constantly collecting and updating material for your air check. Make keeping an up-to-date recording a regular discipline, just like saving money: tough to do but necessary. A current air check also reflects recent affairs and events with which the program director may be familiar. Hearing comments regarding a recent news item is clearly more timely than a line about the Super Bowl from 2 years ago. Historical air checks from your prior places of employment may be included if they are relevant to the new job or demonstrate a completely different style or format from the format in which you are presently working.

The Air Check Should Be a Composite

The best air checks are composites of three or four shows, giving some indication of consistency and variety. If you've been at the same station for a while, just include several samples of work from that station. It's not necessary to go back 15 years and demonstrate every station where you ever worked, other than a relevant prior station as mentioned previously. Also, be prepared to have a standby full, unedited air check of your work. Occasionally, a program director may ask for an hour or two from the past week—music, commercials and all. This might follow a program director's being favorably impressed with your first presentation and a desire to hear more of you in a more natural setting with the other programming elements included. Many program directors listen to air checks in their car cassette or CD players while driving to and from work or on weekends. A full air check gives the feel of listening to a real radio station. Don't fear minor mistakes on a full air check. No one's perfect. How you recover from an error on the air is part of what you will have to do at your new job and a part of demonstrating your naturalness and ability to think and act. Program directors will be suspicious of an air check that is too perfect.

Don't Overedit

Speaking of too perfect, don't overedit the demo. A good program director knows editing when he/she hears it and will be suspicious of something a little too tight and slick. Edit for brevity or timing, not for covering mistakes. It's not the station who's seeking a job; it's a person, so don't be overly concerned with including station promos and production just to prove how cool your present station is. Never edit voice. A splice in the middle of a sentence just sounds bad and suggests that you're hiding something.

10 to 15 Seconds of Each Song

Include at least 10 to 15 seconds of each song in the air check. This lets the program director get a little better, more relaxed feel for the station where you were/are working. It also provides a natural break between talk segments. Try to include portions of the front and back of each song. Edit the middle of the music so you hear an identifiable beginning and the ending of the song. Include a variety of music types and tempos. Air checks tend to flow better and be more listenable if the person listening has time to let each individual element become a complete thought before moving on to the next element.

Make Music Segues Smooth

Make sure that your different audio elements are blended together smoothly. Watch your audio levels and keep disjointed music mixes off the air check. Don't make it "audio-annoying." Clicks, pops, wows, or other technical glitches should be absent from any good air check.

Short Breaks First

Put briefest breaks first. Always include the basics: call letters, time, temperature, weather, slogans, dial position, etc. Slightly longer bits—full weather, promo liners, ad libs—should go in the middle; finish with the longest bit—live spot, phone call, or prepared material. Show up front that you can handle the basics and can be natural with the repetitive elements of any radio on-air job.

Ideal Length: 7 to 10 Minutes

Ideal air check length is 7 to 10 minutes. Program directors say they can hear it in the first minute and, in fact, might only listen that long. You can tell really bad air talent right off the bat, and usually a really good air talent will be equally obvious. First hearing of an air check is only the beginning of the elimination process. Better to have 7 to 10 minutes of additional material should you make the cut and get a second listen. If you've followed the previous suggestion, and have your short breaks and basics up front, you'll have given a very good first impression even if your air check gets only a 2- to 3-minute listen.

Commercials/Production on Another Track

Produced commercial spots and production/promotion work should go on a separate presentation on a separate track on your CD, not sprinkled throughout the air shift presentation. Having your own commercials on your own show may be overkill, as well as ear fatiguing. Production is production and an air shift is an air shift, each with individual qualities and qualifications.

Remember . . . program directors will listen to an air check until:

- They hear something distasteful.
- They hear something unprofessional or amateurish.
- They hear too much repetition.
- The technical quality becomes annoying and irritating
- They get a good feel for your ability and will listen to more later.
- The phone rings.
- The station manager leans into his/her doorway and says, "Got a minute?"

Make the air check count. It's probably the most important single (other than the interview) item in getting an on-the-air position. Use a neatly labeled CD with name, address, and phone information. Do the same with the CD case. Include the total running time of each track so that the program director knows how much time to budget to hear the whole effort (another good reason to make it short). No handwritten labels, ever.

A word about air checks on the Internet. I'm all for doing everything possible to promote and publicize yourself in the job-hunting process. There are several services available whereby you can post your résumé and even your air check on an Internet site. Although this may be a seemingly expedient and relatively inexpensive way to distribute your material, it lacks one key element—your dynamics. Posting your material on the Internet is a very passive way to job hunt. It requires too much focus and effort on behalf of an employer to find and then listen to your material. I think posting material on the Internet may be an excellent way to offer additional information about yourself, like an expanded résumé, several different professional photos, a menu of different formats, air checks, commercials, and outside interests and activities. After you have made a good first impression and have used personal dynamics to gain the program director's attention, it would be an excellent time to direct the program director to the supplemental material available on the Internet. You've cleared the first hurdle and the new station is interested. The Internet follow-up can add an extra degree of professionalism to your presentation, but don't use it or depend on it to open doors initially.

THE RÉSUMÉ

Once the decision has been made to seek a first-time radio position or to upgrade existing employment, it's time to get to the issue of the two basic elements in air talent hiring: the air check and the résumé. Let's look at the résumé. I'm assuming that most readers of this publication are already in or near the radio business in one form or another. Therefore, here are some résumé rules for those already having some broadcasting or related experience. Since entry-level people come from so many different areas of experience, it's really hard to tell what they should and should not include on their résumés unless we could examine them on a case-by-case basis. Does coming from a bookstore look better on a résumé than coming from a bicycle repair shop? Hard to tell. It's a mystery as to exactly what to put on a résumé with one exception: performing. Always include anything that reflects the ability to perform in public: high school plays, band, community theaters, dance, public speaking, poetry, singing, etc.

The aspect of being somewhat familiar with entertain*ment* and entertain*ing* will get a potential employer's attention better than any other skill or quality. Aside from performing, good future radio people come from many different backgrounds. However, the strongest factor, aside from the résumé, is that it appears that entry-level positions are largely granted by the depth of the impression made at the personal interview. Make the best possible impression with clothing, mannerisms, attitude, humor, confidence, and communication. Here are résumé basics that most program directors look for in a qualified job applicant:

One Page

Keep it simple. A single page outlining the highlights of your career achievements and experience will suffice. Should more be needed later, it can be requested. Resist temptation to go for the shotgun effect, that is, putting down everything you've ever done, hoping the program director will find something he/she likes. Program directors know that applicants have done additional things than what's on the résumé and will ask if they want to know more. Avoid getting too specific about job start/end dates, and try not to ramble on when giving job descriptions. Program directors know what all the jobs at a radio station entail, so you don't have to redefine them in your own terms on your résumé. Make the margins neat and wide with easy-to-read typefaces.

The exception to the one-page rule is for the professional who is at the middle or toward the end of his or her career. If there's more than one page's worth of interesting material and experience, go for two or three pages, as long as what you're saying is relevant to the job you're looking for. Remember, the person who's reading your résumé will keep reading as long as the material is interesting and adds to your qualifications for the particular job you're seeking, so be sure that the second page is to the point.

Keep It Current

Include a current address and phone number. If you move, print a new résumé. Don't erase or mark through the old one. Make sure you include an alternate contact number if you may be hard to reach or moving from the primary location. These days, always include an e-mail address and web site if you have one. If you do have a website, it would be a good idea to really keep it up-to-date with a list of your most recent activities, including activities with your present employer or civic and social events in which you have recently participated. This dynamic conveys to prospective employers that you're not sitting back, waiting for the phone to ring, but are keeping busy and acquiring new experiences. Fax numbers are also important. To have all these avenues of communication suggests to the potential employer that you are professional and have resources that may enhance your employment prospects.

Neatness Counts

Résumés should never be handwritten or sloppily typed. Present only a neat, professionally typed page. Avoid erasures, uneven lines, extraneous marks, or flaws on the page. Make sure you have correctly spelled the name of the person you're writing to and that you have his/her exact title. Word processing software is so commonplace these days that it's almost inexcusable to have any errors on a written page. Have someone proofread your résumé, and accept positive suggestions. You might even have your résumé professionally written and then saved to a disk for easier updates should you wish to make additions or corrections.

Alternate Contact

Don't forget to include a work phone or second contact number. More than a few jobs have gone to other people because the employer could not contact an applicant. If you are seeking a new job and don't want your present employer to find out about it, all the more reason to include secondary contact numbers. At least have an answering machine or voice mail to take calls.

Group Similar Items

Sort experience by type. Rather than a running chronology of everything you've done, separate things and list in groups. For example, most radio people have other interests and other employment associated with their primary radio jobs. This may include theater, commercials, public speaking, or civic involvement. Grouping similar items (or thoughts) makes a résumé easier to read. The reader can see a commitment to a particular set of experiences when they are together rather than scattered throughout the page. The image you are presenting just flows better.

Avoid Nonindustry References

Eliminate nonradio positions unless they specifically relate to the business in some direct way (like a recording studio or advertising agency). Do include experience in television, music, theater, speech, journalism, and technical fields if they relate to broadcasting. Computer or database skills are always good, since modern radio has become extremely computer-dependant as an industry. If you have a professional photo (for agencies or voice-over/talent work), send it. Radio is more and more a public appearance vehicle, and the right look in public can greatly enhance your effectiveness.

School and Study

College degrees, majors/minors, certification, licenses, languages, or awards should be last on the page. This is not a place where the potential employer will look for certifications as much as to see what sort of professional and personal discipline you have. It also implies having set and achieved goals.

Guarantee Delivery

It might be expensive, but send the résumé by certified, return-receipt mail if you cannot deliver it in person. Use either the postal service or a variety of private delivery companies such as UPS, Federal Express, and DHL. All these companies' packages project "special" when they arrive at someone's desk. It is another important way to set your presentation apart from the others. It also supplies you with documentation of your job hunting efforts should you need it for tax or unemployment insurance reasons. I recommend sending your material in a brightly colored envelope, preferably red or yellow. While we're at it, take the time to fax a very brief memo to alert the program director to expect your (red or yellow) parcel.

No Form Letter

Each résumé should be accompanied by a personal cover letter directed to the program director. Never use a form letter or Dear Program Director salutation. If you are applying to a station in another city just because of the station's reputation, make sure the personnel at the station haven't changed. Program directors come and go, too, you know. Even if you have obtained your information from a database, to be absolutely sure your hard-earned, important information gets to the correct person, all it takes is a phone call to be certain. While you have the station or receptionist on the phone, double check the mailing address, phone, and fax numbers. In today's consolidated reality, more stations have changed addresses in the past few years than at any other time in radio history. You might even want to be completely sure who the station owner is.

Follow-Up

When you get the return receipt in the mail or the confirmation from the delivery service, call the program director to confirm that he-she has actually gotten the material. You may also ask about the status of the hiring process and the likelihood of a personal interview when you call. If there is a posted job opening, there may be many applicants writing and calling, so it may be difficult to get through to all but the most conscientious program directors. Therefore, be prepared to deal with assistants or secretaries, whom I like to refer to as the gatekeepers. They alone control access to the decision maker. Make friends, be nice, don't be a pest, and don't let your frustrations at failing to contact the program director be obvious.

A Secret

I guess you'd eventually hear it from someone, but I think it would be unfair for me to write this book and not be completely honest about many radio station hiring practices. The truth is that many job postings are made public to satisfy either internal (corporate) or external (government) requirements, policies, and regulations. Frequently, a prime candidate may have already been selected and must wait on the sidelines until the procedural activities run their course. It's a king-of-the-hill game. The prime candidate has already been contacted and has been offered the job, but if a better candidate shows up in the procedural, posting, and interview process, then the prime candidate may get bumped in favor of the new applicant. Sadly, often the prime candidate has already been promised the position, even a start date and salary; but the station's procedural policy requires further interviews and applicants to be sought, with no intention of hiring them. Clearly, this is a waste of time and resources, especially for sincere applicants whose hopes of a career move are at stake and whose financial resources may be limited by an inferior salary or unemployment. Jobs posted in national trade publications or anywhere in print should be investigated further, since all employers (over which there may be government or corporate oversight) build a paper trail to prove the selection process was fair and open.

A Word to Management and Owners

The rudest and most inconsiderate thing you can do is not to reply, respond, or acknowledge material received from a job applicant. We're talking about peoples' lives here. Even if you have to use a form letter as your reply method for each type of job solicitation you may receive, don't ignore peoples' interest in working for you or your company. It's part of your job as a program director or manager. If you're too busy, reevaluate your time management or at the very least delegate the response to someone else. It may be more difficult to reply to unsolicited applications, but if your company actively sought applicants, then a reply or acknowledgment is a professional imperative if not a moral mandate. The more professional and experienced the applicant, the more effort should be placed on giving a reply. Chances are, although applicants may not be what you're looking for, they obviously demonstrated the ability to perform in other situations and you should respect that. The same is true once you have made your decision to hire someone.

Keep a record of your applicants and notify them as soon as possible that the position has been filled.

NEGOTIATING

At some point, an air talent or program director job seeker is actually considered for a job. There is enough mutual interest to warrant further conversation or a personal meeting. In any negotiations, both sides must win (or think they have won) for a successful agreement. When going to the bargaining table, consider the following:

Nonpersonality Stations

Nonpersonality stations have the least flexibility in salary negotiating. They are looking mostly for a compatible sound for their music presentation. They often have a wide variety of applicants since there are more people in radio with good voices than there are with great personalities. These also are the stations most likely to become automated, requiring an even smaller total staff requirement. They may be automated already, so the announcer's duties are primarily voice tracking or program data entry.

Personality Stations

Personality stations often take the longest to select a new staff member. Chances are, more than the program director alone will make the decision; often the general manager must give approval since sales are directly affected by a new personality. Be patient during the process. It's all right to ascertain status reports of the talent search, but don't be a pest and offer ultimatums and deadlines.

Personal Interview

A personal interview is a must for any radio job. Professionals do not hire/are not hired sight unseen based on a presentation and résumé. At some point, during every radio station job seeking exercise, prepare for and encourage a personal interview. The earlier in the process you can have any personal contact, the better. You'll be a real person in someone's memory rather than just another air check or résumé.

Versatility vs Specialization

Versatility is important in smaller markets where you may be called upon to do a variety of functions. Because of consolidation, you may be required to work several different formats simultaneously. Specialization is sought after in larger markets where you simply have to be terrific at what they hire you for.

Know the Difference

There are big stations in small markets and there are small stations in big markets; know the difference. Ask around. Get outside information. Learn where your station prospect stands in its market.

Here are the best ways to learn the market before going for an interview:

1. Check any ratings reports from Arbitron or other ratings company for information about the number of stations in the market and the competitive status of the station you're talking with.

2. Subscribe to (or phone order) the Sunday paper from the market for a few weeks before you go there to talk. Pay close attention to:

   a. Housing (availability and cost)

    b. Salaries of comparable other professions listed in your local paper (for example, how much does a teacher, nurse, tradesperson, or clerical worker make where the job is?)

    c. Advertisements for food, clothing, retail items

    d. Arts, sports, events, names in the news

3. Call the union local. If the station is a signatory to a union, such as AFTRA (American Federation of Television and Radio Artists), call the local office and get the contract scale minimums for the station (or other stations in the market). Nothing deflates a job negotiation faster than asking for less than what they have to pay you.

4. Call the Chamber of Commerce; request information from it as if you are a prospective new resident (which you might soon actually be).

5. Go to the city personally for a sneak preview of the community and the station. Do a little personal research and ask people you meet about the station.

Because of the commercial interaction a radio station has with other businesses, some job benefits may be available for the negotiating table that are not generally available to other businesses. As a consumer, make a list of the top 10 expenses and/or needs you anticipate must be met by your employment. Obviously, all of them can be acquired with money, but money is only the go-between. Then check the list to see if there might be something the station, sales department or management may be in a position to acquire directly for you via trade or barter in exchange for reduced salary demands.

Here is a list of necessities and luxuries various radio personalities have used in job negotiating:

1. Money (always on the top of the list). Include the following:

    a. Salary

    b. An advance on salary to get started

    c. A company loan (to be repaid)

    d. Co-signature on an institutional loan

    e. Escalating salary (built-in raises)

    f. Company stock certificates

    g. Profit sharing

2. Vacation time: Agree on vacation time before you sign up. Don't be caught in the company vacation policy trap. Any employment agreement supersedes company policy. Rather than express vacation time in weeks, suggest in number of days, which could be used for long weekends or full weeks. Agree to nonratings dates in exchange for length of time. Attend conventions on behalf of the station or company, and then take a few extra days of your own.

3. Relocation (moving) expenses

    a. Complete packing and moving

    b. Truck or trailer rental

    c. An allowance for you to do what you want

    d. Lodging until settled

    e. Apartment/house-hunting expense or service

    f. Air fare to a former city to take care of loose ends a few months following relocation

4. Length of work week or air shift: They want 7 days, but you want 5; they want 6 hours on the air, but you want 3. Use in combination with each other for a realistic schedule; include off-air duties, too.

5. Automobile: Station leases or buys a vehicle outright in exchange for commercial schedule for dealer; assign value to this item by which salary may be adjusted.

6. Automobile expenses: Gas, oil, and repairs.

7. Rent: Apartment complexes and real estate agencies need advertising, too. Work a deal on a vacant unit or reduced rate.

8. Travel expenses: Travel agencies love to promote; accept partial payment in airline/hotel benefits.

9. Home furnishings: Furniture and department stores, decorator shops.

10. Home and lawn care: Sometimes seasonal, but everyone from gardeners to housekeepers needs to advertise.

11. Appliances: Home appliances and electronic appliances (new and used).

12. Personal grooming and health clubs: Hair salons and health clubs love personal endorsements from radio announcers.

13. Medical/dental (not insurance, the real thing): Now that it's legal for medical doctors, dentists, and chiropractors to advertise, request a dollar amount of services to have at your disposal. I don't know why more stations don't provide basic dental maintenance to air staff by trade with a dental office. It's cheaper than paying for the same coverage by insurance.

14. Construction: You may need supplies or materials, but small contractors and home improvement folks rarely have money to advertise, yet are often willing to exchange labor for advertising or exposure.

15. Transportation and parking: In bigger cities, commuter rail tickets and parking lot fees are reasonable requests. Even a bicycle or motorbike may be practical.

16. Child care or day care, private schools: Every business needs advertising or endorsements. If it doesn't currently advertise or have any advertising experience, offer to assist it in developing an ad campaign if it means gaining their service for your use.

17. Restaurants: One of the all-time basic perks. Station must already have a restaurant trade somewhere or it's not a real radio station. Get in on it.

18. Clothing: Basic clothing from stores can be traded in smaller amounts, especially with some cash purchases. More stylish stores may prefer a personal endorsement from a radio personality who frequently attends public events (M.C. jobs, TV appearances, talks).

19. Cable: You can't talk on the air about what you've watched on cable if you don't have cable.

20. Schooling: Get your wife and kids jobs as welders, secretaries, hair stylists, computer operators, air conditioning specialists, or a myriad other certified professions. If you've seen them advertise anywhere, they'll usually trade for enrollment. Some privately owned colleges may accept advertising in exchange for tuition for credit courses.

21. Anything else: Don't be afraid. List your needs; examine them as likely targets for a job perk. You'll never get what you *don't* ask for.

Helpful hint: If you are negotiating with the general manager, his/her time is valuable and so is that of his/her sales department. Don't give the new station a shopping list of insignificant items. If you are negotiating with the program director, he will usually have to check with the sales department or general manager before granting non-salary requests. The station makes no money on trade and salespeople make no commission. Set your priorities for those items that, if provided to you, can save the station some money and give you what you want. Unless you are financially secure, don't accept things you really don't need in lieu of salary. It might be nice to have a new room dehumidifier or a canoe with a trailer, but it doesn't pay the rent or meet the other day-to-day needs. Most often, it's the humble things that management is willing to help with, rather than the ego-boosting luxuries. I'd take a couple of cases of toilet paper or canned soup over a pasta maker any day.

Although ratings incentives are often an important part of a program director or air talent contract, they shouldn't be used in lieu of salary necessary to exist day to day. There are too many variable factors that come into play in ratings, most of which have nothing to do with you. Ratings incentives should be thought of as a bonus or icing on the cake, over and above the employment agreement. When using ratings incentives, be very specific, including:

- The exact day parts and days of the week (M-F, M-Sun, etc.)
- If program director, then overall station progress
- If talent, then shift improvement
- If program director and talent, set up separate goals
- The bonus paid on Arbitron ratings
- Spring vs Fall, or Winter vs Winter a year later, etc.
- What numbers?
- Shares, Cume (discussed in Chapter 5), Quarter Hours, TSL
- How is payment to be determined?
- Percent increase? Tenth share point increase?
- Market rank?

Here's a new twist. If a station manager's position is that ratings don't necessarily (or immediately) mean increased revenue, then ask for an incentive plan based on an override of sales or percentage of gross revenue for a given period. Program directors can also suggest a commission on new business (1% or 2%) on top of the salesperson's commission for each contract written during the period following a ratings result.

In job negotiations, do your homework first. Know going in what you need to accept the job. Don't accept a low salary and then try to scale down your life. Be realistic or you'll be unhappy. You'll also be on the manager's doorstep asking for more money in a few months, which will not help you win any popularity contests. Before negotiating for a radio job, know as much as you can about the market (especially if you are from out of town). Demonstrate flexibility and an interest in adapting. Make your personal appearance and body language say positive things about you. Radio personalities make lots of personal appearances, as well as perform radio shows. You'll be judged by how you will represent the station in public as much as by how you sound on the air. Think of radio hiring more like casting and less like "nice voice, runs a tight board."

GETTING OUT OF A JOB: NEGOTIATING

Getting out of a job is sometimes as difficult as getting into one. As a rule, some mention of departure should be included in any letter of agreement between a program director (or air talent) and management. As sensitive as this issue is, the clearer it can be spelled out, the easier it is for both sides professionally and emotionally upon termination. Voluntary departure usually means the program director/air talent is going on to greener pastures. Management should be sensitive to the necessity for career advancement, and program director/talent should not leave without ample notice and a willingness to complete immediate tasks and remain available (at least by phone) for providing information and suggestions for his/her replacement.

It is normal that certain perks included in an employment contract are surrendered if the employee leaves within the first year, including repayment of any advances or company loans. If you are fired for cause, per company policy, there's little recourse if the company has evidence of any alleged impropriety. Firing for cause should usually be explained to the employee first and the employee should be given the opportunity to resign, if he/she agrees with the company position. In all states, companies must prove cause if terminating an employee, so this reason is rarely used except in cases where there is little doubt.

Regrettably, philosophical or artistic differences are legitimate reasons for termination in this peculiar industry. Ratings performance and poor execution of company-directed policies run a close second. Most radio separations should best be mutually settled. Given the fact that the employee would rather stay, little will make him/her happy other than having management rethink its temporary insanity. Short of that, have a reasonable talk with the station manager and come to some agreement on severance salary, terms, vacation pay due, and a mutually agreed upon public statement explaining the departure. If termination is involuntary, be sure that management provides something in writing to that effect, regardless of what the public statement may be. Don't jeopardize the right to collect unemployment by the inference that you quit voluntarily.

A recent legal phenomenon is the term *hired-at-will*. The term is included in many new employment agreements and essentially erases any kind of cause for which a person may be terminated. In simple words, this term implies that you work for the employers until such time as they change their minds, for any reason. In accepting being hired-at-will, you virtually surrender any recourse you may have for your termination. Keep in mind that it works both ways. If you are hired-at-will, then you may leave with minimal notice, for any reason, at any time. Unless bound by other tenets of an employment agreement, you are free to leave, even to go to the competitor in the same market. I'd suggest never accepting at-will employment if there are other restrictions attached that may hinder your re-employment in the same market should termination occur. I regret that the desire to be employed in radio frequently results in people saying yes to anything just to get the job and then suffering the consequences later. Employment should be a two-way event, so be suspicious if the terms and conditions bend too far toward the employer's side. You have value, too. Part of your value is your ability to increase the performance and value of the company for which you work. Don't underestimate your importance to the employers' overall financial goals and success.

If there is an employment contract with separation terms, it might include:

1. Full payment to the end of the contract, if there is a contract and it so specifies;
2. Payment of 50% of the contract balance (this is a compromise that usually is acceptable);
3. 90–,60–,30-day notice or pay in lieu of notice;
4. Anything less than 30-day pay is unreasonable: 1 or 2 weeks' pay and out the door is unprofessional and insensitive;
5. Job search assistance. Opportunities within the company in other markets, or access to phone, office, the copier, production rooms for a specific period of time.

Get it in writing. Have a third party look over the items and act as a sounding board for any questions. If you use an attorney, watch out! Unless the attorney specializes in broadcast or entertainment law, he/she will suggest all sorts of ways to make everything so legal that it can threaten a potentially good working relationship. A simple letter of agreement will suffice, signed by both parties. After all, you're both hoping that the agreement sets down what will happen when the station is a winner, so it should emphasize the positive elements of employment. Be realistic and be specific. Sometimes, however, it just happens. You get fired.

What are the most important things you should do before during and after the blessed event?

1. Most firings are not unexpected. Watch for clues from co-workers, changes in management attitude market rumors, or just that pit-of-your-stomach hunch.
2. Therefore, résumé, air checks, and references should not be done in a last-minute panic.
3. Get a clear understanding about why you were fired and what future status you have with the company.
4. Get any severance offers (vacation, insurance, etc.) in writing.
5. When we get fired, we feel a loss of self-respect, so go out for dinner or take an overnight trip. A pleasant or rewarding event helps restore self-worth and lets our mind clear.
6. Note in writing about getting fired with a few words about how it felt.
7. Develop perspective about it, including the company's possible point of view.
8. Go to co-workers, shake hands, and wish them well.
9. Don't whine. Show some class; the other professionals with whom you have been working will remember it.
10. Register for unemployment (state unemployment offices don't have a clue about radio), even though you must endure the forms and procedures to get benefits.
11. Contact close friends in radio and explain your status and availability.
12. Bank card companies offer a version of unemployment insurance covering monthly payments of your credit account if you lose your job. Their policy kicks in when you get the official word from the state unemployment office that you've been approved for benefits. Call each of your credit card companies and ask if they offer such a feature. Sign up today to remove a potential heavy financial burden, as well as protect your credit status.

Above all, remember . . . it's not the end of the world. From the moment you lose a job, 100% of your focus and resources should be devoted toward the *next* job, not the *last* job.

BEING AN ON-THE-AIR PROGRAM DIRECTOR

Frequently in the interest of economy, it is necessary for the program director also to be a full-time member of the air staff. This practice is almost routine in smaller markets, but the workload and other station responsibilities at a larger facility may justify an off-the-air program director. In either case, the job of programming the station must be accomplished. Largely it becomes a lesson in discipline and time management. Being on the air can help the program director identify with some of the problems faced by the other air staff members. He/she also can identify and correct problems with the operation of the format that others are expected to follow.

With few exceptions, most program directors have risen through the ranks of being on the air in a variety of markets and formats. At some points in their careers they have observed and modeled their potential program director style after someone (or a composite of several people) with whom or for whom they have worked. Station management should be specific regarding the goals of the program director and how doing a regular air shift can accomplish those goals. I've known some very good air talent who became ineffective program directors because they retained more of the artist than the administrator. Conversely, I've worked with some terrific program directors who were very bad on the air. Somewhere, they hooked onto their ability to work more effectively behind the scenes than on the air. Between these two examples is probably where most on-air program directors find themselves. I actually suggest that the program director should be better than average on the air and be used in a more visible position than just doing one of those popular 2-hour mid-day shifts. New York radio legend Dan Daniel (WMCA, WHN, WYNY, WCBS-FM) told me many years ago, "Never give up the microphone." I think the difference in being on the air and off the air cannot be overstated. To this day, regardless of my consulting, speaking, and management duties, I continue whenever possible to be on the air. Having said that, however, being on the air can give the program director a long list of ideas of things to do, but being on the air allows little time to do them. Whether or not a program director position comes with an air shift assignment, it's never a bad idea for the program director to be prepared to fill in on the air, so familiarity with the studio and its operation is very important.

Here is a checklist of possibilities for on-air program directors. Look over them and see if any apply to you or the program director with whom you work:

1. You have the advantage of empathy with the air staff since you are one of them. Use this to find the trouble spots and operational problems in the studio.

2. Take the opportunity to lead by example. Show them how it ought to be done correctly!

3. Professionally, you can advance a career on two fronts simultaneously, on-air as well as programming management. Learn from each position.

4. (This is a toughie!) You must be able/willing to play by your own rules and follow the same directions you require of staff. Self-evaluate air work; share programming rules and regulations (memos) with a trusted counterpart at another station somewhere. Find another program director (or consultant) whose opinion you trust. Let him/her review your on-air performance based upon the rules you have laid down and have supplied to him/her.

5. Listeners deserve total attention while you are on the air. Don't use studio time for staff meetings or personal business. This is one of the best reasons *not* to be on the air at mid-day.

6. Reinforce the sanctity of the air studio by being firm in asking for no interruptions while you are on the air. Include sales, secretarial, other announcers, etc. A sample memo may read:
    SAMPLE MEMO:

    > *As you know, I am now on the air every afternoon from 3 to 6 PM. I would personally appreciate holding any programming or business discussions for times other than those 3 hours, when our listeners should get (and deserve) my full attention. There will occasionally be exceptions. Please make them exceptional.*

7. Ideally, the on-air program director must walk a fine line between representing the interests of the programming staff and those of management. For this reason, it is necessary to always keep the position in perspective. When push comes to shove, you represent management foremost, frequently requiring the creation of a comfort zone between you and other air staff members. Try to accomplish this without appearing aloof.

8. Reexamine personal relationships with other air staff members. Avoid social situations that appear to show favoritism. It is better to develop the impression that your staff works with you rather than for you.

9. Avoid developing an image of using the position for personal gain at others' expense. Don't assign remotes and talent opportunities to yourself or accept station perks that could be shared.

10. You are a conduit of information between management and the programming staff. Never let yourself be compromised by giving the appearance of being a spy for either side. Developing an even-handed attitude that allows you to manage up and manage down will be crucial in establishing yourself as a good program director.

11. Develop and maintain communication with all the other departments at the station. Establish the ground rules for dealing with each of them. Set up rules and options for having them work with you at mutually agreeable times. Make it imperative that non-emergency administrative duties not be handled while you are in the studio and on the air.

12. Document everything. Save copies of memos, budget requests, promotional ideas, personnel concerns, proposals, and meeting notes. The idea is not to build a paper trail for purposes of indicting someone, but to have a record of the many, many things requiring attention. Occasional review of prior notes can give you perspective on what has and hasn't been done toward programming goals.

13. Have occasional meetings away from the station. A home, restaurant, park, or other nonstation environment can be an excellent release from the confinement of the station. A more relaxed atmosphere is more conducive to creativity and conversational exchange.

14. Attend as many conferences and conventions as you can. Never pass an opportunity to compare notes with other program directors from other markets and formats. Similarly, communicate with other air personalities regarding how they can best execute a superior on-air performance. Share these ideas with your on-air staff.

15. Develop a network of program directors elsewhere in the region (or country) to share and exchange air checks and ideas.

Being an on-air program director has challenges, but it also has rewards. In addition to probably making additional salary by being on the air, you have the enviable position of dealing with the listeners on a daily basis. You answer their calls, take their requests, and give them the information they need. At public events, you also get to share in the show-biz status reserved for people on the air. In the office, a good program director must continue to be creative and instructive with the air staff, diligent, and expert with the format and its inner workings, and an excellent administrator to answer the needs of management. You'll be busy, but not getting things done should never be blamed on the job. Getting things done *is* the job. By appearing or feeling too busy to answer calls, do a good show, write letters, complete reports, and schedule vacations, you'll be advertising that the program director job is over your head and you can't handle it.

THE ANNOUNCER: MESSENGER OR MESSIAH

Radio hasn't always been about the music. It hasn't always been about advertising. It has been about the whole package of putting together a broadcasting station that attracts listeners, and the effectiveness of that can be translated into advertising dollars and ratings success. The key element has always been the human element. I believe that radio personalities are on the way back and that the people who have something to say, who set themselves apart from the music, and who have prepared material of interest to the listeners are going to be the next generation of radio superstars. It depends on whether the person at the mike is a messenger carrying out the format designed by the management of the radio station, announcing the songs generated by a music list from a computer music scheduling program, or a Messiah, imparting to the listener something special, something that invites the listener to connect to what's going on at the radio station, community, and world.

There has been a generation of radio broadcasters with little or no appropriate training on how to be the Messiah rather than the messenger. There are so many radio personalities now who really shouldn't be called personalities because there isn't anything there other than a voice, a weather forecast, and fake excitement about the latest contest. A true radio personality is someone who can accomplish all of those basic elements, but who also brings something new and exciting. There should be a twinkle in the voice of the radio personality that compels you to listen and to make you think that if you don't listen, you might miss something. Let's see more station management allow more leeway for talented, entertaining, and funny people to take chances, to take risks, to try things, to do things on the air that break the normal day-to-day routine of announcing the songs and giving the format basics.

Regrettably, in many cases this permission has been given in recent years all right, but to the wrong people. Talk radio has created personalities who have decided to take radio into risky areas using off-color language, sexual innuendo, gossip, and in some cases inciting illegal activities. That doesn't necessarily have to be the only case to be made for personality radio. There is an opportunity to remain clever, to be observant, and to take pot shots at community figures or public personalities without being demeaning, without being negative, or without coming across as a "wise-ass."

Many of the radio personalities to whom I listened while growing up in the 1960s and in my early days entering the business were people who seemed to just converse with me, who acted almost like they were sitting across a room, whose ability to communicate with me was very one-on-one. I felt like I was being spoken to, not talked at, and I appreciated that very much. Unfortunately, although there are notable exceptions, in the last few years we've created a generation of program directors who have not effectively been able to teach people how to communicate because they weren't taught how to communicate. They were taught how to shut up and play the hits. There's nothing wrong with playing the hits, but if you watch hits-oriented music television, you will still see that the hits are linked together with someone saying something interesting in between. So even television does not exist on just pictures alone; nor does music television exist on music alone. The message that the announcers bring can be an important message to provide in-depth information about the music or the artist, and the messenger can become Messiah by adding some thoughtfulness and care. Give the listener something important to think about. Give the listener a cause of action or a plan, a philosophy, or a rationale, or a place to be mentally and emotionally. Catch the listener off guard and create an even more special relationship between the announcer and the listener.

After long exposure, listeners feel a friendship for their favorite air personalities. They even form mental images of them and are actually shocked when they see pictures or see the air talent in person. There's a friendly relationship there that comes only from the establishment of a unique and individual air personality. The air talent's voice gradually creates a mental image, the image of an old and trusted friend or acquaintance, and the station's other personalities, for example, the support staff for the Morning Man, become members of the family, too, playing roles unconsciously in the listener's mind like uncle, grandfather, smart-mouthed neighbor, or whatever. When the listener tunes in, he/she is even more at home than when at home.

Not only do listeners find a friend on the dial, but they find a helpful one. Maybe it's a group of friends, one of whom brings you the news and another the weather. Maybe one of them is in a helicopter advising you on morning traffic. It's this sense of identification with particular air talent that keeps listeners coming back and tuning in. The less personality that is evident in the person on the air, the less the opportunity for listener identification with that person.

Listeners have learned to forgive their friends on the air when the friend tries to sell them something, but I suspect that there's a limit to this. Despite Arbitron's claim that listeners don't mind more and more commercials, most of us don't want a friend who's constantly badgering us to buy this or that. Expecting too much selling and not enough entertainment from the air talent may be counterproductive in the long run.

Messenger or Messiah? I don't know. You'll have to decide which one you want to be. You'll have to decide whether you, as a radio personality or as a program director, or your company, as a station owner, wants to play the role of being the messenger and passively present music coming in from third parties generated by computers and announcers that offer nothing more than a brief break in between the songs to expound station virtues and promotions, or whether you want to uplift and move the community by putting people on the air who can catch people's attention and move them to some course of action.

THE MUSIC AND THE TALK

FORMATS

When considering the commercial viability of a radio station, one of the primary require-ments is to successfully operate the station within a marketable format. Once the decision has been made to either adjust existing programming or select a new approach, the next step is to go shopping for viable format alternatives. Sometimes this isn't as easy or obvi-ous as it might seem.

Here are the most frequently made mistakes in selecting a station format:

1. Copying something from another market because it is a "hot" format.
2. Researching a demographic void in the market and then programming what *you* think that demographic needs/wants.
3. Getting a financial deal with a format supplier to switch to an economical format, or get swept along by changes within other stations in your broadcast organization.
4. Thinking that music *is* the format; ignoring personalities and information that may also need correcting.
5. Ignoring music and information when research shows personalities may be considered by the audience to be the strongest element in the format.
6. Switching to a format preference of the owner's spouse or relatives. (If this is the sta-tion you're in, get out!)

Music Formats

There have always been different formats available for radio stations. Some of the same ones keep recurring, though redefined from year to year. Here are some examples of the most common music formats, with a brief description of each one. This list is not inclusive; it does not address presentation or non-music elements within each format.

1. Contemporary popular music by today's top recording artists, generally appealing to the young adult audience, or music-conscious adults.
2. Country music, either contemporary or traditional, ranging in demographic appeal from young adults to very old. Has appeal musically, especially to the "life group" that frequently identifies with this format and associated activities.
3. Recent hits from the past decade or so. Largely the most highly visible and identifiable songs. Programmers refer to this as "recurrent based" music.
4. Oldies, songs at least a generation old. Now branching into various subformats as the body of available music familiar to radio listeners grows. Often represents various urban preferences. Appeals to mature adults.
5. Ballads and soft, easy-listening music. Familiar melodies by known artists.
6. Adult music from nonrock background. Includes MOR (usually meaning Middle-of-the-Road, or a mixture of various styles), Pop Standards, Lite Adult Contemporary.
7. Rock in any form, either Classic Rock from the 1970s and 1980s or Contemporary Hard-Edge Rock.

8. Specifically ethnic or urban music targeted directly at a certain ethnic group. Often shares with category 3.

9. Background easy listening, mostly instrumental, nonforeground; can represent both newer and traditional selections. Here it's the sound, not the song.

10. Religious or inspirational. Possibly traditional gospel/spiritual music or contemporary artists with religious or moral message.

11. Classical. Orchestral, chamber music, opera, choral, arts-involved, major composers.

12. Alternative. Counterculture, whatever is not mainstream, changes frequently.

These are general categories, but they are the building blocks that tend to make up the many combinations and hybrids at radio stations everywhere. Depending upon how many different radio stations there are in a market, many of these formats can be blended or merged, forming hybrids. With about 11,000 commercial radio stations in the United States, the clear definition of the word *format* can be elusive. What one market may call Rock, another may refer to as Alternative. One market may define itself as Urban, but in another market, a station playing the same music may call itself Dance/Rhythmic.

Billboard Magazine publishes an extensive weekly set of music charts from which the songs for most music formats are derived. Of course, what chart information means to the music and recording business my not be the same for the radio business. Therefore, although there are many different genres of music, none purely reflects a single statistical chart. As of this writing, here are the chart music definitions as published by *Billboard Magazine:*

HOT 100
The Billboard Hot 100
Hot 100 Singles Recurrents
Hot 100 Airplay
Hot 100 Recurrent Airplay
Hot 100 Singles Sales
Bubbling Under Hot 100 Singles
Hot Digital Tracks

HOT R&B/HIP-HOP
Hot R&B/Hip-Hop Singles & Tracks
Hot R&B/Hip-Hop Recurrent
Hot R&B/Hip-Hop Airplay
Hot R&B/Hip-Hop Recurrent Airplay
Hot R&B/Hip-Hop Singles Sales
Bubbling Under R&B/Hip-Hop Singles
Hot Rap Tracks

HOT COUNTRY
Hot Country Singles & Tracks
Hot Country Recurrents
Hot Country Singles Sales

ROCK TRACKS
Mainstream Rock Tracks
Modern Rock Tracks

ADULT CONTEMPORARY
Adult Contemporary
Adult Contemporary Recurrents

HOT CHRISTIAN
Hot Christian Adult Contemporary
Hot Christian Singles & Tracks

HOT DANCE
Hot Dance Music/Club Play
Dance Radio Airplay
Hot Dance Singles Sales

HOT LATIN
Hot Latin Tracks
Latin Pop Airplay
Latin Regional Mexican Airplay
Latin Tropical Airplay

TOP 40
Top 40 Tracks
Rhythmic Top 40
Adult Top 40
Top 40 Adult Recurrents
Top 40 Mainstream

CANADIAN SINGLES
Canadian Singles Chart

So you can see that radio program directors have a lot to work with.

Nonmusic Formats

Among nonmusic formats, the favorites seem to be:

1. All talk. Topical conversation or some combination of local and national, telephone participation, occasionally part of an otherwise all-music station.
2. All news. Nonstop information, combination of national network and local resources.
3. News-Talk. Combination of 1 and 2. Usually divided by daypart.
4. Sports. Primary coverage of all aspects of sports from talk shows to play-by-play. Often sports coverage is included in the formula for station types 1, 2, or 3.
5. Specialized information. Financial, agricultural, motivational, sales or merchandise opportunities.
6. Religious. Often part of a religious music station, but can be standalone, nonmusic.

One of the interesting things about formats is that the definition of them is frequently different, depending upon whom you ask. How a station defines its own format may differ from how its audience defines it. Many stations have given up defining themselves by format and have sought other ways to make their programming remembered and defined, many not dealing with the issue of programming content at all. Slogans, nicknames, catchy call letters, mascots, and dial-position configurations have recently taken the music definition away from describing stations. Now, with many formats splitting and taking different musical paths from the same root format, it is increasingly difficult to synthesize a single word or phrase to define a format.

It's still important to know how the various stations within it occupy the format spectrum in any given market. When deciding upon format strategy and direction, there is still a need to have some reasonable analysis of who's doing what and how. For this purpose, we've devised a "format-search" graph, which you can modify to suit your own market, but it can be quite revealing when it comes to changing formats or exploring possible voids within a market.

Figure 4.1 shows a sample market-research chart to determine format voids:

Figure 4.1: Example of a market-research chart.

Fill In Stations Who Own The Demo	DEMOGRAPHIC						
	12-17	18-24	25-34	35-44	45-54	55-64	65+
WAAA (Rock)	xxxxxxx	xxxxxxx					
WBBB (CHR)		xxxxxxx	xxxxxxx				
WCCC (AC)		xxxxxxx	xxxxxxx	xxxxxxx			
WDDD (MOR)					xxxxxxx	xxxxxxx	
WEEE (Gold)				xxxxxxx			
WFFF (Ctry)				xxxxxxx	xxxxxxx		
WGGG (Talk)					xxxxxxx	xxxxxxx	
WHHH (BBand)						xxxxxxx	xxxxxxx
WIII (Lite)				xxxxxxx			

On a chart like this, it becomes easy to see which stations are appealing to which demographics and where the voids are. Because we live in a highly market-conscious society, any sizeable demographic group, even though it may be in the numerical minority, can be marketed to and catered to successfully by a station appealing to its interests. If the station is marketed correctly, it should operate at a profit.

FINDING A FORMAT NICHE

When searching for a new format in any given market, most broadcasters look at the other stations in the market to see how much of the market share each station/format commands. The prevailing mentality is that any new audience must come from gathering listeners from the other stations. In adopting this philosophy, there is an inherent admission that every listener in the market has already selected a station, the number of listeners is finite, and the market shares of all stations combined will always add up to approximately the same number, allowing for some audience shifting from one station to another. Now, follow this analogy. (You may have noticed that I really like analogies in describing radio situations. Just remember that's all they are, so don't get so deep in the analogy that you miss the radio point.)

Imagine that 1000 people have been invited and all attend a charity ball (in a community of 2500). The event will be held in a 50-room mansion. All things being equal, there should be 20 people per room. As the partygoers roam around the large house, their numbers per room are constantly changing. Perhaps there are 100 people in the parlor where the piano player is, 50 in the bar, and 1 in the bathroom. Equating this to radio terms, with each room representing a radio station:

Parlor station has a . . . 10.0 share of audience.

Bar station has a . . . 5.0 share of audience.

Bathroom station has a . . . 0.1 share of audience.

Some people are in the hallways moving from room to room, but the hallways are not counted as rooms, and so the total room share is never 100%. As the 1000 people attending our party have been invited from a community of 2500 people, there are 1500 people outside the mansion (in the community) not invited to the party.

With the party example in mind, let's turn our attention to an anonymous (but real) radio market example from a recent Arbitron survey. The market chosen has a population of approximately 500,000, which makes the math easier. Both Arbitron and common sense will tell you that there are always more people in the community than there are Persons Using Radio (an Arbitron term) in the community, because there is always someone *not* listening to radio. In fact, some people *never* listen to radio. Therefore, in our example market, the number of Persons Using Radio is less than 500,000.

Here's the total audience 12+, that is, all radio listeners in the market who are at least 12 years old.

#1 station	13.3 share	Country FM
#2 station	11.3 share	CHR FM Contemporary Hit Radio
#3 station	8.6 share	AOR FM Album Oriented Rock
#4 station	8.2 share	N/T AM News-Talk
#5 station	7.5 share	AC FM Adult Contemporary
#6 station	7.1 share	Gold FM Top 40 Oldies
#7 station	7.0 share	AC A/F Adult Contemporary
#8 station	4.8 share	AOR FM Album Oriented Rock
#9 station	4.6 share	Country AM Country
#10 station	4.4 share	N/T AM News-Talk
#11 station	2.8 share	Classic Rock FM Classic Rock
#12 station	0.3 share	Country AM Country

If we go looking for a format niche, we see the existing distribution is:

Country:	18.2	Total share	3 stations
AC	14.5	Total share	2 stations
AOR	13.4	Total share	2 stations
N/T	12.6	Total share	2 stations
CHR	11.3		1 station
Gold	7.1		1 station
ClscRock	2.8		1 station

We can see there are some popular formats missing from the mix, mostly because of ethnic composition of the market or market size. There's no MOR, no Christian, no Urban, no Lite AC. Of course, no one would make a format switch based upon 12+ numbers. So we'd have to look more deeply into the demographics in the market before saying we had successfully found a hole. We might, however, apply some common rationale by a series of questions or statements to consider from the preceding information.

This market likes Country. Is there room for another station here to take some shares away from #1 and knock off #9 and #12?

This market likes AC; is there room for another AC, taking audience from both #5 and #7, who are almost tied, and maybe force one of them off the format? Maybe that Classic Rocker could make a run at it.

This market likes AOR, but it's a tough sell with a narrow target, probably maxed-out here in this market, since there are two of them and a Classic Rocker near the bottom of the pile that can only hope for the audience leftovers.

News-Talk is hot everywhere; could there be a stronger #2 AM in the format? Maybe that #12 AM Country might give it a try.

These are the mental gymnastics that start the format-switch thought process. The decision is not always based upon the ratings, but usually it is. The station revenue potential is an even greater impetus to a format switch, which is a by-product of ratings performance.

Here's something else to consider, but few station operators do:

Statistically, about 96% of the general population will listen to the radio within a week. This implies that 4% will not. In any given average quarter hour (another Arbitron term), only 17% to 20% of the Persons Using Radio are listening, and 80% to 83% are not. Rather than look for a format niche exclusively within the existing format spectrum, consider developing a *new* product that may appeal the present *non*radio listener. Create new motivations and programming to capitalize on the 80% to 83% who have, for one reason or another, decided not to listen.

This brings us back to the creative process and the question of research. Don't be afraid to apply creativity to come up with something new for your market. Even a clever, fresh approach to an existing format has a possibility of success. Reach out to disenfranchised listeners with no particular station loyalty and create an exciting, new, local product for them. In some markets, the percentage of people without a radio station is significant. If the missing 4% of the population all began listening regularly to a station rated #8 to #12 in our sample market, that station could move into the top five. Many of today's most successful formats are actually playing music that was previously introduced on other formats and presented originally in another setting. So, rather than come up with a new format with totally new content, it can often be very rewarding to come up with a new way to package and combine familiar music in a new setting. "Rhythmic Oldies" is just a hybrid of Motown, Urban Oldies, and 1970s–1980s dance music, combined in a high production setting. Even some of today's best classical stations are getting away from playing full symphonies and concert pieces in favor of a fresher presentation of the most familiar movements and sections of classical material.

So whether you are looking at a totally new format concept or at a new setting for previously exposed music product, exploring the existing shares and existing formats is not the only thing to consider when searching for a format niche.

Sometimes it's what people are *not* listening to that may better tell the story.

CHANGING FORMAT

A radio marketplace is an ever-changing environment, with stations moving, shifting, and adjusting their formats, personalities, presentation, and emphasis in programming from different perspectives. Some stations will change personnel. Some will add more news. Some will change their music direction, while others will change their formats altogether. This creates new job openings while causing other stations in the same market to make the appropriate adjustments to their formats. For music-format stations, the music industry itself is extremely fluid. It creates new types of music that are *hot* one year, but next year are not. This creates the need for further adjustments so that radio stations accurately reflect contemporary tastes. When this happens, there's just one, inevitable solution: a format change. The radio station will change its format and, along with that, it may be required to change its personnel. One of the more traumatic experiences in the life of the radio personality or a program director occurs when management and ownership of a radio station have determined that the radio station is going to change format. What do you do?

A number of stations and station managements, in deciding to change format, generally have already made some decisions based upon experience in looking for a new format in the first place. So information regarding the availability of new personnel and other dynamics of the new format generally have already been set by the time the format-change decision is executed. Rarely does station management decide, "let's change format" and then go looking for the music, the consultant, the program director, and the air talent.

In most cases, the format change is automatically accompanied by some of the tools necessary for implementation. This is either a consultant or a program director. Management often fails to acknowledge the flexibility and the range of talents of existing employees already available inside the station. Frequently, some loyal employees may continue to be loyal employees to the radio station and to the company and to other behind-the-scenes people with whom they worked under the old format. In fact, they will likely continue to become the same valuable assets toward the new format direction of the radio station as they have been in the past. However, some managers still insist that severing all ties is the only way to go. I've occasionally sensed a sudden degree of paranoia by managers who may feel that at some point they will become victims of a mutiny by the old staff members. There's also the suggestion that there could be some sort of negative image created by former staff members who are unhappy with the format change and may project that to listeners and advertisers.

Knowing employees better up front is the best way to anticipate their reaction and evaluate their involvement in the new format. General managers and program directors need to spend more time getting to know, in-depth and at a much greater degree of thoroughness, each employee. A manager who knows employees—whether announcers, news persons, or other staff people—has a much better feel about how much of a team player the employee is going to be with a major change like a format switch. It's fear of the unknown that creates traumatic experiences and the need for massive layoffs and firings. From the point of view of air talent, it's also a traumatic experience because they have been comfortable in what they're doing and, in many cases, were hired specifically to execute the current format. With the new format coming, they are not really sure what their status is going to be. The period of uncertainty is probably the most uncomfortable period in most air personalities' lives.

It's the element of not knowing that raises fears and concerns. So many stations over the years have told employees there would not be any staff changes and no staff changes were anticipated. But even those assurances, verbally given, are not taken seriously. Historically, denial always precedes action; and the words said to comfort people, to keep them calm or from doing something radical on the radio, are rarely effective.

Station format changes need to be executed quickly and swiftly. The only exception to this is in the case of a station sale, which by its nature requires an extended period of time for financing, legal maneuvering, and finally for the approval by the Federal Communications Commission (FCC). During this extremely awkward period, incoming ownership is prohibited from contact with the existing employees because contact would assume that the sale has been approved, and the FCC frowns on that. Conversely, the outgoing ownership is in no position to offer any long-term arrangements, promises, or offers to existing employees. It has little to gain by making financial overtures to employees or to suggest that they apply to the new company at the appropriate time.

At these times, it's important for people employed in radio to have some sort of expanded income base. The rewards of working in radio can be great, but they can vanish very quickly with little or no warning and with no personal reflection upon one's ability. Have a savings account, avocation, talent work, or some other sort of outside interest that may be a profit center for you or your family. This doesn't suggest that a comfortable and secure career in radio is not possible, but just that it may not be practical to assume so.

Format changes and the rapidly changing, fluid circumstance of station ownership have added a high degree of uncertainty to employment prospects and length of employment in the industry. Companies can now own many more stations than was previously allowed. Although more liberal multiple-ownership opportunities are proposed for the future, recent rule violations and programming improprieties have brought the whole process back under legislative scrutiny. With the phenomenon of consolidation, whereby companies may own several stations within the same market, there clearly is a strong, sensible management case for cutting staff to eliminate duplication of effort and function. Savings of this sort, however, tend primarily to be available in the office, rather than in the studio. Some on-the-air positions, like production and news, may also become victims of efforts to eliminate duplication. Be a keen observer. Watch what happens around you. When you see consolidation or changes in station ownership or format, it's a clue that tells you to come to a good understanding about your relationship with the management team. It's also a very good time for you to start hedging your bets by making sure your income and obligations are in order. Prepare to ride out the consequences should they negatively affect you.

Remember when you first started to learn about radio? Remember all of the things that you used to do and all of the formats that you didn't particularly care for, but were obliged to work in because they were required in the learning process? To be sure, the more flexible you are and the more format experience you have, the better able you are to ride out a format change. For this reason, broadcasters entering the industry should not be afraid of *any* format. Work AM or FM. Do News. Do Sports. Do Rock 'n' Roll. Do MOR. Do Oldies. Do Country. Do every format you possibly can to gain knowledge of that format so that you can put it on a résumé and call upon that experience in the future. Radio personalities in major markets who have worked in only one format, who are truly in demand, and and who maintain that they have format integrity do *not* represent most people employed in radio in all the other large, medium, and small markets.

Most broadcasters generally make average but livable salaries and are community-oriented people who happen to be in the broadcasting industry. Nevertheless, they, too, can get caught in a format switch and will need to call upon all of their past knowledge about the new format to sustain themselves in the new format environment. It's extremely important to school yourself by having actual hands-on experience with formats that may occur in your future in broadcasting.

Broadcasters who are now part of an AM-FM combo or market cluster are already working in a multiple-format environment and should take advantage of that situation to learn about other format characteristics. Having another radio station just down the hall offers a convenient way to pick up a few pointers about another format. Study its play lists, listen to its music, and listen to the competition in the marketplace for a better understanding of the types of formats available and how each is positioned to create its individual character. Knowledge of a format, the ability to execute it, the ability to present yourself as competent in the new format, and a good relationship with your existing management are the first steps to survival. But more important is the ability to transfer that feeling of competence and confidence to a new manager, program director, or consultant during a station's format change. This is the greatest asset you will have to survive and prosper within the new format. The purpose of making a format switch is to move the station from a position of marginal success to a position of enhanced popularity and profitability.

Being on the new team offers the hope of more success than with the old format and can ultimately involve greater rewards. By staying with the company and the station, and making it a better station, you enhance your own income and professional growth. Radio stations are not people; they are businesses to which some of us get very attached. Sometimes we even assign them personalities. They are, however, just businesses, and as businesses, they need to reflect the atmosphere of the marketplace and tap into it financially. Many legendary call letters around the country have come and gone. They have lived and they have died with a reputation that cannot be tarnished because it is maintained in the memories of the listeners who fondly remember them. To cling to a set of call letters simply for the sake of its former status is pointless if the station cannot compete in the contemporary marketplace. To defend a radio station ardently simply on the basis of call letters and history is not a wise and prudent move.

If stations are to continue their heritage, they need to do so in light of the contemporary changes that must take place. When it's time to let go (like losing a relative or a loved one), let go. Radio stations are not people. They do not live. They are like our favorite Broadway shows, bands, or restaurants. We surrounded them with visual impressions, which we would like to hold forever, but know that this cannot be. Those in the industry who can move on, who can adapt, who can change, who can let go, and who can accept the new order will be the survivors.

MUSIC ROTATIONS

One of the more complicated and misunderstood areas of programming is determining the correct rotations of the music played on the air. Music policies range from a very tight play list of a few selections that are heavily played for maximum exposure, to stations with massive record libraries where songs are heard every few weeks. There's a place for each type of a radio station and record rotation. For radio programmers working with very contemporary music, the speed of the promotional thrust and the incredibly brief popularity of hit records require a music rotation pattern designed to exploit the image of the station as being on top of today's hit music scene. These same stations also know that, when a song is over, it's really over and it's time to stop playing it. The greatest casualties of contemporary music are songs exposed to the public for a very brief time, enjoying intense daily exposure at peak popularity and then vanishing from the station's play list completely. The audience does not become familiar enough with the song to sustain any memories of it.

In the days of Top 40 radio in the 1950s, 1960s, and 1970s, a station could get away with playing 40 or 50 songs over and over. The top songs stayed on the charts for 10, 12, 15, or sometimes 20 weeks. They were on the station for prolonged periods in various rotation patterns, giving the audience an opportunity to become old friends with the music. Today's contemporary music is in and out so quickly that familiarity simply cannot develop. This situation is creating a potential music void down the line. Today's music will not become Golden Oldies in the same way that yesterday's Top 40 favorites are revered today. Contemporary radio has created a generation of music meant for today only and that will likely *not* have another opportunity to be heard. Stations programming to adult audiences have the luxury of not needing to be trendy or contemporary in their music. They may play a wider selection of music and artists. Since they are not chart-conscious, they are not tightly constrained to play the most commercially marketable songs. Instead, they have latitude in choosing songs that they feel are more artistically correct for the format.

Much in today's world is designed to be used once, then discarded. This is considered good marketing because it creates an always fresh demand. Contemporary hits are treated as disposable goods. Although some would argue that the loss is small, it's possible that some very good material may be forever lost through this process. The advent of the paperback book provided us with personal, disposable copies of contemporary literature. Much of the older music is analogous to the hard-backed book: It will be around for a long time. The new music, probably more because of marketing than merit, may go out with yesterday's newspaper.

In the 1970s and 1980s, there was a type of stability in the Country Music format. There were mainstay artists, whose current records were automatically played. These primary artists constituted an almost predictable percentage of the station's current play list. This allowed the remainder of the available play list positions to be divided among newer and lesser-known artists, giving their material and their careers exposure. The flexibility afforded the format an opportunity to continue bringing in new artists who, a decade later, have become established as mainstays themselves. Because of this, country music has perhaps the widest range of known artists, both past and present, which share the same radio station. As host of the nationally syndicated *The Country Oldies Show*, I've seen that the desire for hearing more of the familiar radio country hits has reached huge proportions.

Contemporary stations with short play lists have record company music research on their side, since each song that is selected for air play has been tested, retested, auditorium tested, telephone tested, and market tested to the point that it's hard to go wrong by riding the crest of a song's popularity. Contemporary music has the additional boost of music video. New music often appears nationally as a music video before it plays on local radio. Music video technology has become a major factor in the promotion of contemporary music. Stations that play a wider variety of more vintage music have no boost from record companies, since the artists are no longer contemporary figures. This chapter is primarily directed toward them. If your station has a very wide play list and covers a music span of several decades, I hope you will find some useful information here. You probably won't read this anywhere else, especially from heavily research-oriented sources.

When radio stations were programmed from a combination of single records and LP cuts, most of the vinyl records themselves were in the studio. If each vinyl LP contains from 10 to 12 selections, a few cubic yards of shelving could literally hold 10,000 different selections. In the days of the broadcast tape cartridge, we were very often letting space mandate our format limitations. We arrived at a mentality where each song gets its own separate tape cartridge, contributing to storage, filing, and cost concerns. A station may actually need

1500 to 2500 different selections to offer a complete representation of its intended format. To cart each individual selection can easily be cost-prohibitive, unless management is convinced that such a large selection is necessary to market the station. Fortunately, many of the new technologies for music storage have greatly improved the opportunity for radio stations to assemble large libraries without going broke. Starting with the compact disc (CD) about 20 years ago and going through to today's computer hard drive, there is now ample storage capacity to access a wide choice of musical selections.

The music is, after all, the product. CD players, including historical music, are commonplace in almost all stations, including historical music. Contemporary formats made the transition to CD rapidly, since it is the medium of choice for promotion and retail distribution of new material. Now, as older material is becoming available on CD, many formats can program beyond the Hit Singles or best of collections previously available, no longer depriving those formats of flavor songs necessary to complete the format. Now, a basic hard-disk audio storage system may cost about the same as 1500 tape carts may have cost in the past, but here again, we're back to selecting a technology.

Here's a novel approach I personally think works best:

"The best resource for determining the size and content of a record library is the knowledge and experience of the professional, mature broadcasters you hire."

There is no resource for music knowledge greater than the amassed capacity of a staff of professional, experienced broadcasters. NONE! Their ability, sensitivity, judgment, and taste can provide more insight into the viability of the music on the station than all of the auditorium- or phone-tested songs in contemporary radio. Know what resources you respect, and go with those feelings. Let them guide you.

The best resource for determining the size and content of a record library is the knowledge and experience of the professional, mature broadcasters you hire.

Other chapters in this book deal with research. Before getting to them, I'd like to take a few lines to say that music research, though a valuable tool, has been grossly overrated and overused as the sole criterion for assembling music libraries and determining play lists. I probably could write another entire volume about music research, but it would be a collection of anecdotal information about auditorium tests, song-hooks, call-out, etc. The fact is, I think radio could be a lot better, more entertaining, less predictable, and far less repetitive if music research were used less and radio programmers (and staff) had more freedom to select material. One way or the other, a station's music library and policy are developed. That completed, the mechanics of putting together music rotations (whereby the library is sequentially exposed to the listeners) can be done either manually or by any one of a series of effective music-scheduling software programs. All are designed to be manipulated toward the music goals of the station. We'll discuss actual ratings terminology later, but the goal is to increase Time Spent Listening and we use the abbreviation TSL to denote that.

Delicate decisions must be made regarding music selection:

How do you play the songs in your library?

How can you effectively expose the music that will create the most favorable image?

How can you make the music work for you?

Let's look for the answers to those questions by first exploring the elements that come into play. The process for circulating songs in and out of the music library and in and out of the daily music play list is called *music rotation*. Music rotation is accomplished by using internally defined descriptions for various categories of music. Not only is every song placed in a defining music category, each also is given additional codes that further define the song's character. This may include the tempo, artist, gender, mood, running time, intro time, and sound sodes, which may further place the song in subcategories, such as rap, soft, twang, etc., depending upon the music format. Because we cannot see inside a computer and because today's music scheduling software is actually a more refined and sophisticated version of the manual systems that went before, it helps to see how the music rotation patterns might look on paper. Then we can better understand what's going on inside the computer. Music categories are, in essence, cycles. A group of songs is played over and over within each category. Other groups are similarly played over and over. The positions within each hour determine which categories are being selected and therefore how frequently we hear them.

For a very simple example, divide a clock hour (60 minutes) into 20 segments of 3 minutes each. Of those 20 segments, 10 will represent category positions for today's top hit songs (approximately every two songs), 5 will represent category positions for new and up-and-coming songs (approximately every four songs), with the final 5 category positions being oldies (also approximately every four songs). The hour might flow something like this, starting at the top of the hour:

Hit/New/Hit/Old/Hit/New/Hit/Old/Hit/New/Hit/Old/Hit/New/Hit/Old/Hit/New/Hit/Old

Music rotations are not hard to understand and can be developed in a myriad ways to characterize the music library for the specific format. How songs are scheduled on the air is a day-to-day procedure, and there's more on this subject later in this chapter (see Rotation Cycles). Philosophically, however, radio station active-air-play record libraries are designed for two basic types of rotations, pyramid and rectangle.

Pyramid

The pyramid type of record library starts with a point at the top and works its way down to a broad base. The pyramid record library is designed for stations that play some new releases and current records. These are the songs that are added at the top of the pyramid and that are played initially with higher repetition and shorter rotation so that they can become known. Over time, if a record remains in the library, it slowly filters downward through the triangle and is gradually played less and less often until it arrives at the lowest level of the triangle. Here it joins the bulk of the record library, which is the backbone of the overall, consistent sound of the station. Each song at the base of the triangle has earned a special place among the recognized features of the station. These songs have become the listeners' old friends. Pyramid libraries/play lists are typical in contemporary stations or stations where new music is frequently added to eventually become a permanent part of the overall library.

Figure 4.2: Pyramid

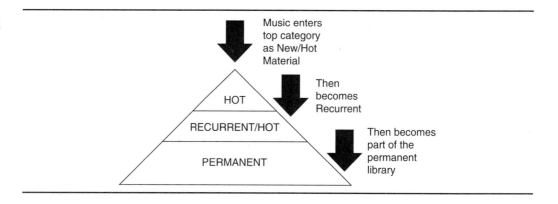

Rectangle

The other type of music rotation library is the rectangle or box. In this case, the record library is divided evenly among the categories that the station plays. The only difference is in slightly varying rotations within each section of the rectangle. The definitions of each section of the rectangle may vary according to format.

Here's an example of a typical Oldies, Classic Country, or MOR format large music library. Consider each category as a pile of songs. The next song played will usually be on the top of the pile in each of the categories. Music is scheduled horizontally, selecting in sequence from each of the available categories of music.

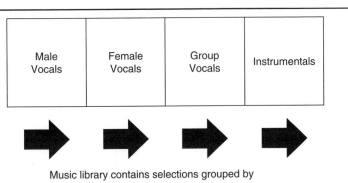

Music library contains selections grouped by Gender/Sound

Figure 4.3: MOR-Oldies Rectangle

In the case of Adult Contemporary stations, music categories usually represent musical eras or years. The scheduling sequence selects the next available song in each category, moving from one category to another for variety and balance.

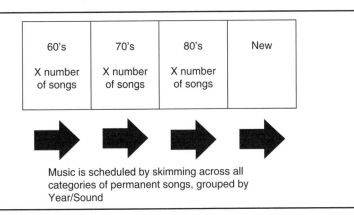

Music is scheduled by skimming across all categories of permanent songs, grouped by Year/Sound

Figure 4.4: AC Rectangle

The same rectangle philosophy applies regardless of how many songs actually are in the record library. It's a matter of how many categories and how far down into each category the scheduling process is permitted to dig to find an appropriate selection.

ROTATION CYCLES

In other chapters we have discussed how radio stations need to have an identity. This identity is most often achieved through the music it programs. How to accomplish this is a radio basic—simple to understand, often difficult to implement.

1. Program management needs to determine what image the station projects musically.
2. It then classifies all the songs in the record library into varying degrees of that identity.

3. If songs do not fit that identity, they should not be in the record library.

4. To carry out the task of projecting the station's image and consistency, *all basic elements of the music library need to be represented in each hour* the station is on the air.

5. If the record library has been divided into four principal music categories, all of which are very important in establishing and maintaining the identity of the station, then all four of those categories must be represented in each hour.

6. In some dayparts, there's more time spent playing music than in others, so the important thing to keep in mind is the ratio of songs from one category to the other, moving from hour to hour.

If only eight songs are played in morning drive:

Three of them need to be from the most highly identified station category.

Two of them need to be from the next highest category, and

One each from the next two categories.

Finally, from the lower categories, select the fill music or optional songs.

When programming other dayparts, where time permits playing 12 to 16 or more selections per hour, follow the same approximate ratio. During these hours, include more selections from lower categories, thereby creating a mood of greater variety.

Segment of Time Cycles

It is not necessary for every hour of the day to be identical. Using the TSL figures from Arbitron, arrive at an estimate of how long each listener spends with the station on average during each daypart. Audience listening habits are rarely broken down into neat, little, quarter-hour blocks as Arbitron has done. Therefore, arrange music rotations based upon a 70-minute, 90-minute, 2-hour, or whatever length of time determined by TSL. Once you have determined the listening cycle of each daypart on the radio station and how long listeners stay with the station during each of them, plug in the rotation ratios accordingly.

Break the age-old theory of programming of developing a program clock that duplicates identically hour after hour. If the station's TSL cycle in morning drive consistently indicates the audience stays with you at the rate of about 45 minutes per morning, then you need to get maximum music exposure accomplished in a period of less than an hour. Conversely, during mid-days or at night when the audience may turn on the radio and leave it on for several hours (statistically verified through Arbitron TSL figures), then determine a music rotation cycle of a similar length or of a time period that is equally divisible into that long TSL segment.

Let's say you have mid-day TSL of almost 3 hours. This could permit you to develop a 3-hour music cycle, two 90-minute music cycles, or three 1-hour music cycles, depending on how creative you intend to be. This is not exactly the most conventional approach for programming music, but for stations with wide play lists, with accurate TSL figures, it works! Not only does it work ratings wise, but the station sounds musically superior to competing stations playing a similar format trying to cram everything into chopped up hour-by-hour block/clock rotations.

As is frequently the case, stations with the best ratings successes have been those that were musically superior to their competitors, not just because of the songs played, but also because of the way programming management successfully mapped the overall music image that the station needed to project.

1. Divide the record library into a few categories, arranging them by priority. There really is no restriction on the number of categories you can have. By classifying the library into a few basic categories, additional category definitions evolve based upon the makeup of the songs in the library.

2. Establish a category of vocal groups. Then, after taking a good look at the number of groups in the record library, subclassify them by male group, female group, or duets.

3. Similarly, create a category of male vocalists, and then subclassify them into male vocalists who represent different time periods or different musical styles.

4. Since each station has its own individual record library, it would be impossible for me to give an established set of categories, but trust me—you'll recognize them the more you immerse yourself in the process of defining the station's music and all the songs in the entire library.

As in the case of determining our record library size by how many tape carts we can afford, we've become so computer-minded at radio stations that we are presently locked in a situation where most computer music scheduling systems are not equipped to handle music rotation patterns in excess of 1 hour. This is a really good feature to determine when shopping around for a music scheduling system. It's also a sensible feature, because you can prove that listening does not happen on an hour-by-hour basis but, rather, over extended periods of time. It's the difference between assigning grades by a strict numerical percentage system or grading on a curve, in which case the full range of student grades is accommodated in the grading scale. The music scheduling system that can schedule on a curve will have a highly marketable product, and you will have the advantage of knowing what to do with it. Even though most music scheduling computer systems cannot accommodate this method of music programming, you can still easily use existing systems by figuring the mathematics required to plug music rotation patterns into the hour-by-hour blocks provided by the existing scheduling system. It's more exacting to set up initially, but you'll probably agree that it's worth it when you hear the results.

Music is sound. Because it's sound, the overall image of any station needs to project a sound that is consistent and representative of the musical promises you make to the audience. The preponderance of today's radio stations classifies music by era, exact year, and chart positioning. None of these relates to the sound of the song. What *does* relate to the sound of the song are its sound qualities, which include tempo, instrumentation, male, female group, vocalization, and the subclassifications having to do with the musical style. One can identify whether a song is choral, country, acoustic, or orchestral by its sound rather than by knowing about the artist, the song, its chart position, or the year it came out.

When setting up the music rotation system, determine both the variety and range of sound qualities that are available within the library. Give each sound quality a priority ranking. Then classify songs by those sound qualities. This should be your primary consideration. Reserve the nonsound characteristics as secondary. If two different songs represent a similar sound, even though they may have been recorded 20 years apart, it would be wrong to play them back-to-back. A music scheduling system with no sound priorities would not recognize this, which is the greatest flaw of computerized music scheduling. A computer can know everything about a song except what it sounds like. That's why assigning a musical identity must depend almost entirely upon the human element in charge of classifying the library song by song.

At the beginning of this chapter, I mentioned how space and economy seem to be determining factors in the length or size of the record library (an undesirable, but inescapable, reality). Then, consider this (and here's where some of my engineering friends cringe). If a station has a priority record library of 800 to 1000 carted selections, a simple turntable and a few more yards of shelving can provide double or triple the number of selections to be played on the air. Considering that record albums, the LP variety, were state-of-the-art technology for almost four decades, we might be oversophisticating ourselves to think that there cannot be a practical application for that technology in today's CD, DAT, digital high-tech radio studio.

Wide-play-list radio stations play songs from the era in which high-quality vinyl was produced. If there are still reasonably high-quality recordings available, use them, playing low rotation material from a turntable if it can greatly enhance the musical image and complexion of the radio station, which I believe it can. If you're really lucky, you might convince station management to go ahead and spring for the additional carts or hard disk storage necessary to contain the whole record library. Also remember that you don't have to keep 100% of the library available for play all of the time. Some selections, or groups of selections, can be phased in and out of the play list library every few days or few weeks.

As a station consultant, program director, and air talent, I must admit that music programming to me is an extremely intimate thing. It can't be reduced to mere technology and research. I have often been accused of being a gut-reaction program director because I prefer using people skills, intuition, and the knowledge and experience available to me from my own background and the backgrounds of my staff members over researched and tested material.

If I am called one of those gut-reaction programmers, then I feel obliged to respond that programming music does not come from the gut; it comes from the heart. A radio station that has no heart will have a difficult, if not impossible, time establishing a lasting relationship with its listeners.

MUSIC TEMPO

Except for length, the tempo of a music selection is one of the most important bits of programming information. Through the correct usage of tempo, the entire rhythm of the station can be altered from a slow-paced, easy-listening approach to hot, contemporary delivery, with essentially the same record library.

Typically, stations use SLOW-MEDIUM-FAST or DOWN-MEDIUM-UP designations for record tempos. Occasionally, there is a combination of two different tempos (usually when the Music Director can't make up his/her mind), such as MED/FAST. Determining the actual tempo of a song has usually been left to the whim or daily mood of the person dubbing the music or typing the cart labels. Now, here's a foolproof way to get accurate tempo information for a station's music.

Long, long ago, before Radio, a musician/scientist somewhere in history invented a *metronome*, a device that ticks like a clock and can be adjusted to tick at variable tempos. Later on, these ticks were assigned numerical values that in turn were put in writing on sheet music to give conductors or musicians the desired tempo of the composition. Well, wouldn't you know it? They're still making metronomes today, both mechanical and electronic. They can be purchased at any music store for about $15 to $50, depending on the type you want. All metronomes have the same numerical scale that corresponds to the tempo of the ticking sound it makes.

Here's the best way to correspond the music values to numbers:

Beats per Minute	Tempo
40 - 72	1 (Slow)
76 - 100	2
100 - 132	3 (Medium)
132 - 168	4
176 - 208	5 (Fast)

When adding songs to the music library, dubbing to cart or hard drive, have someone (preferably, with a slight musical ear) listen to the music while adjusting the metronome to the overall tempo of the music as it plays. Then assign the appropriate numerical value to the song. From this, indicate through the music-scheduling system (manual or computer) the tempo rules and regulations desired for the sound of the station. The chart is a recommendation for most music. Develop more gradations in the scale if station music policy needs tighter definition. Although every significant brand of music scheduling software has a variety of characteristics that can be assigned to every song, the tempo seems to be consistently on a 1 to 5 scale. Resist the temptation to guess about song tempo. A simple metronome is mathematically accurate and defeats any personal prejudice of a person's mood at the time. I just had a great day, so every song sounds happy and bright. It's raining and my rent check just bounced; every song is a downer. Get the idea? No opinions are expressed, there is only the actual numerical value of the music tempo as determined by the metronome. There is absolute consistency in determining music tempo by this method. I am also of the opinion that, subjectively, this process reinforces the fact that we're dealing with music, a highly creative and technical art form.

While we're on the subject of music tempos, I offer this word of caution. Frequently, there is some concern about the tempo of song "intros" vs the overall tempo of the whole song. For instance, a song may be a 4 on the music scale, but the intro is about a 2 for the first 12 to 15 seconds or so. For purposes of good sounding segues, some programmers and music-scheduling software will allow indicating both tempos, such as 2/4 (song's opening tempo is a 2, then the overall tempo is a 4). Segues are important, especially when there is no scheduled production elements or liner to assist with the flow from one song to another. Some song segues are so bad that I refer to them as "audio train wrecks" and they are as hard on the listeners as they seem. Abrupt changes in level, tempo, or style can distinctly alter the perception of the desired sound of the station.

Be careful! Since most songs run 3 to 4 minutes in length (at least), you should be more concerned for the *overall* music "feel" of the station rather than the few seconds at the beginning or end. So don't get too caught up in ideally matching segue tempos, if it is at the expense of the total hour-by-hour sound of the format. As air staff become familiar with the music, the segues should take care of themselves. One disadvantage of automation or computer-generated programming is that the computer can never "hear" the song. Only a person knows what a song sounds like.

A computer always depends on the reduction of every song to a series of mathematical values and rules. Most music-scheduling software has gotten more sophisticated over the years and can now include additional song values for each selection in order to "tell" the computer more information. This assists the computer to tune the way songs sound more finely when programmed next to each other or throughout the hour. This is certainly closer than a simple, single-digit value, but still not perfect. Of course, each individual song is only a fraction of each hour, so how the entire hour is programmed and the values assigned to each song position within the hour is equally important.

In developing the overall tempo rules for the station, here's a good way to see the total hour by "averaging" the tempos into a numerical scale.

1. Add the tempo numbers (1-5 each) of all the songs in an hour.
2. This gives a total for the hour.
3. Divide by the number of selections scheduled.
4. This gives the "average" for the hour.
5. For example, in a 6-song AM drive hour:

   Song #1   Tempo 3
   Song #2   Tempo 5
   Song #3   Tempo 4
   Song #4   Tempo 2
   Song #5   Tempo 3
   Song #6   Tempo 4

   Tempo total = 21 (6 songs = 3.5 average hourly tempo)

6. Assign a minimum hourly average for each hour or daypart, in this case, for the AM drive we might have a rule requiring a 3.8 hourly tempo average to keep things brighter, in which case we would exchange for songs #1, #4, #5 for songs with higher tempo values to get the hourly average up to the 3.8 rule.
7. Let the hourly-tempo-average rules reflect the changes in the mood of the station throughout the day, probably permitting a lower average tempo during mid-days and at nights, but higher in drive times.
8. Most computer music scheduling systems offer this feature as a built-in rule-setting opportunity. It's important to use it as an important part of designing the music-scheduling requirements for the station.
9. If you have a manual system, just do the math.
10. Consistently monitor the sound of your radio station. Don't be afraid to make frequent "fine-tuning" to your music scheduling and rotation pattern. They are imperceptible to the audience and add variety to the sound of the programming.

THE GREAT MUSIC SHIFT

Shifts in music are not unlike shifts in spoken languages. Both the English language and the German language early in their development underwent a great consonant shift. That is, certain unvoiced consonants shifted to voiced consonants, and their unvoiced counterparts shifted to set them apart from their derivatives. We still see/hear this today when comparing languages from these roots. In the same way, popular music in the United States underwent a strong shift in the 1960s. This shift marks a divide between those who grew up before the shift and those who grew up during and after it. Many of the older group still don't identify with postshift music. It should be noted that the shift affected popular music almost exclusively; country, classical, jazz, and other types of music continued their slower, more natural evolution.

The great music shift involves almost all elements of popular music.

- Big bands and big orchestras shifted to smaller, stand-up stage bands.
- Horns and strings gave way to electric guitars and bass.

- Wholesome gave way to a grungy, doper image (Doris Day became Janis Joplin).
- Lyrics shifted from simple to complex.
- Lyrics shifted from sentimental or romantic to harsh and realistic.
- Voices shifted from smooth and mellow to harsh and naturalistic (Bing Crosby became Bob Dylan or Rod Stewart).
- Articulation shifted from clear and accessible to difficult and sometimes obscured.
- Vocal power shifted from strong to amplifier boosted and sound processed.
- Love and romance became more frankly sexualized.
- Rhythms that may have been slow or moderately fast became faster.
- Emphasis on melody shifted to emphasis on rhythm.
- Lyrics became more poetic in the sense that they became more personal to the artist and, often, more sophisticated. (Moon and June gave way to contemplated and dilated.)
- Pieces as a whole became less immediately accessible but more rewarding during repeated careful listening.

The Great Music Shift didn't happen overnight. Its roots are in the Rock and Roll of the 1950s, but the 1960s were one of the richest periods of popular music ever. A short listing of who was on the scene gives you an idea of the variety and depth of what was on the dial. There were Peter, Paul, and Mary; Joan Baez; the Beatles; Jimi Hendrix and Janis Joplin; the Mamas and the Papas; Bob Dylan; and so on. Probably no other decade rivals this period as a period where the popular musical salad bowl had so many ingredients.

If there's anything sad about it, the sad thing is that the diversity didn't last. Perhaps because of commercialization, the rock bands all settled into business as usual and into more or less imitating one another. Folk faded from the scene. Groups like the Bee Gees, the Beatles, and the Mamas and the Papas left town and were replaced by single vocalists backed up by their band members. Innovation slowly faded, and pop music on the airwaves became dominated by Disco. Disco's strength was that it invited people to dance to the radio, something they hadn't really been able to do for a long time.

Whether all of this was good or bad, I'll leave for you to decide. What you need to be aware of, however, is that there isn't any American lifestyle. There are people in America today who are living just as they lived in whatever decade they grew up, and their musical preferences are rooted in the same place. Nothing is set in stone, however, but 9 will get you 10 that pre-Great-Music-Shift-People won't have much tolerance for Dance or Urban or Contemporary Hits, while younger people equate Swing with opera and classical music. It's both silly and accurate to describe a singer like Sinatra as classical, but in the real sense of the word, the work he did has become classical.

DAYPARTS AND DAYPARTING

Radio listeners have different listening patterns. People listen to the radio at different times for different reasons. They may want more information in the morning to help plan their day: weather, time, information about the day's community events, or news from overnight. Morning radio has always had and always will have the highest listenership of the industry. In the morning, most people feel the need to be caught up on what they might have missed while they slept. From the time the late evening TV news goes off until waking the next morning, most people are in a news and information blackout. Therefore, there is an imagined (if not actual) urgency or at least curiosity about what went on around the world and down the street while they slept.

Let's do another analogy. Imagine a radio station as being like a restaurant. Each time segment of the day has specific items available on a menu that is designed to meet the customer's demands, whether for breakfast, lunch, or dinner. Continuing with the radio/restaurant analogy, one can expect more than just breakfast, lunch, and dinner specials. There are substantial offerings of selections available, interspersed throughout the menu, which offer some basic, dependable, always-in-demand items that are available around the clock, while at the same time offering variety and special items only available at that time of day.

Radio stations do the same thing by the highly sophisticated term *dayparting*. Based upon researched or estimated listener levels, the broadcast day is divided into segments called *dayparts*. A slightly different menu is served during each of those dayparts, reflecting the likely environment of the listeners and their preference for entertainment and information at those times. Even though the menu changes through the dayparts, it still delivers the basic, consistent elements on which the audience has come to depend and by which the station is identified or defined. Although there are distinct changes throughout the day, there also is consistency in the overall expectations of the listener toward the radio station.

Most stations are defined by their formats, most often music. Therefore a station's music is generally its defining element. A station may infuse more information in the morning and less influence later in the day, but it always plays the songs that identify and sustain the format image. It just plays them in different numbers at different times. In other situations, the station may wish to designate certain songs to be played only at specific times of the day or night, because the audience targeted by those songs is available in greater numbers at night or on weekends. Thus, a station may sound substantially different from one daypart to another. This type of programming takes advantage of assembling parts of several different available listening audiences. If it is not done carefully and the dayparts are too different, a station runs the risk of alienating its audience and sending them to a competitor.

Here again, it is necessary to retain some identifying elements throughout the station's menu, even though the music and information balance may change throughout the day. How a station decides to daypart itself is largely determined by the needs of the marketplace. Often, those needs are dependent on the number of stations that serve the market. The fewer stations for the listeners to select from, the safer it becomes to include more diverse programming elements throughout the day. The more stations, the greater the need to pick a single objective, then narrow the format to include only elements that identify the station's image, and avoid including too many outside diversions. In either case, the programming complexion of a station falls into some typically similar patterns, as shown next.

Let's take a look at a few other examples of dayparting. From the examples listed here, write the call letters of one or two stations in any market that follow the patterns described. By the time you get to the end, you will most likely have listed all the major stations in that market:

- Strong morning personality with minimal music; music intensive thereafter.
- Music format all day; talk mid-days and nights.
- Music or talk shows with regular long-form sports or play-by-play.
- Regular programming weekdays with special weekend programming including countdowns, religious or public affairs, interviews, retrospectives, etc.

- Information-intensive morning show with talk and interviews thereafter.
- Music varies widely depending on daypart, but personalities all sound similar.
- Consistent music balance 24 hours with different personalities for each daypart.
- Ethnic programming. Music mixed with special shows.
- Full service; puts together music, interviews, public affairs with no loss of identity.

The opportunities and variables in dayparting are limitless, but the important thing is to be sure the dayparted programming accomplishes the goals for which it is designed. All ratings services throughout the history of radio to some degree have encouraged stations to explore dayparting by publishing their ratings reports using dayparts as part of the ratings analysis. Although ratings services suggest specific hours to be designated as "standard" dayparts, there is an increasing tendency toward more "custom" dayparts. Be sure that the dayparts you establish for your station are based upon the true listening habits of your listeners and really reflect some parallel between your station and the market overall.

In many countries outside the United States, *block programming* is the rule. Both long-form and short-form programs are scheduled throughout the day, mixing widely varying types of music and information. Radio is scheduled more like television on a program-by-program basis. To a degree, this is a form of dayparting, since the programming reflects the time of day and the listeners' environment (i.e., a soft jazz program late at night, an extended news program in early evening, and an entertaining talk show during midday). However, as countries develop more radio stations with full-time 24-hour formats, the practice of dayparting within the format will naturally occur.

Arbitron and most other ratings services have divided the regular weekday into dayparts:

6 AM-10 AM	Monday-Friday	Morning Drive
10 AM-3 PM	Monday-Friday	Mid-day
3 PM-7 PM	Monday-Friday	Afternoon Drive
7 PM-12 AM	Monday-Friday	Evenings
12 AM-6 AM	Monday-Friday	Overnight

These time periods are referred to as *standard dayparts*, although new ratings software now allows an infinite and creative opportunity to define dayparts in every possible configuration. However, the standard dayparts remain a ratings staple. Regardless of how they are eventually defined, let's not just look at these only as periods of time; let's consider them as performances, like a movie schedule. Let's also then consider that each of these performances will appeal to a different audience, since different people are available to attend at different times of the day, as it suits them.

So we apply some research, ratings analysis, and common sense and come up with the probability that the 6 AM–10 AM performance will have the largest audience, so let's give them the works with a multifeatured morning show and high-profile personality. By 10 AM, the morning audience has left, so let's do a slightly different show for the mid-day crowd, and so it goes. Opening and closing the doors several times a day permits entry of new audiences for each daypart.

To avoid confusing the audience, especially the listeners with ratings diaries, it is generally thought that we should not change the personnel in mid-show. This sort of thinking is the primary reason for assigning or hiring announcers to work shifts that coincide with ratings company standard dayparts. But as mentioned, computer technology now permits custom design of any daypart configuration, whether or not it follows the

Arbitron dayparts. Arbitron still retains the basic five-daypart daily format for its printed quarterly report book. For stations not blessed with the computer information, the ratings companies' defined dayparts are gospel. This is also the way advertising agencies and buyers of radio advertising time have come to define a radio station's success or lack of it. The rationale for the use of predefined dayparts is that these daypart breaks appear be the ideal times to change announcer shifts or phase-in dayparted programming elements. Having the programming follow predefined dayparts suggests that success or failure can be isolated and identified with whatever (or whoever) is on the air within that specific daypart.

Problem: The predefined daypart policy runs into trouble when it fails to take into consideration the times of day the *listeners* actually tune in and out of the radio station. If the morning audience is already out of its cars and at work by 8:45 AM, what's the purpose in continuing the morning personality and the information until 10 AM? Similarly, drive time in the afternoon in many cities is over by 6 PM, yet the afternoon drive air talent hangs in there until 7 PM. In such circumstances, the ratings for a 3 PM to 7 PM shift may be compromised because the audience drops off drastically at 6 PM, averaging three strong hours with one very weak hour. By the same token, in an early-rising "shift-work" community, many listeners are up and going by 5 AM or earlier. A 6 AM to 10 AM morning shift might only truly represent a portion of the morning audience, but 5:30 AM to 9 AM may more accurately represent the reality. There may be significant advantages to developing the station's daypart structure on ratings presentations and a sales strategy that is defined by listeners' actual habits.

It is very possible that scheduling announcers across predefined dayparts can help to even the difference between stronger and weaker air talent: For example, how about keeping that morning man on past the morning audience because the mid-day talent is weaker? Radio air talent are rarely chameleons (despite their claims), and many personalities do not effectively change with a different shift. Some are more flexible than others, but a station should always tailor each daypart with the right person. This becomes something to consider when promoting from within the staff. We can all certainly appreciate company loyalty and rewarding someone for a job well done, but never lose sight of the ultimate goal of the radio station: Be a successful business.

A good program director may be the most popular person at the station, but it's not a requirement. A person working overnight in a factory may seek to get a day shift, and via seniority and merit, get such a shift when one opens. Is this a practical way to reassign radio air talent? Despite all the things that can be said for boosting station morale, the winning programmers say no. However unpopular this might make them internally, they usually get better results by seeking a specially qualified person for the shift rather than upgrading someone who is less qualified, because he or she is already on staff. In baseball, you wouldn't give a shortstop the open position at catcher because he wants a better view of the game. If someone on staff really is qualified to move up, then the programmer should recognize this and make the staff upgrade. The harsh reality is that no one survives if the station is a failure. The necessity of putting the human element aside for programming and daypart needs is often a difficult but critical element in successful programming.

Make sure that you do your homework and study the actual times and quantities of audience flow. Position the station to the advertising community this way as well, and generate support through sales presentations. There will always be advertisers or buyers who will routinely base station value/worth on the predefined daypart averages. There's nothing you can do about this, since the numbers are the numbers. But you can develop and promote a significant position that the station represents in the market by providing information about the station's real dayparts. It may indicate the ability to maximize an advertiser's dollars. Go ahead. Raise some doubt in the mind of an advertiser about whether they are buying efficiently when they select a competing radio station using predefined dayparts.

It's also important to note that most commercial advertising scheduling software now interfaces with ratings data. Modern stations with up-to-date technology can now generate extremely exotic and custom-designed dayparts for the purpose of getting maximum exposure to a particular audience for a specific advertiser, regardless of what the programming happens to be at the time. Ultimately in ratings-driven advertising buys, it's the numbers of listeners and the demographic they represent. How those numbers are generated through programming is of little consequence as long as they exist. The practice of "selling by the numbers" has extremely practical business and revenue ramifications, but it also can be another factor that can alienate any mutual understanding between sales and programming.

VIRTUAL PROGRAMMING

Virtual programming is a fancy word for automation, and automation (satellite or local) has allegedly had an impact on the employment status of thousands of people in radio for the last several years. Automated programming is nothing new. If we look back at the history of radio, we can see that almost since the beginning of the industry, technology has been used to make programming simpler, cheaper, and with greater control of content and time. Since the very beginning of radio, the industry has gone through change after change to streamline programming, any one of which could be considered the virtual programming of its time. There's really nothing new about creating "walk away" time at a radio station for the purpose of making the job of keeping programming on the air easier or allowing the operator to do more things during the time he/she is responsible for the programming. So, while we are dazzled by the accomplishments of today's technologies, if we look back, we'll see a series of other benchmarks in radio that were (in their time) the building blocks of what we are today calling virtual programming. I've generalized the dates (remember, this is not a history book), but you'll get the idea about the evolution of the process.

- In the 1930s, the members of the studio orchestra, fired from a radio station, left grumbling about being replaced by the use of recordings of bands and singers, rather than live music.
- In the 1940s, announcers doing live commercials and actors on live programs were replaced by "electrical" transcriptions, recorded in advance or shipped in from outside sources.
- In the 1950s, audio tape was widely used to provide programming to FM music stations, with clunky, automated reel-to-reel machines doing all the work.
- In the 1960s, tape cartridges, easily mounted in racks on the studio walls all but completely replaced vinyl recordings for playing music, thereby eliminating cuing up records, slipping them in and out of their pasteboard jackets, and refiling them to the music library.
- In the 1970s, we got more sophisticated with our cart machines and taught them how to sequence from one to the other, creating seamless stopsets, using audio tones on the tape to trigger the next cart to play the next spot. Later, this was also accomplished with songs, allowing significant walk-away time from the studio (depending upon how many cart machines you had).

- In the 1980s, the computer became a routine tool for scheduling music, spots, and serving as the controller for the playback of programming.
- In the 1990s, it was all about hard-disk storage. Mechanisms and machinery with moving parts have given way to hard-disk digital storage of everything from music and commercials to the insertion of announcer voice tracks. An entire 24-hour, 7-day-a-week radio station can be programmed from a device about the size of a microwave oven.
- Now, in the 2000s, if we're not careful, the programming of the first decade of the new millennium will also have the personality and the creativity of a microwave oven.

Get the point? The logical progression of radio technology has led us to the place we now are in developing new ways to generate programming. The concept of using any form of mechanics to sound live was always the goal. Although the goals internally at the radio station were for maximizing quality control and time efficiency of staff, the audience has been largely left out of the process except to be bystanders and witnesses to the programming. As formats have become less and less human, requiring less and less personality and more music, strung together with production elements, it has become far simpler to create virtual programming to replace it. It is as if the industry has been gradually, over the past decade, bending programming into a shape that will easily fit into the necessary limitations for easy duplication by a computer.

Think of it. Listen to most of the contemporary radio formats. Can you really tell which ones are live and which ones are not? How many radio stations operate by lengthy much-more-music sweeps and minimal announcer presence? How many stations today offer clusters of 10 to 12 commercials in a row at a specific time each hour in order to claim they are playing more music?

Consolidation and the related economics of paying for and operating radio stations have played a huge part of the accelerated development of virtual programming. Almost every major player in today's radio megacompanies has announced the development and use of extensive programming technology to operate more effectively and economically. Simultaneously with the announcements of acquisitions of group after group of radio stations have come parallel announcements of the development of in-house networks, inter-market sharing of announcers and resources, as well as consolidation of facilities.

Let's step back for a reality check. It's still all about the listeners. As we have said throughout this book, the success of radio results from the development of an intimate relationship between the radio station and the listener. How we combine, consolidate, engineer, or otherwise manufacture programming still needs to accomplish that goal. The assembly of the audio elements is not the same as communication, nor does it guarantee the development of a relationship. Another aspect of the impact of virtual programming is the reduction of staff for promoting and representing the radio station in public or in the community. Unknowns, who may be not-on-the-air members of the promotion department, are now handling jobs and responsibilities once held by announcers and radio personalities, with whom the audience had a personal kinship. In many cases, these same people do similar duties for every station co-owned within a market. Virtual programming has yielded virtual promotion.

The long-time benefit of radio has been its localization. Even by law, each radio station in the United States is licensed by the Federal Communications Commission to serve a local market. Local traffic reports, sports coverage, weather, and community events have been the mainstay of local radio since its inception. As radio has become more homogenized and the personal aspect removed, the ability to be responsive to local needs diminishes geometrically. Further, no matter how slick, tight, high-tech, or seamless virtual programming may be in a local market, the relationship breaks down at the simplest moments. Who will answer the phone when a listener calls? Who will follow up on the traffic accident on Main Street? Who will say a special hello on the air on Monday morning to people met over the weekend at a station event? Who will answer the letters, play the requests, and be a part of the local market every day?

Don't get me wrong. I love all the new technology. But I'm seriously concerned that the ability to do so much more has resulted in the desire to do so much less. If we could have continued the development of effective personalities and intensified local involvement and coverage of local events or community issues, that could have resulted in magnificent results for local radio with the addition of the new technologies. Rather, it has apparently lessened the obligation to accomplish those things as a trade-off for profitability.

On the one side, we have heard our sales and industry organizations expounding the virtues of radio over print or television for advertising. Yet the percentage of advertising dollars nationally allocated for radio, although finally growing in recent years, had remained stalled in single digits for decades. At the time when the technology to do so much more with our radio facilities finally kicked in, a counterevent, consolidation, became the law of the land. The tools that could have made local radio absolutely unbeatable and a formidable venue for advertising and promotion were diverted to tools designed to save operational expense and reduce staff.

> A missionary taught the starving natives how to plant seeds, water them, pull the weeds from around them, watch them grow, and from the resultant crop, feed their village. Following the teaching, the missionaries gave the natives a bag of seeds. The starving natives ate the seeds.

I am hopeful that one by one, programmers and owners in local markets will be able to reassert the power of local radio. Perhaps the development of satellite radio, designed to provide national radio service for the first time in U.S. history, will be the catalyst that compels local radio to focus on its strengths and economic base (i.e., the local market it serves). Regardless of what it takes, getting back to the development of the radio station/listener relationship will be an imperative for its survival. As a program director for a radio station using the best available technology, you may be in a position in the future to direct this change. In the design and implementation of any form of virtual programming, heed this advice. Regardless of:

How good it looks on the computer screen

How well timed the hour is

How seamlessly the announcer's liners fit into the sequence

How effectively the commercials are scheduled

How balanced the music-scheduling software has designed the song list

Remember, someone is listening. It's all about that person!

ABOUT COMMERCIALS

In June 1999, the Arbitron Company in cooperation with Edison Media Research conducted a "Spot Load Study" to determine the tolerance of radio listeners to commercial interruptions. Apparently since the very first commercials were broadcast on radio, there have been ongoing issues of how to best mix commercials and programming. One thing for sure is that as an advertising medium, radio does an excellent job when the messages are effective, and the demand for radio inventory has never been greater. Radio has also been a fast growth area for advertisers as conventional wisdom now suggests that radio works best when combined with other media such as billboards, direct mail, and television. Advertisers who may not have used radio in their media mix are now including a budget for it apart from their investment in other media.

There are only so many radio stations in any given market and there are only 24 hours in a radio station's broadcast day (less if it's an AM daytime-only station), so we are confronted with an increased demand for a limited resource.

According to the goals of the Arbitron/Edison study, listeners would be expressing their perceptions toward radio advertising to determine the degree to which an increase in commercials would be noticed and how listeners would prefer to hear the presentation of programming and commercials, together. The survey was conducted nationally in Arbitron's continuously rated markets to arrive at a national viewpoint of the subject. Listener responses were matched to their format preferences and radio usage. At the conclusion of the survey, six dominant messages were drawn from the exercise:

1. There is a perception among listeners that the number of commercials on radio has increased, although, interestingly, they did not perceive their favorite station as playing more commercials than other stations. Time spent listening was also not affected by the increase and the perception that TV played more commercials than radio was noted.

2. The majority of respondents found commercials to be mostly informative. Eight out of ten said commercials are a fair price to pay for free programming.

3. Listeners seem to be more bothered by the quality of commercials rather than by the quantity of them.

4. Younger listeners seemed less tolerant of increased commercials and, perhaps not coincidentally, radio listening by 12- to 24-year-olds has diminished.

5. In the 6 years leading up to the 1999 survey, radio listening was down by 9% as part of an overall gradual decrease in listening, which continues. There was no direct correlation, however, between the two. We suggest that an increase in the influence and availability of other media was a greater factor.

6. Listeners generally preferred more frequent, shorter commercial breaks rather than a long sequence of programming followed by a long cluster of commercials.

I use this Arbitron/Edison study as an example of an important concern. To have determined a need to conduct such a survey in the first place suggests a preconceived notion that there might be a problem. Similarly, CD Radio (now Sirius) conducted similar research to determine whether a noncommercial programming service such as satellite radio could propose a successful business model, based upon people's willingness to pay a cash premium for commercial-free programming. On the strength of interest in paying for such a commercial-free service, the satellite radio industry was born. To some degree, the inclusion of music programming within cable-TV service has answered the same concern, as has the plethora of commercial-free Internet radio stations.

Radio programming and commercials are both going to be around for as long as radio exists, and it is essentially a good match as long as the goose doesn't eat its own golden egg. We may discuss and argue and quantify and factor all sorts of minutes-per-hour tolerances, but in the end, the message I see in all this is the tiny little section about quality vs quantity.

Commercials are most effective and most tolerated when they are perceived as part of the programming or entertainment rather than when they are perceived as being set apart from it.

Stations and advertising agencies should work constantly to develop better commercials. The priority of hiring better creative and production personnel to attend to the needs of writing and producing commercial messages and campaigns should get moved up a notch. Too frequently, commercial messages have been banged out by the sponsor, or the receptionist, or one of the station DJs after an air shift. As a part of any station's ongoing audience research, finding out listeners' feelings about its commercial should be just as important as finding out about its music or its contests.

At this point, I'd like to bring up homogenization. Good, if you're a dairy product. Bad, if you're a radio commercial. Commercials are generally divided into two types: local and national. Local spots extol the virtues of the furniture store on Main Street, the lunch special at Morty's Diner, or this week's hot deal at Paul's Pre-Owned Plymouth Place. National commercials are purchased, in bulk, by agencies to run in markets throughout the country and promote national brands: Procter & Gamble, Ford, General Electric, etc.

Local advertisers, particularly in small markets, are less concerned with audience demographics, station ratings, or quantitative analysis of listenership than they are the personal relationship they have with the radio station and the effectiveness of past advertising. National advertising is based completely upon the numbers. Ratings, demographics, format, and time-of-day are all crunched and squeezed before the first dollar is spent buying time on a radio station. Most national advertising is placed by advertising agencies that must, in turn, justify the cost of placing such commercials on the selected stations. It's called "buying by the numbers." National advertising is also likely to be the same identical commercial heard everywhere, regardless of the region or locale. What we get is a homogenized commercial, something that is supposed to fit everywhere it plays. Often such homogenized commercials reinforce a TV campaign or newspaper campaign about the product, which is also run at a national level.

Radio, however, is not a national medium. It is local. Its audience varies widely from Maine to California, Alabama to Wisconsin, and Idaho to Texas. How people feel about a product or even something subtler like the announcer's accent (or lack of one) may affect the effectiveness of the commercial. I am sure that most radio stations look forward to getting included in national advertising buys. That revenue is a sought-after resource and few questions are ever asked about what the commercial sounds like and its compatibility with the station programming. It is my opinion that the gradual erosion of listenership in radio at a national level may be related to the gradual increase in national advertising over local in many markets and the disconnect starting to occur between regular local programming and the content of its commercial breaks. I am pleased that many advertisers are sensitive to this issue and will create a different commercial in a different style and different announcer to run in different national regions, but they are not the majority. The money-saving economics of producing a single one-size-fits-all commercial are too compelling.

Finally, an additional comment on national advertising. Many agencies do extensive testing of their commercial messages before submitting them to stations for national exposure. Several versions of the commercial are written and produced and played for sample audiences to get their reaction. The commercial copy is discussed and questions are asked. Responses are measured, sometimes verbally, sometimes galvonically. Many times respondents listen to the commercial in a conference room, an auditorium, or sometimes behind a two-way mirror in a focus group. Some agencies even play the commercial to respondents on the telephone or send it to them on a CD. Unfortunately, as scientific and empirical as this may seem, it's not the way people actually listen to the radio. Perhaps the better way to determine a commercial's effectiveness is to put an entire hour of programming on a CD containing programming similar to the stations being selected for the ad buy. Include 25 to 30 minutes of music followed by a 6- to 8-minute commercial break containing somewhere therein the commercial being tested. Since dollars are at stake and accuracy is important, the commercial should be tested in the identical environment in which it will actually be heard. Right?

PUBLIC SERVICE ANNOUNCEMENTS

The commercial should be tested in the identical environment in which it will be heard.

Public service announcements (PSAs) have been a part of radio since the very beginning. Prior to actual commercial radio, stations provided information regarding civic and community events. Through the years, PSAs have embraced nearly every type of nonprofit group, fund-raising event, information distribution, or community activity. The need to serve the community to which a station is licensed (or coverage area) cannot be overstated. Previously, a station could run any PSA by any agency, add up the total, and consider itself in compliance. Even with the deregulation of radio station activities, the smart owners are still paying close attention to their commitments to community needs. In most markets, stations now (individually or collectively) develop a list of community priorities ascertained from information acquired during interviews with civic and community leaders. The stations then list the leaders' priorities in terms of ascertained community needs and proceed to address those issues through PSAs targeted toward them. There are no real restrictions in the types are of needs to be addressed as long as there is community ascertainment to back them up. For example, suppose a station determines that unemployment is a high-priority issue in its community. This goes on the station's list. Then, the station seeks, develops, or accepts PSA material from agencies directed toward unemployment (e.g., job counseling, hiring information, financial assistance, psychological counseling, unemployment benefits).

In the Forms Appendix of this book, I have included a "Public Service Personal Apperarance" form. This form and others we'll be using are available in the Forms appendix or online at www.radiothebook.com. The form is helpful in documenting when and where members of the staff actually attended and participated in public service events. Public service events are too numerous to be attended every time, but when you do attend and participate on carefully selected occasions, that should also be documented.

All PSAs are written as liner cards. Each should include:

• Name, date, time of event

• Brief description of event

• Official name of sponsoring agency

• Station phone number (always give the station's easy-to-remember phone number).

People don't listen to the radio with a pencil and paper in hand. Let them contact you, and then you provide them the additional information about the PSA event including the phone number(s). Have the organization number on the card, but don't use it on the air.

At this time, let me remind you that a lot of this accountability and record keeping can now be handled by computer. There are many database programs, as well as some popular commercial traffic and music-scheduling software programs, that can do a fine job of tracking your PSAs. I'm also aware that a lot of the information is now available on a computer monitor in the air studio rather than on cards or paper. Further, all of your PSA information should be readily available on the station web site. But remember, we are playing the low-tech end of the game plan. I'll keep letting you know the things you need to take care of, and you find the best way to handle it, manually or technologically.

Here are a few tips to help in determining the best use of PSAs:

- Make PSAs matter. If done live, give the credibility of air talent to them.
- People don't listen to radio with a pen or pencil. Don't give phone numbers for PSA agencies, just a station number. Have the complete PSA material available when they call.
- Keep them short: 10 to 15 seconds maximum. Radio works by repetition, not length.
- Make PSAs that conform to target demographic interests. For example, if the station is:
  - An older adult station, PSAs regarding children should be directed at grandchildren.
  - A male-teen station, don't try to offer services common to middle-aged women.
  - Offering assistance for senior citizens at a contemporary country station, direct PSAs toward listeners' parents or grandparents.
- Use common sense. Make the language match the listener. Seek and use events or sermvices aimed at target listeners. There's never a shortage of them.
- Seek PSA opportunities to stroke advertisers. Find out the civic involvement of key advertisers. It can give you an edge when the time comes to considering the station for an ad schedule. Be able to say "yes" if the bank president asks, "Weren't you the station who supported the hospital fund drive last year?" Recorded PSAs can be a waste of time unless they are very clever or tied in locally. Local involvement in public service activities can be a very valuable tool at making inroads to the community, particularly if your competitor does not.
- Never use specific or restricted announcements. Ask, "Can every member of my audience, man or woman, old or young, attend this event and feel comfortable?"
- For this reason, avoid soliciting membership for social or civic clubs who restrict membership or who announce meetings or events that are open only to club members. It's not that these organizations don't often perform great civic functions, but airtime is precious. Don't speak to a selective audience and leave out more people than you attract. The past presidents' meeting at the Moose Lodge may be important to the past presidents and to the Moose, but otherwise you're better off promoting the cookie bazaar and crafts sale presented by the Moose auxiliary and that is open to the public.
- Participate in community public service events. Look for opportunities to participate in them actively. Attention to a civic agency (that has to go begging most of the time) can work wonders for image.
- Create unique public service events sponsored by community organizations. Approach them with co-sponsorship opportunities. Visually, position the station prominently at the event, especially those where large crowds might be expected. Get to know the people who run the event. Develop relationships while gaining actual understanding of the purposes and goals of the organization.

Mark these important elements with a highlighting pen. Put them at the top of the liner card. Elsewhere, put all the other specifics and things to tell a listener who calls. Consider this just one more opportunity to speak with a listener one-on-one. Also suggested is a date box, which is a simple rubber stamp, made at any neighborhood rubber stamp store. A date box consists of 10 (NOTE) square horizontal boxes. As each announcer reads the PSA, he/she dates and initials the next open box. Subsequently, the announcer should look for the last date and time each was aired, being especially mindful of his/her own usage. This provides a certain amount of control and avoids repeating the same PSAs during the same shift. It also identifies PSAs that are receiving less airtime than they should. Every new liner card should be stamped with a date box to immediately indicate that it is to be read 10 times.

After the first run, you can add an additional row of date box stamps for longer exposure of that particular PSA. Here's a typical date box with notations indicating the date read and announcer initials:

Figure 4.5: PSA Date Box

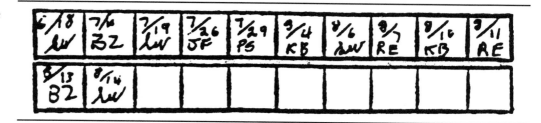

If each PSA was read 10 times and there are 10 to 15 different PSAs in rotation, then they will not be overly repetitious. Depending upon how many are scheduled per day, offer a wide variety of interesting opportunities for listeners each week. The events in which the station is involved get double or triple the exposure. Have the traffic department include this line at the bottom of each program log page:

"This hour's PSA_____"

The blank line is for writing in the name of the PSA agency. The announcer then logs his/her own PSAs, one per hour, as the cards rotate through the number of available PSAs. After the PSA has run 10 times and the date box is filled, remove it from rotation and replace it with a new one. File the old liner card under the appropriate community needs to keep a record of it. Completed cards provide a dated, documented record of actual performance of community service.

To get the most out of PSAs, relate station efforts to the agency sponsoring the event. In the Forms Appendix of this book, there is a sample invoice to present to a community organization on station letterhead. This attaches a value to PSAs and indicates, in financial terms, their value. The invoice shows how much it would cost a commercial client to receive the same amount of airtime. Additionally, staff attendance at public service events should also be noted. Therefore, we have also included a form designed to outline and document such attendance. Copies of this form should be included with all other documentation concerning the issues to be addressed by the station's public service ascertainment policies. This form and the others we use in the book are available in the Forms Appendix or online at www.radiothebook.com.

Whew! There you have it. It took some time, but we have delved into the basic elements of a music format radio station, including the mechanics of the music and the rotations. We've studied the announcer and the spoken word and public image. We acknowledge the realities of format changes and business decisions that trigger them. All these components mesh together to provide the dynamics in play behind the scenes of a typical radio station. Now, we'll dig deeper into some of the underpinnings of how and why radio acts and reacts to a variety of influences.

RESEARCH

MARKET AND MUSIC RESEARCH

In this chapter, we look at the role that market research plays in the mission and operation of a radio station. Smart programmers need every bit of information they can lay their hands on to assemble a winning combination. I have no fundamental problem with any sort of research to develop a plan. I do disagree with many aspects of modern radio research companies. It's not their fault. They really do gather, collate, and distribute information for use by radio stations. Ultimately, however, they are all sellers of products; therefore, my greatest disagreements lie in:

1. What to research?
2. How to go about it?
3. What role does research play in decision making?
4. What other interests does the research company have?
5. What other resources does the station have?

Who even needs market research? The use of outside market research firms is almost universal today. These firms are expert marketers who employ persuasive speakers, show compelling data, and can provide reams of documentation to support or deny. Research is *big* business, with established companies gaining in sophistication and expertise and with newer companies springing up every day to fill in the cracks. I have had the pleasure of working with several major research organizations on a variety of radio station projects and am impressed by the degree of detail achieved by modern radio research. Being a realist, I also know that research is here to stay. However, we in America fear the danger of a one-party system. Therefore, the prudent manager avoids relying too heavily on any one source of information.

Professional market research is a useful management tool, but its value can easily be overestimated. There are alternative sources of market information that can be employed, including the effective use of staff talent and raw creativity. Collectively, the research companies spend millions of dollars on promoting and advertising their services, so they don't really need me to tell you about who they are and what they do. I am not antiresearch, but in the interests of presenting another side of the question, I'll advocate for alternatives. Besides, since this book winds up in the hands of programmers in very small markets and in foreign countries, we cannot assume the research resources are available, affordable, or appropriate for those situations. Therefore, let's position ourselves in a situation where research is *not* the best option.

After all, it's my book.

Without negatively prejudicing the case for professional market research, let me point out that in 10 of the top 50 markets I've examined in preparation for writing this chapter, there are anywhere from 25 to 40 stations per market. Thirty percent of those stations were involved with or had recently undertaken a research project of some sort. As a rule, the stations on the bottom stayed there, the stations on the top stayed there, and the challengers occasionally either won or lost a few points. If two top stations are pitted against each other (signal, funding, talent, and all else being equal) with both doing major research projects, one will win and the other will lose. But how can this be? Maybe we need to look deeper into the research process and how it is applied to each case. Things to remember, however, are:

There are just as many losers who used research as there are winners. Market research is no guarantee of victory. Hones market research should be used to get or keep listeners, not to justify prior decisions.

- There are just as many losers who used research as there are winners.
- Market research is no guarantee of victory.
- Honest market research should be used to get or keep listeners, not to justify prior decisions.

Most music research is based upon the premise that if people tell you their preference and you give it to them, you'll win. That's research in a nutshell. Supply and demand.

The problem with that premise is that people can only tell you what they are familiar with, or about items and events to which you have just exposed them. For instance, suppose a new song comes out and you play a segment of that new song down a telephone line for test subjects to hear. They hear only a very small portion of that song; they don't hear the whole thing; they don't have a chance to get familiar with it or know much about the artist. For most music, it takes time for a song to be accepted. Even the biggest all-time hits got their reputations from gradually becoming familiar to and preferred by listeners. Much of a song's popularity also depends on the other music against which it was in competition for listener attention during its initial exposure. Mediocre songs sound very good next to terrible songs, but in a really good musical era, there may be a glut of excellent material.

A few songs have immediate appeal. On first hearing, people like them. In the past, people liked the songs of George M. Cohan the first time they heard them—and who could blame them? Songs of that era had to be immediately appealing because, without radio, sheet music was the basic medium. Tin Pan Alley hired piano players to play and sometimes sing the songs so that people, on hearing, would like and buy the sheet music. And some artists have immediate appeal. Barbra Streisand's "Happy Days Are Here Again" was an overnight hit. People liked her and liked the song the first time they heard it. But for every song and every artist who's an immediate success, there are hundreds who must slowly build an audience—a following, if you will. On Broadway, the overture contains all the melodies so that, when the song comes along in the show, the audience will already have some familiarity with the tune.

Familiarity varies with the listener, too. Some listeners can hear a tune once and sing it again immediately, but most people must listen over and over before they really *hear* the song. Songwriters know this; so popular music is deliberately written with a great deal of repetition, both in melodic lines and in lyrics. Of the 10 people who heard a bit of a new song by way of telephone, maybe only 1 or 2 actually even heard it at all.

Most songs from 30 years ago were played back-to-back with other songs of the same era. They were not competing with music 10 to 20 years newer or older as in many of today's formats. It took time for a single music selection to work its way up the charts (and back down). This gave every song several months of public exposure through continual, but not constant, airplay. Some were on the national charts for almost a year. There were no television videos, and music fan magazines were few and published only every week or month. Even most radio stations didn't program music all the time. Music shows were interspersed with dramatic or comedy series and news.

The people from the research company stood in front of the art museum all day, asking people their favorite color. At the end of the day, the majority of the respondents said, "Blue."

That night, results in hand, the research team and the museum management went into the galleries and added 50 more blue paintings.

There are just too many variable factors that come into play when people make their ultimate like/dislike decisions in every aspect of their lives. Each single event, whether it's a song, a food, a place, or a person, comes with a whole set of conditions and circumstances that guide and determine the eventual opinion. We feel differently about a walk in the park on a rainy day than we do about a walk on a sunny day. We like liver and onions for dinner, but not for breakfast. Therefore, the research and recall of opinions and impressions are incomplete without all of the ancillary input that creates those impressions. Music is particularly vulnerable to outside influences, yet those influences are rarely considered when doing music research.

One of the most important variables is the associations one makes with a particular piece of music. A love song may be associated with a person from the past and a set of circumstances that might have created a different impression if the person or the circumstances had been different. People go through happy times and tough times, and the music they first heard during those times carries with it subtle connotations that can't be measured by any known form of music research. In the same way, what is currently going on in a test subject's life is likely to influence his or her reaction to new music. The power of suggestion is very important, too, in how carefully one listens and how open one is to new material. When air talent introduces a new recording, we rarely hear, "Well, here's another cheesy nature song by John Treehugger Colorado, who, come to think of it, looks a lot like the raccoons he celebrates." No, we hear, "Here's a new song by that terrific new singer, who's really in tune with the natural world and celebrates it in all his songs, John Colorado!"

Read This

Today's music has a shelf life of a few weeks (months, if really lucky) of maximum exposure. Then, once it hits the top of the charts, it vanishes. This minimal time exposure for today's material will create an entire era of music with so little popular familiarity that there will be virtually no market for it in future years. Contrast today's hits with today's oldies. Those songs are still popular because they became familiar to the listener over a longer period of time. With few exceptions, this simply will not be so for contemporary songs in today's popular formats. Even the record companies are alarmed at the lack of familiarity the public has for many of today's most popular performers.

Another problem with "testing" music that has been around for 20 to 30 years is that the listener's opinion of the music has already been set from the time the songs were first exposed. The memories evoked by the song are usually more significant than the music itself. Because memories are so subjective to the listener, different people for different reasons will favor a particular selection. Comparing them to one another on overall popularity is comparing apples with bananas.

Now, Read It Again

The #1 song on a popularity list of tested songs may be more familiar overall than the #30 song on the same list, but #30 may be a better song for evoking memories and may be generally more durable within a format. Music research in these cases actually measures something that has already been done to the listener at some time in his or her music-listening history. Music tests of older selections do not predict audience reaction. They measure only the recognition level a song achieved within a target audience. A station may have played a significant role in exposing music to its audience in the first place. How that music is ultimately remembered is up to each individual listener. The audience may like or dislike the song, but both feelings are fixed by history and you cannot change that. We cannot forget the notion that, of all the songs a person has ever heard, he/she will select only a few as favorites. Some songs just may not "test well" when played alone, but are perfectly acceptable in the company of other songs where they fit as part of the overall mix.

Music research is always based in the present. It asks, "How do you like these songs today?" This attitude presupposes that present opinions are the road maps to the future. This is not the case. Again, the subjectivity of music preference allows for songs to have established meanings to the listener. How they like a song now has no effect on the original memory of the song, and that may never be changed.

With older songs, the time, charm, and impact of the music have already occurred. Songs strike familiar chords in different people for different reasons.

For example, at Golden Oldies formatted stations, the appeal is to persons who attended high school in the 1950s and 1960s. That type of music had a sound and a feel that are not only musical but paint a picture in listeners' minds of the times they lived and enjoyed (or not) when the songs were new and had maximum public exposure on radio and juke-boxes.

All the songs simultaneously popular (not just the top 20) from the particular year helped create the mood and ambiance that created the overall image of the era. To select only the so-called top songs from a year or era denies the listener the remaining music necessary to complete the picture. Comparing the musical portrait being painted by a radio station to an oil painting by an artist, the researchers will ask the audience their favorite colors, and then paint a picture with only those colors, whereas, in reality and in creating the more lasting image, a true artist, without benefit of research, will create a picture using all the colors as well as subtle shades for an overall impression. To restrict a play list to strictly numerical favorites fails to give the total complexion of the music/era you are programming and will ultimately be deemed incomplete by target listeners. It denies them the total atmosphere needed to relive the era and times you are trying to evoke favorably.

In the case of even older music—MOR Adult Standards, Country or Top 40 Oldies—there are literally thousands of songs. From a merely physical point of view, it's impossible to store, much less play, every song. Now, with the creation of CD, DAT, CD-ROM, and other audio storage technologies, it is possible to devise a system that includes an incredible number of songs necessary to create the total atmosphere of the era. Here again, the problem with music research is its insistence on taking the same tried-and-true several hundred songs that were the top "chart" songs at the exclusion of the other material necessary to complete the format. Obviously, there's more than one way to perform a hit, familiar song. Music researchers routinely deny this. Hundreds of the most hummable, singable, memorable musical selections of all time have *no* original hit version.

Here's a list of familiar songs from an Adult Standards play list. Chances are most people over the age of 40 can hum the melody to many of them. Can you recall who had a "hit" with each?

"What Now My Love"	"My Favorite Things"	"Summertime"
"Heart and Soul"	"When My Sugar Walks Down the Street"	"The Second Time Around"
"Dancing In the Dark"		"Tenderly"
"Love Is a Many Splendored Thing"	"It Had to Be You"	"Lullaby of Broadway"
	"Anything Goes"	

"The Greatest Love of All"	"On a Clear Day"	"Embraceable You"
"Yesterday"	"Somewhere"	"Deep Purple"
"Solitaire"	"Time after Time"	"My Funny Valentine"
"Dancing Queen"	"Just One of Those Things"	"I Write the Songs"
"Where or When"	"Put on a Happy Face"	"Misty"
"Smile"	"That Old Black Magic"	

You can "hear" in your imagination several different singers doing their own versions of each song. Look at the list again and "hear" Frank Sinatra sing any of them; then "hear" Celene Dion, Harry Connick, Jr., or Ella Fitzgerald. If you are familiar with the music and the artists, you can even let your imagination run wild and "hear" versions of these songs by artists who would never record them. In your imagination you can "hear" Michael Jackson, Elvis, Madonna, or Elton John singing these same songs.

Music researchers, who usually pick one version and rank it numerically, almost always discount simple facts of music versatility and variety. It then becomes the total representation of that song in their format.

Many different artists for many different reasons recorded these songs. Record buyers in the 1940s, 1950s, and early 1960s bought records, not just because they liked the songs, but also because they were fans of the artists. A record buyer would purchase a Frank Sinatra, Johnny Mathis, Peggy Lee, Ray Conniff, or Vic Damone album because he or she wanted to hear that artist's version of a popular song. Even in the days of the big bands, each band would feature, as part of its show, songs made popular by other bands. This gives strong evidence that there has always been a significant pool of listeners with a high preference for artists who perform a variety of songs, not just the exclusive handful of selections that became charted hit records. Regrettably, research seldom takes this into account.

To further illustrate the timeliness of this philosophy, there is a current phenomenon that mirrors the earlier practice of recording alternative versions of established, familiar songs by today's artists. Today's Modern Country and Lite/Soft Adult Contemporary are including re-recordings of older songs by newer artists. Following the "only-play-the-original-hits" theory, there would be no market for this product. After several generations of remakes and new versions of today's popular music, the invalidity of the "original hits only" theory will finally become clear to those who now haven't the experience to appreciate it.

The phenomenon of the very contemporary "American Idol" placed the talents of Clay Aiken in front of the TV audience week after week, but following the competition, Clay's first breakout hit was "Solitaire," a 1975 hit by the Carpenters written by Neil Sedaka, who himself had million-selling records throughout the 1960s.

There has (in more recent times) been a love affair between the radio and record industries. Both industries are immeasurably intertwined and interdependent. Radio listeners— regular, ordinary, everyday people who use radio for basic information and entertainment—are not aware of the radio industry or the record industry with any clear understanding. They are aware only of a little electronic box that delivers talk and music in a variety of formats. Their knowledge of the industries behind those songs and radio stations begins and ends at the radio on/off switch. Rather than cram industry jargon down listeners' throats, what we really need to do is entertain them. They like songs they may hear in a nightclub, on TV, in an elevator, in a movie or play, or hummed by a co-worker, or wherever they may be exposed to music. To use only the record industry version of hits means to miss an enormous body of available music. Not all hit songs became hit records.

Many diverse elements go into making a song a hit record. A song may become a hit due to:

1. The immediate popularity of the artist
2. The money behind the record
3. The promotional thrust of the record company
4. Its being part of a movie soundtrack
5. Timeliness or lyric content
6. Trendiness or popularity of a type of music
7. A popular video on music TV

Because there are so many ways for a song to become a hit, it does not necessarily follow that the material is superior. It may be a great record, but not a great song. Even today's Grammy Awards include a "Song of the Year" as well as "Record of the Year," acknowledging a difference. The love affair between the radio and record industries has made music researchers believe that the only music they ever need to research are the hits. Radio stations that seek to create an atmosphere of familiarity and companionship with audiences are impeded by research that spews out the same identical list of safe records that "test well" in market after market, city after city, station after station, year after year. Yet there are owners eager to throw their money away on testing this music. Excessive music research, executed by contemporary research organizations, often obstructs the creativity of talented programmers by limiting the music available to complete the format.

Music testing is an expensive item. Owners and managers, who want to use what they've bought, mandate the use of the researched music within the format. The results of a music research project often override the preferences of a good program director. Ideally, music research should be used to supplement an existing format concept, while the selection of all other music should be the left to the program director.

The classic songs of all time do not need to be researched. They have been recorded, sung, and sold for 20, 30, 40, or 50 years. They sell sheet music, records, and tapes from catalogues long after their original popularity is over. Why reinvent what's already there? What is the purpose of taking these same songs we can all sing or hum and subject them to auditorium or phone "hook" testing? It is a wasteful and useless expense that ties up staff and revenue. The hits are the hits. The more you play them, the closer you get to duplicating the atmosphere of familiarity listeners need in order to identify with the station. Programmers should use extreme caution in researching material that already has a proven track record with the public. Moreover, they should not determine arbitrarily to restrict the music that is played on the air because of research results. Don't assume that the material you *did* research has a higher priority than that which you did not.

RESEARCH CAN GIVE YOU RESULTS ONLY FOR MATERIAL YOU DECIDE TO TEST

Research can give you results only for material you decide to test.

Since it is too big (or too costly) a job for most stations to test every song, only rarely can accurate results be achieved that fairly serve a wide list, variety, older demographic format. With contemporary stations, the hype, drive, and promotion behind getting songs played are a far more fluid and ongoing process. Programming contemporary music becomes a daily or weekly chore that demands the concerted efforts of record promotion people and music directors or program directors, with an eye toward song and artist reaction in the marketplace. There is no exact answer to selecting new music for a contemporary station. The whole matter is directly related to the accuracy of the combined talents and perceptions of the people charged with the responsibility. It's odd and contradictory that when music is new, the experience and expertise of the music director are relied upon heavily. Yet when a song has already had its run and earned its merit, then it can be played only when the research reports allow it. Selecting new music is not so much a question of what to play as it is in what rotation to play it. Since most contemporary stations do ongoing music research (at least some form of audience call-outs qualifies), the rotation and frequency of a song can change daily or weekly. This requires flexibility in formatics to accept updated music selections and yet remain consistent in overall sound. If you are considering a music research project and you want to know what to research, here's my rule:

> The older the demographic you seek in targeting the radio station, the less likely it becomes that you will need massive music research and the more likely you'll need a skilled music director.

HOW TO USE RESEARCH

Modern radio research can take a variety of different approaches in gathering data. For the sake of simplicity, let's talk about a hypothetical radio station that is:

1. Trying to locate a format in its marketplace
2. Trying to secure it musically in the minds of listeners
3. Trying to secure it through nonmusical elements (sports, news, traffic, weather, personalities, etc.)

The primary concern, once the decision has been made that the situation demands the input of some sort of research, is how to go about getting the information required and from whom you will get it. Will you ask existing listeners about their preferences and perceptions of the station, or will you ask the general public about the station's overall impression in the community, even among nonlisteners? Also, will you ask the public about overall listening preferences and tastes with the goal of determining a programming void in the market and how the station may fill it?

In any case, you will discover some revealing information about the station. The basic caution in asking "how to do it" is raised by what radio is all about in the first place. Because radio is a very intimate and private medium, attempts to test radio or to ask for responses about radio's impact from listeners in a blatant and less-than-intimate manner can often defeat the confidential attitude listeners hold about their relationships with their favorite radio stations. If one betrays this confidence, one is likely to get misleading results from audience research.

Let's suppose we are going to ask a listener about the radio station. Let's also suppose that this person listens to radio in one of these places:

1. The comfort of home (maybe the bedroom, the kitchen, the garage, or even the bathroom)
2. A car (in traffic, on a long drive, shopping, conducting business)
3. A place of work (companionship, set a mood, entertain)

A listener selects a particular radio station for whatever reasons, whether for music, information, or personalities, in order to be a part of one or more of these private environments. Then is it fair, or completely representative, to ask this same listener to sit in a round-table focus group with 10 to 15 other people, or in an auditorium with 50 to 100 other people, or on a telephone with an interviewer and make judgments, statements, and comments regarding very intimate and private feelings about the radio station?

The telephone itself is a very impersonal medium of communication, so telephone interviewing can be distressing to some people. Even though the interviewee does have the benefit of a certain degree of anonymity while on the phone and can avoid physical confrontation, it is common for the person interviewed to be hesitant and guarded about the information being solicited.

Radio listening covers every possible age group from preteens to quite elderly. Clearly, each type of person on this age scale will respond to different types of inquiries in a manner that is comfortable to that person. Currently, no type of radio research attempts to approximate the listening environment while soliciting listener response. In the case of younger listeners, peer pressure is a primary life influence. It is demonstrated in their clothing, their social life, their attitudes, their values and their self-expression. Why then would it not be wise for a station that wants to research this segment of the audience to conduct the research in peer settings and situations? A school classroom rather than an auditorium? A pizzeria rather than a conference room?

Put the listener in a research environment that replicates the listening environment. If other people must be present, let them be peer-group members. Keep in mind that *same demographic* does not always mean peer groups. It may be necessary to subclassify groups down to the clubs or cliques with whom they frequently socialize. All age groups are composed of parochial subgroups. These distinctions more clearly define the group members than does common chronological age. Research information from these groups can provide a more accurate collective, as well as individual, opinion. Not to consider these divisions when soliciting research information removes a basic deciding element in determining radio listening habits.

Suppose it were possible to broadcast chess games by radio. (It's possible, but unlikely, at least in the United States.) What the listeners would have in common would be an interest in chess, but they would be of all ages, sizes, shapes, and persuasions. Grouping them by age or by some other characteristic would not necessarily tell you anything about their common interest in various opening gambits or favorite players. They would be from all social and economic groups, racial and ethnic groups, and even educational achievement groups. They might all be rather smart, but even that's not a given, because ability at chess is a specialized talent that is correlated with other talents but does not always co-occur with them. If we are trying to find out whether or not chess listening is related to a demographic group with buying power, the answer would be no, but there would undoubtedly be people with buying power in the group.

It's the same with music and music research. There are, for example, teens who like only contemporary hits, but within this group there are many others who are country music fans or who have discovered old-time Rock and Roll or even older music. Tony Bennett is currently popular with some youngsters who were a long way from being born when he first appeared on the scene. Go figure.

So it's dangerous to assume that all of any group will like the same things. When it's preferences for this type of music or that, the only safe assumption is that what these people have in common is that they like this type of music or that. ("People who like this kind of thing will find that this is the kind of thing they like.") This also ignores the fact that most people like several different kinds of music and switch freely among them. One day, a typical listener may feel like listening to light jazz, the next, easy listening, and the next, something else. People are not locked into formats, nor are formats locked into demographic groups.

All that being said, let's now march into the field of research as it is, realizing that the tools may be faulty and the methods somewhat suspect.

As listeners mature and radio station demographics get older, research personnel should be asking themselves, "What is the environment in which these people are comfortable listening to and appreciating radio programming?" I suggest that the one-on-one personal interview might be the best interview technique with mature adult audiences. Our experience clearly indicates that information useful in the programming of the station's music can be obtained by individual, personal interviews conducted informally at station events, promotions, or even when a listener stops at the station (perhaps to pick up a contest prize or for some other business). This research technique can be extended to formalize some questions for listeners who call the station for comments, requests, and general information.

The best research companies are the ones that provide a sliding scale of research techniques that can be applied to the rainbow of listener types, tastes, and ages rather than the type of research company that is trying to sell the latest fad or buzzword in research technique. Remember also, if you are looking for honest, fair information, especially about existing programming, the best environment is one that is as compatible as possible with the listener's everyday listening environment.

In the case of a radio station looking to fill a void in a marketplace, this area does not lend itself to research as much as might be originally imagined. It really does not take a radio wizard to look at a market of 15 to 25 radio stations to see where the format opportunities are.

Sometimes, there *is* a case for using common sense.

Population and census information is available from ratings services, chambers of commerce, public and college libraries, and on-line computer services. An idea of the demographic spread in a market should be overlain on the actual ratings of the stations already doing business in the market. This will give a good idea of what population cells are or are not being served by existing stations. This can be done simply by formulating a chart of demographics and listing each station that appeals to those demographics. Since discussions of radio formats are integrated into every aspect of radio, you'll find mentions of and comments on formats in just about every chapter of this book. Each market is different, but the basic approach and the understanding thereof are simple to grasp.

Sometimes, there *is* a case for using common sense.

Too much attention has been paid in the last 10 to 15 years to the so-called *hot* demographics. These are young, attractive professionals with readily disposable income who are upwardly mobile. Usually they are grouped between ages 18 and 34 or 25 and 54. It should be understood that this audience is fickle and can be swayed by marketing. They're seldom "brand loyal" and will try new products when influenced by advertising.

As listeners mature, hot demographics of the past become more settled, consistent, and established demographic groups of the present. Their incomes have leveled. They have become more brand loyal through a decade or more of trial and error. They are more concerned with home and family than with the impulse buying that peer pressure induces. They have saved money and invested it. For the most part, they have dug in for their life careers, and their preferences have served them well.

Recently, there has been growth in the number of stations appealing to mature adults, especially the 35- to 64-year-old age group. An even more dynamic demographic is 35+ or 45+. By raising the ceiling on the demographic with no maximum age, the demographic allows for service to viable consumers/listeners regardless of age. This trend toward serving older demographics will become even more critical as the median age of the population rises. This former "no-man's-land" of senior demos will command greater attention in the future. More competitive marketing and creative programming strategies will need to be developed to garner their attention and include them in radio's contemporary marketplace.

If any merchant in any city in America had 10,000 people show up at his or her store at one time, the merchant could not handle the business, much less care about how old they are. As little as 3% or 4% of any major city's population could represent a number of listeners that large and create this sort of reaction if they could be motivated. For a radio station to be effective, it does not have to offer something for everyone; instead it has to be something "special" for a particular segment of the audience. An effective station can motivate and mobilize the audience to patronize businesses, to show up at station events, and to respond to promotions. Essentially, the station must make its audience visible in support of station activities, commercial or otherwise.

A few professional broadcasters with a broad range of experience and expertise can most often perceive almost immediately where market voids exist. And often they must swallow hard and superserve the target audience, even though personally they may not like the selected format. If you own the station and have the luxury of turning it into a private jukebox, then go ahead. Otherwise, you're in business for profit. Too frequently, station managers, program directors, and even sales managers create a station after their own tastes and in their own images, only to fail because they did not serve the market segment.

Radio is a business. Businesses survive through their customers. Any influences that change the station's direction or the focus of the station's business opportunities are disruptive to the station itself and will contribute to its lack of success and ultimate downfall.

WHAT ROLE SHOULD RESEARCH PLAY?

Too often, research plays 100% of the role in decision making. This is unfortunate. It creates an environment wherein the research organization can take improper advantage of a broadcaster. Radio station owners, especially new owners with large loan payments to make, spend a lot of time looking over their shoulders to see where the next expense might be hiding. They always keep an eye on the station's financial bottom line, sometimes to the degree that the creative process itself is crippled. It is for these people and their financial backers (often from outside the broadcasting industry) that requirements for excessive documentation seem to have a purpose.

More time, money, and energy are spent trying to justify an expense than is spent on the expense itself. This is the corporate version of CYA (cover your ass; you'll be hearing it a lot!). A situation develops in which decisions cannot be made based on any type of artistic or creative judgments simply because they do not have the support of any data or documentation to show that they are viable. Enter the research team.

Here is an organization, already in place, highly promoted and advertised, that can sample hundreds if not thousands of persons in the community.

They can:
• Collate
• Cross-reference
• Classify
• Identify
• And otherwise document
• Or establish (!) the sought-after opinion or proposed station decisions.

They can present:

- Volumes of printed data
- Narratives
- Charts
- Graphs
- And buzzwords on a variety of subjects

Armed with this information (or data), the decision-making process becomes easier to sell to the station stockholders, directors, or owners. This might be referred to as research for its own sake. The spirit of researching audience information should be to come up with a viable business plan. This spirit is often pushed aside or made secondary.

Many of today's radio stations are supported by money from investors who are not broadcasters. Also, a few years ago, in different economic times, radio stations fared better than they might today. Therefore, there have been some astonishing losses in the value of radio stations. In being accountable to the investors, all decisions are supported by volumes of research. The precious limited financial resources are spent more to justify than to entertain. As a result, much of the immediacy and responsiveness of radio has been removed by oppressive financial concerns, with research companies being the primary benefactors.

WHAT OTHER INTERESTS DO RESEARCH COMPANIES HAVE?

In seeking to understand the function of research organizations, we need to understand that they, too, like radio stations, are businesses. As such, they must sell products to new customers as well as enhance their product lines to keep existing customers. Rarely will any research company advise you that you need its services only once. The most desirable circumstance is the development of ongoing relationships. An ongoing policy will better benefit the station in the long run, but the caution here is to not be sold on the next product offered by the research company simply because it attests to being new and improved. My favorite breakfast cereal has been "new and improved" about 10 times over the years and still tastes the same to me as it did in 1975.

Selecting a research project cafeteria style (depending on what's on the menu from month to month) ultimately may actually detract from the credibility of the research. As in the case of radio ratings, selecting one policy that works and sticking with it will give a more consistent long-term view of the station rather than criss-crossing a variety of methodologies that could frequently give misleading and incomplete information, aside from being costly.

In an industry where there is a constant mingling of media interests, it is common to see research companies involved in providing additional goods and services above and beyond the initial agreement to conduct some form of audience research. Today, many research companies provide either a full range of programming or access to vendors who can contact the station to pitch their services. This can also include actual station consultants to work with the station on adjusting its programming needs in compliance with the outcome of the research. Most contemporary research companies operate with the utmost honor and in an atmosphere of respect, good business conduct, and integrity.

Concern should be focused, however, on those occasions where the results of a research project lead that company to an opportunity to pitch to the station additional services at additional cost to address the station needs as determined by the research. Their expanded product line often includes providing a complete, new format. Similar conflicts might also exist at research companies that distribute or sell promotional items or programming assistance services, such as music-scheduling systems. Clearly, a research company should be able to offer its clients some help as they address the legitimate concerns and needs that the research may have uncovered. An alarm should sound when the results of the project almost perfectly define a specific service, format, or policy that the research company has for sale in its next tier of station assistance packages.

The goal of doctors is to cure all disease, thereby putting them out of business. In the same way, the goal of research companies is to achieve desired results with client stations and become obsolete.

I suggest that this is *not* the way it happens, so the "new and improved" product line extensions continue to be available for stations. The hope is for legitimate research organizations to be vigilant regarding where to draw the line at potentially taking advantage of and exploiting a station's vulnerability and selling them unnecessary products and services. At some point the credibility of the quality of the research can be questioned by virtue of their overinvolvement in the selling and merchandising of other products.

Many radio companies have hired experienced research people away from research companies to set up their own in-house research departments. At the smallest level this might take the form of someone from a marketing company working for the radio station part-time, doing call-out music research. Eventually, the job may evolve into developing research and marketing material to be distributed within the market or to core listeners. As long as the spirit of doing research is really to find the answers to questions and solutions to programming problems, then any outside input should and can be an important part of the process. However, if the development of an in-house research team has the job of justifying programming expenses, or documenting programming decisions, then it's hard to take its role seriously; this becomes further apparent if the results of the research are circulated to corporate and ownership on a regular basis rather than to the programming department for consideration and implementation.

Research designed for radio programming should not be part of any kind of accountability process. It is to learn and uncover information that may strengthen the listener/radio station relationship. The results of research should not be designed as an excuse for program directors to say no to programming ideas, new artists, local events, or nontraditional programs, but as a reason to further examine and understand how those things might be effective under a different set of conditions. Here are two interpretation of the same music research.

Interpretation #1

Our research has shown that a majority of our audience prefers newer songs to older songs; therefore, we will not feature an Oldies Show on the weekend.

Interpretation #2

Our research shows that most of our audiences prefer newer songs, but some of them like the older songs, too. How may we benefit from having an Oldies Show on the weekend?

So, which of these scenarios will lead the station toward becoming more creative and responsive to all of its listeners, and which one stops the process? How we use and interpret programming research defines how strong we are as creative people. Programming radio stations is hard work. Using research to take the easy way out instead of making decisions and creating compelling programming won't do much for the industry, your company, or your career. A successful radio programming career means never surrendering the ability to be creative to a pile of research results.

ALL ABOUT THE RADIO RATINGS

There has probably already been enough written about the various ways radio stations are rated over the years, especially regarding Arbitron, the dominant ratings service at present. Most of what has been written has been from Arbitron itself. In spite of the giant steps in technology, the increase in sample sizes, the incentives to get people to respond, and the multitude of ancillary products now available from Arbitron to interpret and decipher its data, it all ultimately boils down to asking people what they listen to on the radio. Still, regardless of the foregoing, the radio station with the most aggressive and effective listener-getting and listener-keeping tactics wins. Completing weekly diaries to register listening has been Arbitron's measurement method for several decades.

However, I'm trying to cover all bases in this book, especially for program directors who are attempting to learn things they might have missed during their prior training or to refresh their memories about information that they might have forgotten or not fully understood when it was first learned. Although there have been and are alternative audience measurement companies, a fundamental understanding of Arbitron basics and language provides a good place to start understanding the process. I'm going to use the example of Arbitron as the ratings service simply because, to date, it remains the most used, and because the terminology that is used generally is the same terminology used in other ratings services as well.

Arbitron is not some giant independent agency that drops down out of the sky and hands out free radio station ratings. Arbitron Inc. (NYSE: ARB) is an international media and marketing research firm serving radio broadcasters, cable companies, advertisers, advertising agencies, and outdoor advertising companies in the United States, Mexico, and Europe. The Arbitron core businesses measure network and local market radio audiences across the United States, surveying the retail, media, and product patterns of local market consumers, and providing application software used for analyzing media audience and marketing information data. Arbitron Internet Broadcast Services measures the audiences of audio and video content on the Internet, content commonly known as webcasts. All radio stations wishing to use Arbitron ratings data and results in sales pitches and publicity must be subscribers to Arbitron. Only subscribing stations, paid up and with an Arbitron contract in hand, may legally access and distribute the information about the station and its competitors. Many smaller stations, in specialty formats or with limited resources, may opt not to subscribe to Arbitron. Those stations will be listed and ranked among the other stations in the surveyed market, but they will not be able to promote or publicize their positions. Essentially, the payment of Arbitron fees from the radio broadcasters in each rated market constitutes Arbitron's income. Each Arbitron-subscribing station must adhere to a code of conduct regarding how the station may be promoted during a ratings period and an agreement not to illegally or subversively influence the persons selected to participate in the survey.

In addition to the rights to use the Arbitron data, the company provides a series of proprietary software products to interpret and decipher the data for various users from programming (P.D. Advantage) to sales (Maximi$er, Tapscan).

If a station is a full-fledged Arbitron-subscribing radio station, Arbitron will provide ample explanation, documentation, and training to interpret and understand the information it provides. There are also periodic seminars and lessons at various broadcasting conventions to explain Arbitron terminology and methodology. As mentioned previously, if anything, Arbitron writes and publishes extensively about its products and services. If your radio station/company is not yet an Arbitron subscriber, but plans to become one, Arbitron provides a comprehensive training period to acquaint the staff with its techniques. Let's briefly review some of the key terms that are important to know and understand about Arbitron as it relates specifically to programming and to information a program director can pass along to members of the air staff so they can better understand the mysteries of audience measurement we call the *ratings*.

It's not imperative that all members of any air staff *completely* understand every aspect of Arbitron. The sales aspects are useful only to understand the sales department at the station. It is helpful for staffers to understand the terminology and the procedures that underlie those on-the-air activities designed to influence Arbitron diary keepers and rating services generally. Key ratings terms that will be helpful for air-staff members to know and understand are discussed next.

Cume

Think of the cume of a radio station as an abbreviation for cumulative, which means the total audience, the body count, the absolute top number of *different* people that listen to a radio station. Every diary keeper who listens to a radio station for just 5 minutes in any quarter-hour period is providing enough time listening to give the station credit for one cume-person. Cume is sheer numbers of people. Cume tells you how many potential listeners you have reached during the listening survey period. It does not tell you the quality of the listening, how long they listened, or whether they liked what they heard.

Compare cume to the number of shoppers that go into a supermarket. Let's imagine that the station has no listeners and the supermarket has no shoppers. When the station comes on the air, it is the same as opening the doors to an empty market. As listeners tune in the radio, so do shoppers enter the store. For every shopper who enters the store, the store is credited with a cume of one person. For every listener who tunes the radio to that station, it too is credited with a cume of one person.

At the end of the survey period, the total number of diferent people who have gone through the doors of the supermarket, regardless of whether they bought anything or how long they stayed, would be that store's total cume. Similarly, all of the listeners who tuned in the radio station, whether they stayed long, remembered anything, or liked what they heard, can still each be counted as a cume-person *one time* each.

If the shoppers in the supermarket or the listeners of the radio station come back a second day, or a third day, or a tenth day, or every day during the survey period, they can still be counted only once for that first time they visited. Cume is all about the number of *different* people, not about the number of times the same person visits.

Each cume-person is one smiling face—no more/no less—and can be counted only one time. The length of time the cume-person stayed, a demographic description, place, and quality of listening habits or shopping habits are determined by other data in the survey.

Using easy-to-remember figures, if a thousand people listened to a radio station—a thousand *different* people, a thousand *different* smiling faces, whether male or female, a thousand *different* social security numbers—then the station cumed a thousand people. Cume is useful in determining whether a station is effectively asking people to listen. It's called *sampling*. Cume is often an indication of the total radio audience inclination to sample/try the station. Cume can be indicative of progress or lack of progress after a radio station has launched a major promotional, visibility, or advertising campaign to generate new listeners. It can tell whether the radio station is effectively attracting new people to the store, at least for a short visit.

Once you've established that the sampling or cume of the radio station is increasing, make sure the product being sampled is interesting enough to hold the attention of the audience. In our supermarket, a shopper may go into the store, but if the shelves are in disarray, the selection is poor, the lights dim, and prices are too high, he or she will exit, taking no positive action toward the establishment. Although the store counts that person as a cume and has asked the person to sample them by shopping in their store, the customer is not likely to return. The customer found the product to be inferior and not worth spending any more time on the first visit, much less a second visit later.

A cume-building campaign is needed to first establish or turn around a radio station. Get as many people listening as you can! External station promotion, although it may be a luxury, is the only way to access people who aren't already listeners. Cume building can be economically generated by simply passing out flyers at supermarkets, by trading television or newspaper ads, using billboards, cable, or door-to-door canvassing. Some stations put staff members on telephones after their shifts to call numbers randomly from a telephone book and literally ask people to listen. A successful cume campaign is a campaign that asks people to listen and actually gets them to do it. Cume becomes more important when the station can successfully translate the listeners who cume the station into listeners who will stay with the station over extended periods of time.

Average Quarter Hours (AQH)

The building block measurement used by Arbitron is the Average Quarter Hour. To gain a quarter-hour's worth of listening, a person who cumes the station (listens to it) must verify and document (in a ratings diary) evidence that he or she listened for at least 5 minutes within any particular quarter hour of the broadcast day. Those quarter-hour periods are identical to clock quarter hours:

> Top of the hour
> :00 to :15 minutes after
> :15 to :30 minutes after
> :30 to :45 minutes after
> :45 to :00 top of the hour

Therefore, any listening for 5 minutes or more within any of these time periods credits the station with a quarter hour. Obviously, there are four quarter hours up for grabs in every hour.

If listeners write down that they began and stopped listening for any period that covers 5 minutes completely *within* any of these four segments, then the radio station gets credit for a one-quarter-hour building block. If that same listener listens for two documented quarter hours, then the station gets credit for two quarter hours and so on. Even though a station can cume a listener only once, the number of quarter hours to be accumulated by long listening can vary greatly from listener to listener. Therefore, it is to the station's advantage not only to assemble as many different listeners as it can but also to keep them listening for long periods to acquire additional quarter hours.

If a listener tunes in for a while in the morning, turns off the radio, then turns it on later in the same day, the quarter hours will continue to be added to the station's total, even though this listener can still be counted only once as cume. For this reason, stations should continually cross-promote to other events and other dayparts to reinvite the listener to tune in several different times. The same is true from day to day. So, if a listener turns on the station on Monday morning and documents listening for 5 minutes within a quarter hour period, then listens at the same time every morning through Friday, the station gets credit for 5 quarter hours even though this listener can account for only one cume.

A single cume listener, therefore, may account for dozens and dozens of quarter hours during the rating period. The mechanics and mathematics of cuming new listeners and then translating them into listeners who listen for extended periods of time and who return to the station repeatedly become the dynamics by which ratings are created. The higher the cume a station has, the more opportunities it will have to extend listening from each individual. In its simplest form:

$$1 \text{ cume listener} \times 5 \text{ Average 6} \times \text{Quarter Hours} = 5 \text{ Average 6} \times \text{Quarter Hours}$$

$$5 \text{ cume listeners} \times 1 \text{ Average 6} \times \text{Quarter Hour} = 5 \text{ Average 6} \times \text{Quarter Hours}$$

The best scenario, however, involves multiples of both cume and quarter hours working together:

$$5 \text{ cume listeners} \times 5 \text{ Average 6} \times \text{Quarter Hours} = 25 \text{ Average 6} \times \text{Quarter Hours}$$

As mentioned, to be counted as cume, a listener must listen for at least 5 minutes within one quarter hour, so for every cume person, the station automatically gets credit for at least one quarter hour. High cuming stations, therefore, have a built-in advantage in having at least those single quarter hours, even if they fail to keep listeners very long. But realistically, it's the extended listening that develops the number of quarter hour building blocks, which eventually determine a station's ultimate ratings success. The types of promotions that generate cume are promotions that literally ask people to listen to the station or to ask the nonlistener to listen to the station. Cume campaigns use television, billboards, or newspaper ads. Cume-building campaigns by necessity must take place outside the radio station through outside media.

The only way a station can generate cume from its own listenership is by the tell-a-friend strategy in which existing listeners are encouraged to share information about the station with people who don't listen, in hopes that they will be converted. The Average Quarter Hours the radio station generates are broken down into the same demographic cells as the station is generally: male, female, time of day, and age—all-important elements in composing the station's ratings profile. For most practical applications, the quarter hour is the basic building block, and accumulating them becomes the full-time job for the station staff and management. The types of activities, format, and promotions that the station programs directly affect quarter hour acquisition.

Time Spent Listening (TSL)

The third major ratings term (and maybe most important from a programming perspective) is TSL or *Time Spent Listening*. We have referred to this term previously. This is the actual length of time a listener spends with your station. Although AQH and TSL are interrelated, mathematically, TSL is usually expressed in terms of actual hours and minutes. Certain radio formats are almost entirely defined by their TSL. Any station with an exclusive listenership by virtue of the demographic or listener characteristic it appeals to (i.e., Spanish, religious, older audience, classical, background music) enables them to extend TSL. In fact, small, highly specialized format stations often have the longest TSL in most markets.

Having the market's highest TSL is often used as a bragging-rights tool for such stations, but it does not define the quantity of these stations' audiences and therefore has little effect from a sales perspective. On the other hand, very popular stations, often with several competitors, tend to chop up/share the audience with one another and fail to retain the same listeners for extended periods of time. Typically, car radio button pushing is an example of how very popular stations with many listeners can suffer from low TSL and thereby low AQH. Getting listeners to listen for longer periods of time by creating compelling and entertaining programming is the ultimate challenge for programmers. If the station is well promoted and is generating new cume, and if the amount of time being spent listening is extended longer and longer, clearly the quarter hours will continue to mount.

The Arbitron Portable People Meter (PPM)

For many years, Arbitron has invited program directors and consultants to their headquarters in Maryland to bring everyone up-to-date on the status of their technology, methodology, and policy. I have personally been attending that event for about 20 years. In the early 1990s, Arbitron revealed that it was developing a new technology to measure radio listening electronically rather than by diary entry. The device was called the Portable People Meter. The project was in response to cries from advertising agencies and radio station owners for a purely scientific method to measure audience apart from the potential inaccuracies of diary keeping. After all, A.C. Neilson, the TV ratings company, had used a box attached to a TV set for years in monitoring TV viewing, so why not something similar for radio? Each year, those of us attending the Arbitron "fly-in," as it was called, was given a status report and actual demonstrations of prototype PPMs.

Unlike TV, radio listeners are mobile and listen in multiple environments. As mentioned previously, as a secondary medium, radio is always competing with some other compelling activity that takes place while listening occurs. Thus began a long series of trial-and-error experiments on how best to monitor listening with a device. That process involved the following:

1. Develop a device that was minimally intrusive, to be worn or carried by the respondent.
2. Develop a code that could be embedded in each participating radio station signal, so the PPM could uniquely identify it. This required the cooperation of all radio stations wishing to participate.
3. Develop a system whereby the collected data could be retrieved from the device and fed back to Arbitron for analysis.
4. Field-test the meter in various markets to determine the similarities and differences between diary reporting and PPM reporting.

At the current time, several market reports have been issued offering the PPM data for review by stations, but, as I said earlier, anything I write about technology is subject to become outdated far sooner than the underlying concepts and philosophies. Generally, however, in comparing metered data to diary data provided by the same respondent, a greater number of stations were heard by the meter than were reported on the diary, and there were numerous discrepancies between the electronically monitored and diary-written TSL.

To its credit, Arbitron has stuck with this program, although is has not yet been accepted by most radio station owners and agencies. Nor, at this writing, have the PPM data been fully integrated in any official market report; rather it is offered only as a source of adjunct information. The Arbitron web site can give interested parties a very exhaustive and in-depth accounting of the current status of the PPM.

As for my take on the PPM issue, I have serious reservations regarding the concept, which is flawed intrinsically by the difference in the definition of the terms *listening* and *hearing*. The detection of audio sound is far different from paying attention to compelling content, conversation, and entertainment. Radio is not a sound-delivery device; it's an entertainment and information medium that uses audio. The PPM concept plays into the hands of sound rather than content. After years of attempting to develop radio content that matters, it's disconcerting to see the audience measurement technology reduced to what one machine hears encoded from another machine. Millions of dollars and years of research will eventually tell Arbitron that its PPM cannot be effectively integrated into American listening measurement. Aside from issues concerning the requirement of every station in a market to have its signal coded and participate in the survey (some are not), it may be impossible to get a statistically accurate measurement. In every experiment thus far, there have been measurable differences between diary-reported listening and PPM data; therefore there may always be an apples vs oranges situation where the data cannot be accurately combined or averaged.

In other countries eager to get any audience measurement (and with known proclivities toward technology), the PPM will be embraced more readily. Commercial radio is relatively new to many countries as is the interest in measuring audience for the sake of selling advertising. Since audience measurement has experienced parallel growth alongside the commercial radio industry in many countries, there is no established track record or recent history of audience measurement with which to compare the PPM technology.

Other Ratings Data

Apart from the numerical ranking of individual stations, formats, demographics, age, sex, and geographical cells, another key element in ratings gathering is called the *qualitative data*. Arbitron has partnered with Scarborough Research for many years to ascertain other information from the ratings respondents to gather information about product usage, brand loyalties, buying decisions, income, social or recreational preferences, and a myriad of other bits of information directed at achieving a deeper understanding of the listeners, as well as greater accuracy at marketing to them. As a sales tool, qualitative information can more effectively guide or determine the best stations in a market for advertising a product or service, whereas a strictly numerical ranking might not. For example, a car dealership wants to advertise on radio. Station A might be the #1 ranked station among women ages 25 to 54 and station B might be ranked #3 in the same demographic. However, station B can provide qualitative information that its female audience is far more likely to purchase a new car in the coming year, making it a viable contender for the advertising buy. Today, qualitative information is almost a required element of any effective sales presentation.

Another company called International Demographics has also been aggressively on the qualitative research scene in recent years via its product, The Media Audit. The Media Audit is a multimedia, qualitative audience survey that covers over 450 target items for each rated media's audience. These qualitative data points cover things such as socioeconomic characteristics, lifestyles, business decision makers, product purchasing plans, retail shopping habits, travel history, supermarket shopping, stores shopped, products purchased, fast-food restaurants frequented, soft drink consumption, brands purchased, health insurance coverage, leisure activities, banks used, credit cards used, and other selected consumer characteristics important to local media and advertisers. The Media Audit is distributed to subscribers as a syndicated product, but The Media Audit database is also marketed in a proprietary software program, third-party software packages, and on-line delivery systems. International Demographics also provides custom-designed research studies and specialized data processing services.

The Media Audit is a telephone survey, conducted in markets throughout the United States. One person per household is selected and a variety of questions is asked of the respondents. Not specifically designed for radio, The Media Audit is sold to retailers, investment companies, banks, and an assortment of users desiring a qualitative profile of a surveyed market. Among the responses are preferences for favorite radio stations in the market as well as other consumer products. The Media Audit does not pretend to sell these radio preferences as ratings, but it does sell its qualitative information to radio stations. In fact, as pricing has become an issue for gathering and using qualitative information, several radio companies have either considered or have already selected The Media Audit as a source for qualitative information rather than the Arbitron Scarborough package. Therefore, if a station feels it has a strong story to tell based on the quality and preferences of its audience, a numerical, quantitative ranking is not necessary. Those stations may wish to forgo their relationship with Arbitron and subscribe to The Media Audit as their resource for audience information. As of this writing, The Media Audit is making a strong challenge to the Arbitron qualitative data, particularly in markets where the pricing for Arbitron participation is perceived as too costly.

Summary

Now that we have examined the three basic terms in radio ratings, let me state that there are dozens more, but none as important as those three, as far as understanding ratings is concerned. We've also touched on the qualitative aspects of the radio audience. Any library or bookstore has shelves and shelves of information on various research techniques, terms, methodology, and computation, including margins of error and respondent sample size for effective measurement. Beyond that, there are other shelves of books and college courses in statistics and demographics. My goal is to suggest to future and current programmers that their elements are overlain on the radio business, just as any other. Knowing about your audience in quantity and in quality is an imperative in directing your programming efforts and effectively measuring the results, which in turn will gauge your degree of success. If you're not clear on my definitions or descriptions, then contact the appropriate companies for literature on how they define them, or spend some time with someone who works with ratings on a regular basis and let that person share his or her definitions and utilizations of ratings data. Many of the newer terms are created for the purpose of understanding new software programs and enhanced definitions of listeners and listening. For a more complete list of terms and definitions, you may write to:

The Arbitron Company
Marketing and Communications
9505 Patuxent Woods Drive
Columbia, Maryland 21046 (US)
410-312-8000

OR

The Media Audit
10333 Richmond Ave., Suite 200
Houston, Texas 77042 (US)
713-626-0333

Other Ratings History

Throughout the 1980s and into the early 1990s, the Birch Research Corporation was the primary competitor to Arbitron in the radio ratings business. The methodology of the two services was what set them apart. Arbitron relied on people to recall what they had listened to over a 7-day period in a written diary. Birch used phone interviews to gather its data. Respondents were asked to recall their radio listening over the prior 24 hours. Because the phone methodology often yielded higher listening estimates for stations that targeted younger listeners, Birch became the favored ratings service in the eyes of Top 40 and rock stations. Birch also used its phone interviews to gather detailed qualitative information through Scarborough Research. This allowed stations to obtain a clearer picture of the audience that was listening. After Birch's demise, the Scarborough division was purchased by Arbitron, which we previously mentioned, and still produces those annual qualitative reports under that name.

After the demise of the Birch ratings, Strategic Radio Research launched a service called AccuRatings to fill the void. Like Birch, AccuRatings used phone interview methodology and also provided more detailed demographic information than Arbitron. Unlike Birch, which queried people's listening habits over the previous day, AccuRatings asked people to name the station they thought of as their "most listened to." Also unique to AccuRatings was the fact that no trending data were listed in its reports. Instead, respondents were asked what station they most listened to 6 months in the past; the resulting figure was listed as the *Recalled Former Share* (RFS). This gave an idea of a station's rise or decline based on listeners' perceptions rather than simple comparisons to past raw data.

Setting up and administering a full-fledged ratings service is not for the weak of heart or pocketbook. Strategic Radio Research, also operated as Touch Marketing Services, Recall Marketing, Strategic Record Research, Strategic Media Research, Accurtrack, and Star, filed for Chapter 11 bankruptcy protection on January 9, 2001. This proceeding was converted to Chapter 7 on May 8, 2001. SSR, which changed its name to SMR Liquidation Corp., was involuntarily dissolved on December 1, 2001, by the State of Illinois.

Anyone reading books on the history of radio, particularly during the later 1950s, 1960s, and early 1970s, may also encounter other ratings companies that have come and gone, including Pulse, Trendex, and Hooper, among others. Many of these services overlapped and provided results to stations at the same time. It was entirely possible that one station may have bragged about being #1 in Hooper while a cross-town rival took credit for being #1 in the Pulse. Because neither came with much qualitative information, the most convincing and persuasive sales representatives from the respective radio stations usually got the advertising orders. In those days, the ratings services offered very little in the way of audience breakdowns for various demographics. However, during the boom of Top 40 radio, the stations in that format achieved huge overall listening, since all listeners of all ages were lumped together. At the urging of adult format stations, the ratings companies started to break out the ratings by age groups, so that those Top 40 stations getting massive overall ratings could be dismissed once it was determined that their audience was all kids or were too young for most advertisers, returning the adult ratings advantage to the adult format stations. The youth audience had yet to become a power in advertising as it has become today, but such was the mindset of radio in that era.

RATINGS SECRETS AND STRATEGY

Now that you're a little better acquainted with the terms and the companies, let's move forward. The most effective tool to achieve extended listening is a *time target*. A *time target* is anything you say or do on the air that invites the listener either to listen longer or listen at another time. Another chapter deals exclusively with time targets, but as an integral part of audience building, a brief explanation is necessary. Time targeting includes promotion of upcoming songs, promoting a personality in another daypart, promoting an information event (e.g., weather, news, and sports). A time target is most effective when promoting a benefit to the listener. The pleasure of a favorite song or the satisfaction of current information is an all-important target. Contests usually involve a potential for an immediate and tangible benefit to the listener and for that reason are extremely valuable time targets. Contests that can be interestingly spread over several quarter hours are even more effective quarter hour builders.

HEY LISTENERS! ALL ABOARD!

How announcers are instructed regarding how to keep the listener listening is the most valuable direction they can get. All other programming elements should be addressed to that purpose, whether it is music, humor, information, or contests. It's helpful for announcers to understand the importance of this end result, but they are often lacking in management direction. Explain AQH to the air staff. It's helpful to know what it is. Staff members are responsible for the execution of quarter hour building promotions. Excellent quarter hour building promotions such as the following are the sort, of promotions that extend listenership:

- The amount of money in the jackpot is increased by a certain amount each hour
- Adding a new word to the mystery phrase
- Giving an additional clue to today's question
- Listen for an upcoming song
- Call when you hear . . .

All of these generate continued interest and continued listening, which extends quarter hours. If the air staff understands this, then they are motivated to be interesting and clever in convincing the audience to stick around. As far as a radio station's air staff is concerned, generating cume and quarter hours and knowing the types of promotions that do each are important pieces of information.

The other term we talked about earlier, that comes into play with respect to the air staff is *TSL (time spent listening)*, a term that is self-descriptive. The TSL tables from Arbitron can tell the interpreter of the data how long specific listeners stay with the station during the total listening day or during each specific daypart. TSL is a product of extended quarter hours. Stations that achieve substantial quarter hours with their listeners generally have long TSL, too.

As we mentioned in the last chapter, ironically, some of the stations with the highest TSL end up with the lowest ratings because these are stations that program a very specialized type of radio program and have a very small cume. Religious stations, ethnic, foreign language, or other special interests tend to generate high TSL because their audience generally listens to no other station. Even though the cume is small, it has enormous quarter hours. The combination of the two do not generate a high rating for the station, but you can see that on a national level, these stations have very high TSL ratios. So it's deceptive. *A good TSL for any station is really only significant when accompanied by substantial cume.*

Sometimes, it can be helpful to a program director (in reviewing ratings) to see how TSL may vary from one daypart to another. These statistics may be helpful in determining whether air talent is effective. The overall staff may perform well on the TSL, but certain times of the day or certain personalities may have a TSL that is noticeably less. This could be considered warning signals, and some additional direction may be necessary to take corrective measures. Otherwise, TSL is a secondary function to cume and average quarter hours. Those are the big three in Arbitron terms needing interpretation to the air staff. These are active terms that explain what is going on while it is going on.

WHEN THE RATINGS BOOK ARRIVES

You already know the terms that are important to the air staff; here are some additional definitions of those (and other) terms that are specifically used when analyzing the results of a rating book.

Cume

Find the cume for the selected station. Under total persons, the cume figures should be the first thing you look at in the results of a rating period. This figure shows how many people sampled each station during the survey period or during the daypart or in the demographic.

Share

Share is interesting because it is actually a percentage of a percentage. Let me explain. Going back to our example of shoppers in the supermarket, let's say there was a man with a clipboard taking a survey inside the store. Therefore, he could survey only the people who came into the store. If he stayed inside the store, it would be impossible for him to take a survey of all the other citizens in town. In radio ratings, share is arrived at as a percentage only of the people in the survey area who were listening to a radio at the time. Share is not representative of the total population, but only of the population who is listening. Because radio listening changes from hour to hour, day to day, and week to week during a survey period, the total number of listeners who comprise the persons using radio at a time also fluctuates. Let me repeat, *a share expressed in a percentage is a percentage of the persons using radio, not the population of the survey area.*

If a radio station has a 7.1 share, that means that 7.1% of the persons using radio during the survey period (or the time period or demographic being examined) were listening to that station. Because share is a product of the amount of audience that is available at any given hour of the day, the percentages of share can change drastically from one part of the day to another and can often give misleading data about listening.

> For example: The population of the city is 50,000 people.
> 10,000 people listen to all the various radio stations each morning in this city.
> These 10,000 people are called the Persons Using Radio (PUR).
> 1000 of them listen to the morning show on a specific popular station.
> So, 10% of them are listening to this station every morning.
> Therefore, 10% of the Persons Using Radio constitute a 10.0 share of the audience.
> On the other hand . . .
> Late at night when the listening levels traditionally are lower,
> The population of the city remains 50,000 people.
> But only 1000 people are listening to radio throughout the city at night.
> And this same popular station may only have 100 listeners (or 10% of them).
> So it's still a 10.0 share.
> But the audience is only 1/10th of what it was in the morning.

Therfore, explaining share it is also necessary to explain the cume and the quarter hours that establish it.

Rating

The share is expressed in a percentage of the entire market population. The rating figure is gaining in popularity because it expresses the station's listenership in terms that are easy to understand to the layperson or not-necessarily-media-wise advertisers. A station's rating is always a lower figure than its share because the entire market population represents everyone, including those people not listening to radio, whereas share only represents persons actually using radio. It is therefore a smaller universe. A complete glossary of all Arbitron terms and an excellent interactive tutorial called Arbitron 101 is available on their website at www.arbitron.com

OTHER THINGS TO WATCH FOR

Other interesting items to watch for in an Arbitron ratings quarterly report is the hour-by-hour listening where you can track how the station's audience changes from hour to hour. If you map this information over extended periods of time from rating period to rating period, you'll notice perceptible dips or jumps in listening during certain hours of the day. This is helpful in programming during weak hours to help increase listenership or design a promotion specifically to run during that weaker hour. From a sales point of view, you can use stronger showing hours to justify getting higher advertising rates for those hours, because the listening levels are traditionally higher.

ABOUT ROLLING AVERAGES

The previous information has been specifically about Arbitron quarterly reports, "the book," that comes out four times per year. Oddly enough, there are what are known as monthly ratings, which are not really that at all, but are rolling averages of three 1-month periods. When a station receives its "monthlies," what it is actually getting is a 3-month figure with the most recent month (just completed) added to the average and the oldest month dropped. For example:

- A station will get a rolling average for January, February, and March; these data will be given to the station as a monthly figure sometime during the middle of April.
- A month later, in the middle of May, the station will get a new monthly report that will drop January and include February, March, and the new month of April.
- In June, the station gets another monthly report that has dropped the February figures and averaged March, April, and May.

And so it goes, continually adding the new month and dropping the oldest.

The term *rolling average* describes monthly reports. If a station has a good month, those figures can inflate the rolling average figures and give the deceptively euphoric feeling of success. Several months later, when the good month drops off, the station gets a big letdown. The ratings appear to drop. I frankly wish there were no rolling averages. It's nice to see how you're doing, but because of the high potential for fluctuations in the mathematics of rolling averages, I don't find them to be a good programming tool and would rather use some more immediate type of direct in-market research to gauge a station's monthly success.

These monthly rolling-average data are frequently misused, and stations have made important decisions and ultimately critical mistakes based upon rolling-average performance, rather than riding out the storm and basing the station's progress on a series of quarterly reports. Arbitron and other ratings services spend countless hours, days, and years developing their methodologies and their mathematics, refining and sophisticating them even as you read this book. But some basic common language that conveys to the members of the air staff the essence of what is going on with station ratings is an overlooked piece of information. When properly understood, this language can add meaning, importance, and impact to the promotions on the air and the way the station is programmed. The air staff should feel they are a part of a process in which, by properly executing the programming opportunities desired for that purpose, they could affect the person filling the ratings diary.

Anyone seriously interested in programming at a major market level really needs to participate in a professional-level training course given by the ratings companies, as well as to participate with, subscribe to, or learn from other experts in the field. Many have taken audience measurements statistics to new heights by sophisticated interpretive techniques and by applying additional information and insight to factor more creative meaning into the raw ratings data.

A final note on radio ratings. What I have presented here is very basic. Today's radio ratings data can be developed into an unlimited number of reports. From any ratings report, literally thousands of different sets of information can be extracted from the audience and listening data. The multitude of reports for both programming and sales is daunting. Specific reports can be generated for individual advertising clients, specifying the preferences of their client base. Reports by age, sex, location (down to the smallest postal route), and place of listening can be printed and made a part of the advertising and programming strategy. As ratings services have sought to bring new clients into their customer bases and continue to serve their existing clients, they have added more and more enhancements and services to the overall package sold to radio stations. Beneath it all, however, are the basic questions: Who listens to what radio station, and for how long?

DIARY KEEPING

Arbitron uses diary keeping as the primary tool to measure cume, TSL, and AQH. Let's just take a little break here to look at the whole notion of diary keeping as a human process.

First, we have to ask what kind of person would voluntarily keep a diary of his or her listening habits? Would such a person be a typical listener—if there were any such thing as a typical listener? What would be that person's motivation for keeping it carefully and accurately?

Second, if radio is a secondary medium, is what's being recorded actually *listening?* Or is it just when the radio is on? People have developed great senses of selectivity when it comes to what is actually heard as opposed to what is just part of an audio environment. If someone is interested in getting some particular information (Will it rain today?), then he or she may be inattentive until that bit of information is presented. Some people have selectively tuned out what they don't want to hear, but they probably won't push the off button unless they're actively offended. Still, if they're not listening, then the radio might well be playing to an empty room.

Third, how accurate is the information? Many of us have had the experience of keeping time sheets or time logs so that management can figure out how much time various parts of a job take. We are required to record every phone call, every conversation, every meeting, every bit of time spent on this or that task, including coffee breaks and restroom breaks. Information from these time sheets is notoriously unreliable.

It often takes longer to record what was being done than the actual time on task. Keeping these records becomes an onerous chore. We start with the best of intentions and keep fairly accurate logs for the first day or so. Then we forget, and rely on memory to reconstruct the day's events, estimating time. We may be motivated to conceal from management just how much time some things took. After a few days, the actual record keeping has slipped over into a form of creative reality. We construct a time log that reflects something more or less than the reality of the day's work. The task becomes more and more bothersome because nothing seems to be achieved by keeping the log. The whole thing slips over from fact to fiction.

I suspect that something like this must happen to radio listener diary keeping. Instead of keeping the log up-to-date hour by hour or day by day, it may be reconstructed from memory at week's end, with a degree of accuracy that may or may not reflect what happened in reality.

The diary keepers are not intentionally being dishonest. It's just human nature to assign little importance to something like this. They know that it's important—that someone cares—but how can they make themselves care?

Much of the TSL must be reconstructed from memory anyway. Suppose one was driving to work and switched between two stations during the drive. That person would probably just guess how long he/she spent with each. Or maybe the listener was doing something—chopping wood, taking a bath, feeding the baby, writing a report, or bird watching—that limited access to paper and pencil.

We'd have to conclude that diary keeping is an inexact science at best, influenced as it may be by the personality of the keeper, the keeper's ability to remember, and the keeper's motivation to be accurate. Still, maybe the data we get from this source are the best we can get. Probably these data are better overall than what we might get from an electronic device that only recorded how long the radio was on and what station it was receiving.

If a radio plays in an empty room, does it make any sound? I'd say, only if the children's toys or the figurines on the mantelpiece slipped over to listen to it, or if someone left the PPM nearby.

WORKING WITH A CONSULTANT

Now that we have marched through a very long chapter covering all the basic elements of programming, audience measurement, and interpretation, there is one more factor to potentially impact all those elements. The consultant. It is said that American radio has consultants like cathedrals have rats. We thrive on second opinions. Therefore, let's spend a little time on that relationship as it may relate to the day-to-day workings of the radio station.

The term *consultant* has been used in radio for several decades. I can't really recall exactly when the term became popular, but I suspect that in the 1960s, Top 40 radio began to make incredible inroads into most American markets. Many of the Top 40 stations took their role models from successful major-market stations. Some of the names that surfaced during this era were the likes of Todd Storz and Bill Drake. Their particular programming formula was adapted to hundreds of stations by dozens of consultants who seemed to have evolved during this era as program directors or air talent. As America was ready for the excitement and uniqueness of Top 40 radio, many of the formula stations enjoyed tremendous success, and much of the credit fell to the consultants who had worked with them.

Since then, there has developed a corps of professional broadcasting consultants, generally specializing in specific formats, although there are a few mega-companies with a one-stop-shopping approach. The advantage of having many different consultants within one company is the company's ability to combine research, marketing, and administrative resources. I suspect that there is also an advantage in having access to other consultants' opinions and ideas when working with a problem station. The disadvantage may be that the company handles too many clients and may be more impersonal in its style and have less time to invest in each station's individual needs.

In any event, Consultants (now, I'll spell it with a capital C) have become a regular feature on the radio scene with some spectacular success stories and some dismal failures (which you will not likely hear about). As explained earlier in this book, I began consulting radio stations after more than 20 years of being a program director and an air talent. It wasn't something I just woke up one day and decided to do. In fact, it happened inside out. As I continued in whatever position I had at the time, former employers and acquaintances in radio began asking me for my opinion about what they should do in a particular situation. The advice given had been developed through my many years and many formats' worth of personal experiences. Many of my suggestions did prove valuable and rewarding to the stations. At this point I decided that all I needed to do to technically be a Consultant was to charge a fee for my services.

Consultants generally begin their practices by having some specific area of expertise, usually in a format or demographic. As radio has splintered into so many different formats, the spectrum of experienced Consultants has likewise grown. With those 11,000 commercial radio stations in the United States, it is impractical to believe that every station can employ a full-time programming expert as part of its local staff.

It may be possible, however, to hire (or out-source) a Consultant, who, on a regular basis, has an exchange of communication with the less-experienced local program director. The Consultant's primary advantage is the ability to watch multiple markets and share that information with local programmers who, by the nature of their position, remain anchored in their local markets. I think of a good Consultant as being a facilitator, a middle-person, exchanging ideas and providing resources to client stations. Consultants also have the advantage of experiencing the evolution of new ideas (and failures) in many different markets, whereas the local programmer may be a witness to only one.

The best role of a Consultant is as a third party—another set of eyes and ears that may impartially evaluate the client station and its personnel. Consultants are mostly removed from the day-to-day influences that taint the opinions of those who work there on a daily basis. Because the Consultant doesn't know or care about the various personal influences that may impact the sound and effectiveness of the station, judgments can be made impartially. Since the listeners also don't much care what the personal influences are, a Consultant is more like a listener than a staff member.

It would be correct to assume that Consultants have had a hand in determining hiring and firing issues. That thousands of jobs have been lost due to Consultants' decisions is probably true. Those victims probably have not saved a warm spot in their hearts for the "Consultant who fired me." On the other hand, radio stations, as businesses, must succeed or fail overall regardless of the feelings or situation of one employee. More sweeping changes may also result from the Consultant's appraisal, including a format change that may involve dismissal of an entire staff and/or the dismantling of years of work in the old format. It would also be fair to say that Consultants have been the fall guy and given responsibility for decisions not necessarily made by them. The "good cop-bad cop" philosophy has taken its toll on the image of Consultants.

As mentioned earlier, a presumed advantage of an impartial Consultant is the distance from the market and lack of being influenced by local factors. On the other hand, some attention and compassion for the local market, its citizens, and the station staff might also have a place. No doubt, the talent and ideas of many worthwhile employees went unnoticed while management was too busy listening to a Consultant. When hiring or thinking about hiring a Consultant, like anything else, check references and success stories. Take your time. A personal meeting with the Consultant is imperative since he or she will work intimately with the staff.

A good program director will acknowledge the need for a Consultant as a resource and weapon against the competition rather than a threat to his/her job. Choosing a Consultant should involve the input of the program director. In situations where a Consultant is inflicted upon an unsuspecting program director, chances are there are ulterior motives known only to upper management. Be cautious, however: Occasionally, bringing in a Consultant generates rumors in the market about staff and format changes, particularly if the Consultant has a strong identity with a format other than that which the station currently programs.

When first opening MOR Media, I sought to work exclusively in the area of adult standards music and older demographics. It seemed that most Consultants were scrambling for the "Hot, Young" demographics, while stations attracting the 45+-year-olds were pretty much left to their own devices. Having grown up around adult music and having been the youngest member of the staff at some of my earlier stations, I had (what I thought) was a fairly extensive working knowledge of how an adult standards station should sound. I quickly found several client stations needing some direction in their adult programming, since many were working with young staffs who did not have experience in the format. Thus, my consulting company MOR Media International was born. Later, I found the same qualitative material applied to Country-listening adults, as did non-Country, so we also entered the Country format as consultants. This tactic was successful because of the timing. It came at a time when Country ratings were deteriorating nationally and there was increased interest in programming more Country "Oldies." From this need, expressed by dozens of stations, came the motivation to produce our syndicated "Country Oldies Show." This was not a part of the consulting services, and most stations had a beefy oldies library gathering dust. Many had local personalities eager to host a weekend oldies-based show. In addition to my consulting work at the time, I was also still on the air in New York, hosting my own Sunday Night Oldies Show on New York's Country station, WYNY. I did the show live every Sunday night for over a year, with excellent results. I started to get requests from my client stations to send them tapes of my New York show, and thus the syndicated Country Oldies Show was born.

Similarly, although not providing a syndicated program, many Consultants do provide the necessary materials to allow a client station to carry out the directions given. It's one thing to say, "Here's a suggested list of songs for your library, now go find these songs," rather than, "Here are the songs, play them." Frequently, Consultants attend national conventions and conferences and have established a network of relationships with every type of radio-broadcasting supplier. The list includes syndicators, networks, sports, jingle companies, music libraries, promotional materials, advertising companies, and research organizations. A good Consultant should be able to fulfill or address just about any of your station's programming needs, including the necessary technology and personnel to get results.

Maybe there are still a lot of pseudo-Consultants out there, but I don't believe they enjoy the exposure they once received. By pseudo-Consultant, I mean an unemployed program director or air talent who got some cards printed and called himself a Consultant while waiting for the next full-time job to materialize. During a time when good Consultants were in demand, and their price tag was beyond the reach of many medium and small stations, pseudo-Consultants used the opportunity to make some fast money. Many actually had some success and eventually became real Consultants, because they quickly learned what was necessary to do the job. It is clearly more than phone calls and free airline tickets to other cities.

Many Consultants I have come to know personally throughout the years are very bright and perceptive people. They quickly study a situation and know when and when not to take action. The very best are the ones who can write well, since expressing ideas in writing is a most effective way to convey explanations and strategies. A written analysis is something tangible that can be used to document the need to take a course of action, should authorization be required from officers or owners. A Consultant's other favorable characteristics should also include the ability to understand and operate a variety of industry data programs, including music-scheduling software, automation systems, and ratings analysis. The ability to work with these programs also enhances the written report to station management, because it can provide additional documentation, facts, and figures in support of a plan of action.

Now that ownership of multiple stations is a reality, many companies are using Consultants on a regular basis to provide the expertise and experience lost by downsizing the combined station operation. It's now also possible for a Consultant to work with a variety of stations in a similar format throughout a company owning many stations. For example, a company today may own, say, 50 stations, but use only one consultant to work with 12 of them that are in the Country format. Obviously, the combined resources of a good Consultant and 12 stations within the same company can be a formidable opponent to the company's competitors in its respective markets.

I have thoroughly enjoyed being a Consultant, not only because it's fun and rewarding to participate in successful strategies, but because my many years at so many stations have endowed me with more knowledge than I can apply to a single situation. Since each station and each market is different, I call upon many layers of personal experience in seeking a solution. Somewhere in my brain there is archived just about every radio experience I have ever had. Sometimes it surprises me when I find a solution to one of today's radio problems by recalling a 20-year-old personal experience at a radio station.

Use a Consultant wisely. Determine your expectations and limitations. Let Consultants know what their role will be and with whom they should and should not be working. Above all, explain to the staff who the Consultant is, including the Consultant's background, role in working alongside the staff, and the nature of the working relationship.

Use a Consultant wisely.

BRANDING AND MARKETING

THE STATION IDENTITY

No matter what the format is, what kind of music you play, what city you're in, or how many competitors you have, the one thing that is absolutely necessary for the successful business operation of a radio station is to establish an identity. The radio station's identity needs to be a combination of all the things a station is to its listeners, synthesized into one or two highly identifiable elements. A station identity is the one thing that, when people see it, hear it, or think of the call letters of the radio station, provides essentially a snapshot of the station itself. Station identity can be obtained primarily through what is given to the listeners in terms of programming.

One of the things that leads to effective station identity is consistency. Develop and use slogans, sayings, ways of doing things, and consistent programming so that the audience is exposed to the station's identity on a day-in, day-out basis. There should be a thread of familiarity and similarity that runs through a radio station's sound no matter what time of day or night the listener chooses to tune in. Many programming elements can vary from hour to hour or day to day, but there should still be something familiar—something the audience can't quite put its finger on—but something that says to them that this station is different, that it's unique and has an identity all its own.

Effective station identity is consistency.

First, work to achieve the identity of the radio station on the air through the use of slogans, phrases, or consistent terminology. Use it in newscasts and announcer's material. Then reinforce that image on the outside of the radio station by using those same identifying slogans and statements in newspaper ads, in television spots, on bumper stickers, or on billboards. Internally, the radio station in its day-to-day function as a business also needs to be consistent. The station should have:

- business cards
- envelopes and stationery
- sales presentation folders
- internal station signs
- signs at remotes
- banners carried at events
- station vehicles
- a logo
- website with e-mail

All should reflect the same visual identity.

Many radio stations present highly conflicting identities simply because they did not feel it was worth the effort or the expense to convert from old identities to new ones. The kind of station identity that works is the kind that you build from consistency. The image projected is something that cannot be bought; it can only be developed and built through careful reinforcement of the idea that you wish to project to listeners. You simply cannot do this if you break the listeners' focus with a variety of different and conflicting identifying features and images for the station.

Here are examples of identities a station can have. Develop an identity immediately:

The Fun Radio Station

Carry this fun image through by the music that you play. Reinforce this fun image through the types of personalities who are on the air and the nature of materials they talk about. Develop a fun image with clever contests, with more tongue-in-cheek humor, with perhaps a station mascot or image that is humorous. Have feature material or special programming that indicates the station likes to have fun. Contests should be fun and taken lightly, requiring less effort to win but being more entertaining in their operation. This is a terrific identity if you have a very structured format competitor.

News and Information Identity

Provide excellent news and information, and constantly remind the audience during the music programs that they are only moments away from one of the basic information elements. Don't forget weekends, overnight, and late evenings. At times when you may not customarily have many of the information elements, you should still be talking about them. If you have a station identity, talk about it even when not doing it. If you have a music identity, then talk about the music when you don't happen to be playing it. If you have a news, traffic, information image, talk about that image between songs.

Contest Image

This image is easily reinforced with newspaper ads, with dollar signs, and with lists of prizes. Talk about a contest even when you're not running one.

Public Service Image

Identity takes on a more general approach because it is hard to be too specific when serving the entire population of the market. Therefore, give specific examples of the station's current public service activities. Reinforce that verbally on the air and in outside media: If you are the station that helps with the Easter Seals telethon, help with the telethon, promote it on the air, and then tell the audience after the fact what you have done. If the station works on a particular fund-raiser for some sort of other event, similarly, participate in the event, promote the participation, then after the event, brag about it. If you seek a public service/public affairs image, project your station ahead 2 weeks or a month to things you are going to be participating in; start the anticipation. If you have built a public service image, continue to remind the public service agencies themselves, as well as government leaders and persons with similar civic responsibility of the station participation, so that they can help by word of mouth to project the station's identity.

Negative Identity

In a few cases, some stations have managed to make a good business effort out of a somewhat negative identity. This mostly has to do with music programming that runs contrary to popular values and taste. Stations around the country are making good money, selling advertising while at the same time playing extremely distasteful music as announcers use offensive and off-color material, or by being a blatantly obtrusive radio station through their advertising techniques. But it sells, and in a business sense, it works.

Other Identities

There are other identities, so look at the competitors. Start a list on paper and see if you can determine the identity of each competing radio station.

Here's a list of some identities (good and bad):

News	Cheap and Unprofessional
Sports	Ethnic
Contest	Been There Forever
Old Folks	Visible
Teenage	Invisible
Community-Minded	Everyone Grew up with It
Most Prestigious	We Can Dance to It
Keeps Changing	Has That Funny Morning Guy

If you cannot identify or come up with a short, precise identity of each station in each market, then you might well imagine that those stations are vulnerable. Stations that have no identity are subject to the worst type of vulnerability. Those are the stations the listeners will fail to remember. Those are the stations the listeners forget easily. Those are the stations that have not conveyed an image of consistency and have left the listener confused. Sometimes, simply by establishing radio station identity, you can win. In memory training courses offered by memory professionals, the professionals use systems from word association to making absurd connections between the thing to be remembered and some other visual imagery. Establishing an identity for a radio station is no different from this. If the identity is different enough, if it is not to be confused with any other business or station in town, the audience will remember it because of the unique identity. As you establish the identity of a radio station, choose something that you can stay with for a while. Don't change a station's identity too frequently. Good strong station identity imagery is difficult to build. It is even more difficult to change. Many radio stations around the country are still identified by slogans and imagery that they projected to their listeners 10 or 20 years ago. You don't want to be the radio station that has a higher identity of what it used to be, rather than what it is.

Chances are, if listeners haven't given a station a try lately, they still think it's doing the same things it did the last time they listened and that might have been 20 years ago. When establishing station identity, make a profound statement in the market. It's an excellent time to test the effectiveness of station marketing techniques by doing some on-the-street research or focus groups of listeners to see if the intended message is penetrating the audience at large.

One final note on station imagery and identity: Many radio station audience-survey companies rely on the listener's memory in writing down ratings information in diaries or even in telephone interviews. Therefore, it is often better to be the station that is remembered than it is to be the one that is listened to. We would like to have everybody in town listening to our station, but if everyone doesn't listen to us (or they don't listen very often), let's give them something to remember us by. When they are asked to think of a station during a survey period, our station is the one they recall. Make the proper statement in identifying ourselves.

As competitive broadcasters, our goals are to:

• Be confident that OUR call letters come to mind rather than our competitor's.
• Develop station identity.
• Sell the benefits and virtues of our radio station to listeners and advertisers.
• Stick with it.
• Don't promise anything to your listeners that you can't deliver on or off the air.

STATION RESOURCES

In another chapter, we address the importance of formal research, as presented by institutional research organizations. Turning away from the research company approach long enough to see what the station itself has to offer is sometimes a difficult task. It would be common for radio station management to completely overlook the talent and capabilities available on its own payroll in order to accept information coming from an outside source or research company. It would be my hope that most modern radio operations have the good sense to exploit in a positive way what is already theirs. Many radio stations have enormous, untapped resources at their fingertips. Without involving a research company, it is not unusual for great radio stations to use their listeners to find needed music, for determining the types of promotions that best work effectively, by determining what type of programming is needed at certain times of the day, and by providing the station some measure of its success in sales and promotional matters.

This is not a long section, but it states a valuable principle, which is often overlooked. Radio stations, above and beyond all else, need to hire talented and skilled programming management people, equip them with the best tools possible, and let them use the creativity. Mistakes will be made, but great ideas come from good ideas, which come from bad ideas, which may have originally resulted in failure. This is how the process works. Give talented people the opportunity, even the opportunity to fail now and then, and they will create a product that is unlike any other in the market. Station management that repeatedly bypasses its own staff to import data and information from the outside is doing it and its ownership a great disservice.

While it is worthwhile to get a fresh view of the operation from an outside source, such an audit cannot and should not be considered a substitute for the inestimably valuable insights into a market that staff members possess by virtue of their daily participation in the process of executing the format. After all, it is the waiter and the bartender who are the restaurant, not the owner. It is the sales help and checkout clerk who are the store, not the shareholders. It is the front-line, customer-interface people who hear all the suggestions, all the complaints, and all the congratulatory comments. Without even knowing it, the staff of a radio station have a market awareness that no outside consultant can match with structured, formal, time-restricted interviews or demographics. Unless really drastic (read format change) measures are contemplated, it is simply a waste of talent to leave in-house staff out of discussions that relate to listeners and listeners' attitudes.

A radio station speaks with a big voice in the community it serves. Unlike any other form of business, it can attract resources to its doors that can in turn be used successfully. This is the business of communication, and communication is the exchange of ideas. Not only should a radio station be defined by its own format and staff, but every one of its listeners is also a part of the composite radio station identity. Communication with those listeners is a daily external process. Therefore, a business built upon the exchange of ideas can actually be very successful, but not if it fails to exchange ideas among its own staff. To facilitate this internal exchange of ideas, frequently hold brainstorming sessions with the station staff. Start by setting up a list of topics, including proposed topics, promotions, and needs that may arise within several months. Each person at the session is given a sheet of paper with 10 blank lines and a blank topic heading, which is filled in at the direction of the leader. Then, open the topic and have the participants write as many ideas as they can about the subject on the blank lines. The three basic rules for the session are:

Rule #1: There are to be no negative ideas or discussions of why any idea won't work.

Rule #2: We are just looking for ideas; nothing about the ideas is actually discussed in detail. That comes later when the ideas have all been collected and arranged by project.

Rule #3: There are no bad ideas, so write down every thought about a topic. Often what may appear to be a bad or poorly developed idea may yield a better idea that would not have occurred without the original "bad" idea.

Radio stations attract all kinds of talented, diverse people. Brainstorming sessions should include persons from outside the programming realm who work in other departments at the station. Their perspective resulting from being slightly away from the intimate day-to-day programming team can bring fresh insight. Key nonprogramming people may include the reception person who meets the listeners face-to-face daily, or someone from a demographic inside or outside the format target. Let people from the sales or technical side of your operation be participants once in a while. They not only have ideas to contribute, but they become aware of how the creative process works by being a part of it. Watching creative people create is like watching salespeople sell. There's a time to appreciate what the other "guys" do and how they do it.

It is said that a task will expand to occupy the time allocated to it. Therefore, a good brainstorming session should last exactly an hour. Making the session a time-bound event forces thinking and speeds the process of getting the maximum number of ideas written down. In the weeks after the brainstorming session, when the time exists to actually review and organize each of the projects, you'll have a stack of ideas, contributed by the entire staff, from which to choose the direction and methods of execution of the plan. As you execute the new ideas, the members of your staff will recognize where they came from and acknowledge the person making the contribution. Brainstorming is not new. There are books in the library and at bookstores dealing with enhancing the creative process in some form of structured thinking process. Refine your brainstorming sessions with new ideas from other authors in advertising, marketing, business, technology, and commerce. Apply the good ones to your sessions. Let participants make suggestions on how to better exercise future brainstorming sessions or let them hold sessions of their own for solutions and ideas within areas of their particular expertise (e.g., a promotions' brainstorm, a production brainstorm, a remote-broadcast brainstorm). Ultimately, there's no bad way to come up with a good idea (although the invention of the parachute may be an exception).

ADVERTISING: PRINT

Ever since regular, commercial radio started in the 1920s, the relationship between it and newspapers has been one of love/hate. Many early radio stations were owned by newspapers. During the heyday of program-oriented radio (1930s-1950s), many of the largest and most influential radio stations in the country were part of major newspaper publishing groups. Today, most of those associations are gone, mostly by legislation prohibiting cross-ownership of radio-television-newspapers except in cases where the ownership had been "grandfathered" under the legislation. Although very few cross-ownership situations exist today, most markets enjoy some cross-promotional opportunities with area newspapers, usually on a reciprocal trade basis. Television, cable, and Internet operators also take advantage of this relationship by involving both newspapers and radio in major promotions.

More than any other medium, newspapers have also been the adversary of radio sales. Even now, most radio station sales departments position the newspaper as their biggest rival for advertising dollars (including revenue spent on other radio stations). Although the two media compete for advertising, they rarely compete for audience. It's safe to say that nearly 100% of all radio listeners also spend some time regularly with a newspaper and vice versa. To that purpose, it is realistic to expect that using newspapers to promote radio stations makes sense.

These are the primary benefits of newspaper advertising:

1. A wide variety of ad sizes and shapes are available (and newspapers are never "sold out").
2. The size of the ad and the frequency with which it is scheduled determine cost.
3. Specific placement within the publication can be targeted to specific reader interest.
4. Normal black-and-white ads are relatively inexpensive to create/produce.
5. Newspaper ads are tangible, so they can be copied, clipped, reread, or passed along.
6. Using multiple publications can increase diversity and reach secondary audience targets within the primary audience.

Let's break down these benefits and look at how they can best be used for the station.

1. Wide variety of ad sizes available.
    a. Full-page or half-page ads are for major "breaking" events like format changes, major contests, or kickoff of major programming or community events.
    b. Medium ads are for personality profiles, music positioning (lists of songs or artists), contest rules.
    c. Smaller ads are for reinforcement of formats, slogans, sports events, personality dayparts, phone numbers, call letter/dial position.
2. Size and frequency of ad determine cost.
    a. Best time to buy newspaper space is annually, when station budgets are developed and to guarantee placement for key issues. Longer contract length, and high frequency of ad usage can bring rates down.
    b. Reinforcement ads can run daily or minimum weekly, small reminders of station identity to keep call letters visible on a regular basis.
    c. Full-page and half-page ads should be scheduled quarterly, unless a major event (such as format change), then weekly for 5 to 8 weeks before, during, and after event date.
    d. Medium ads provide more in-depth information about station feature, personality, or event.
3. Placement can be targeted to specific reader interest.
    a. Newspapers have a wide selection of sections, if not daily, then weekly dealing with a variety of subjects of specific interests, for example, sports, financial, gardening, travel, food, automotive, comics, books/literature, weather, politics, events, entertainment, cultural, international, police beat, education, environment.
    b. Establish life-group or listener profile of station's target potential listener, and then cater to that interest by exposure within a specific newspaper section. Note: This is a key, important benefit of radio advertising in newspapers. Do not accept substitute sections or random placement. Make section placement a part of your contractual deal.
4. Ads are relatively inexpensive to create/produce.
    a. Most papers offer basic art/layout services as part of package. Usually very inexpensive, but also usually very plain and simple. Not particularly recommended for creative work. Suggest station work with graphic artist or ad agency to develop artwork/copy and provide copy-ready art to newspaper. Stations should use graphic/layout skills as part of the job description for someone like the Promotions Director.

b. Stations should also have an in-house desktop publishing computer or art/graphics program and at least one employee skilled in its operation. This can save lots of money in the long run and can provide versatility and flexibility. Graphics can also be used for flyers, mail pieces, internal forms, sales presentations.

c. Many ads can be reused at other newspapers, both daily and weekly.

d. Ads should not be cluttered with copy. Call letters and dial position should be prominent and often included more than once in each ad (once on the logo, once in the small print). The purpose of a newspaper ad should be singular, selling one benefit per ad. Rotate different ads to expose multiple benefits. Some experts suggest lots of white space for the printed message to be more prominent.

5. Ads are tangible, can be copied, clipped, or reread.

a. People like things they can use as tangible reference. Coupon clipping is a national consumer epidemic. Newspaper ads containing information about sale merchandise is often carried to point of purchase with the instructions, "I want one of THESE!"

b. A simple dotted line around a print ad suggests that it can be cut out and saved. Example are sports team schedules, talk show lineups, contest hours, weekend programming, and phone numbers for requests, weather, newsline, etc. Articles or informational ads can be duplicated on a copy machine for readers to share.

c. There is opportunity for rereading or multiple reading by other family members.

6. Multiple publications can increase diversity.

a. Explore publication opportunities with all possible types of print media distributors. Initial reaction is to think only of the major daily papers, but the specific nature of radio lends itself to several other types of publications worthy of consideration.

b. More esoteric publications are usually dirt cheap for advertising, and many accept trade in exchange for publicity, exposure, and pick-up/purchase locations.

Here's my list of types of publications to consider:

1. Regional, state, or national newspapers with local inserts; include union publications.

2. Major daily newspapers. (Big announcements need all dailies involved; most readers subscribe to only one daily, so at least alternate among several dailies for complete exposure on reinforcement ads.)

3. Weekly newspapers, including:
Black, Hispanic, or other ethnic groups
Senior citizen
Trade newspapers for key employers in the community (real estate or legal journals)
Suburban newspapers (if in your hot Zip codes or specific target neighborhoods)
Shoppers, special publications, car buyer, Pennysaver
Trading posts (automotive, household)
Lifestyle papers, directories, and magazines (gay, hobbyists, retirees, travel, clubs)

4. Monthly or quarterly publications, including:
Arts and cultural
Community or neighborhood newsletters
Recreation (bowling, square-dance, softball, etc.)
Religious

5. Call print shops that specialize in newsletters or newsprint publications. Ask them for the names of some of their clients for whom they print material. Then go directly to those clients and inquire about getting your station message included.

6. Several successful stations have started printing their own newspaper/newsletter or producing a seemingly local station paper from nationally prepared shells. This gives the station regular print exposure (providing the station secures distribution or circulation numbers of its publication readership) as well as the opportunity to sell its own newspaper advertising. So, if you can't beat 'em, join 'em!

Elsewhere in this book, we talk about street-fighter promotions called "guerrilla" promotions. We discuss ways to get the word out about the radio station in less conventional ways. In both guerrilla and regular promotion, using another kind of publication is extremely important. I don't mean newspapers; I mean printed material for direct distribution or review by listeners. Generally, in every market, there are a number of print shops that are amenable to some sort of trade/barter arrangement, or at least some low-cost, ongoing relationship with a radio station.

There are flyers and simple notices, but the most effective printed piece is "The Radio Station Program Guide" handed out at every radio station event. This print piece contains the station logo along with a list of representative musical artists heard on the station, as well as other featured programs, the times they are on, the air staff lineup, and perhaps a sponsorship logo in case a sponsor would like to contribute to the printing cost of the piece. These are very effective for leave-behinds at all kinds of station functions, from concerts to street fairs, at sponsorship locations, mailed or picked up at the station. They can be included in all station mail sent to advertisers, listeners, or in casual correspondence. People do get to read them, and they're more effective than a refrigerator magnet, key chain, pen, or some other thing that people tend to discard or overlook.

Even though the Radio Program Guide may ultimately be discarded, it can create a number of impressions before it is. Print on the top, bottom, back, and front, and include as much information as possible. This item should be presented as something a listener might want to stick on the refrigerator door or thumbtack to the bulletin board or something to use as a reference for special programs. A program guide also reinforces the correct spelling of announcer names and useful phone numbers to the station such as the news or request/contest line. Print pieces can reap benefits in some unlikely ways, such as being used as scrap paper while jotting down the phone number of a new acquaintance from the event.

Successful promotions have used print for small tabletop tents. These are little signs that are put on tabletops in restaurants where people sit for 30 minutes or more, have their meals, and get a chance to look at a tabletop presentation by the radio station. This can be done with a restaurant that has an advertising relationship with the station. Also, if the station has any sort of event or function at a restaurant itself, or at a banquet hall, then these tabletop tents could be simple single-fold tent pieces of paper with radio station information and the logo on it. They also can be used as raffle tickets. By being numbered, people attending certain events can take them home or, better still, win prizes. One of the other unlikely uses of paper supplies and printing would be with napkins: Either cocktail napkins or dinner napkins (more especially cocktail napkins). There it is: a cocktail napkin with the station logo on it, staring at them every time they take a sip.

These methods are subtle, but they are frequently overlooked and inexpensive reinforcement opportunities to make your station a winner. A station seeking every aspect of every opportunity to promote itself will be far more successful and memorable than a station that assumes everything and does nothing to hammer home its image to listeners and non-listeners. Reinforce the station logo, the dial position, and a one- or two-word format description. Elaborate printing may include photos of featured artists or even the station lineup.

There's always a cost advantage in printing these things in large quantities, but if there is any chance that the print subject affiliated with the station might be moving on, then don't commit too far ahead. Basic, unchanging information like names of artists and features likely to be a part of station programming for an extended period of time should be included. Most people attending station events like to have a good time. Therefore, it's always important to reinforce the radio station logo, its image, and its dial position at the same time that the audience is having a good time. Simple psychology: Associate the good time with the call letters and name of the radio station and make that positive impression re-create itself every time listeners hear about the station or when they see the station logo. It's a case of simple psychological reinforcement from Pavlov's dogs to modern communications. The more opportunities you can create to put the call letters and the dial position and the station logo (or any other small bits of information) in front of the audience, the more opportunities exist to create an extended impression beyond what is accomplished on the air.

Occasionally, for the aggressive station programmer, a printed item can be useful for diffusing a competitor's event. In a typical guerrilla operation, hand out printed matter regarding your station as attendees leave a competitor's concert. I can recall more than one occasion when a competitor (in the same format) got to host a major event. Armed with numbered program guides, our staff politely greeted each person as he/she left the venue after the concert, thanking him/her sincerely for supporting the format (Country, in this case) and presenting him/her with a numbered program guide for our station. Then, we requested them all to listen on the way home and in the morning, because we'll be announcing the guide numbers on the air and awarding prizes and cash.

ADVERTISING: TELEVISION

For any radio station to succeed, the word must be spread throughout the community about the benefits of listening. While it is true, as we have illustrated in other chapters, that many stations do not take full advantage of their own resources, still there's only so much you can accomplish talking only to existing listeners. At some point, the station needs to reach out to nonlisteners with a plan to bring them into the station family.

Every program director dreams of creating a format that will spread like wildfire due to its sheer popularity, one that will enjoy a 100 share by exclusive virtue of word-of-mouth advertising. Real life seems to fall somewhat short of this ideal because, even if everyone did talk to everyone else, the message would be diluted and/or distorted. When a radio station makes use of other media to promote itself, it is hardly an admission of its own ineffectiveness. Rather, it is an exercise in common sense that amounts to attacking a target with an array of weapons. Just as we tell advertisers that radio makes a good complement to TV and print campaigns, so must we also make use of all our opportunities in order to achieve our own objectives.

Radio and television are both broadcast media. After that, they have very little in common. Radio survives by formats, TV by individual programs. No advertising package for TV is put together based on the station, but rather on demographics delivered by individual programming. An advertising agency is more likely to buy a greater selection of TV stations than radio stations for an ad campaign. For example, four or five TV stations may be selected using several different programs on each station to put together an effective advertising campaign. Each program appeals individually to the lifestyle or demographic in the target. In the same market, there may be only one (or maybe two) radio stations delivering the same demographic, but they do so exclusively and at all times.

In selecting television as a medium to advertise radio, the lifestyle issue is often as important as the demographic. There are lots of folks out there between the ages of 25 and 54, but which ones are likely to listen to your station? The TV programs watched by a country music fan may differ widely from a classical music lover or a talk show junkie. By carefully selecting the placement of your station's message with the TV programs closely linked with your potential listeners' lifestyle, the message will be far more effective than if the ad placement were selected on the basis of demographic criteria alone.

Cable has further fragmented TV schedules into even more diverse and specific programming selections. Cable advertising has benefited from the same general advertising opportunities as periodical magazines; that is, it caters to specific interests. As cable saturation in every market continues to grow and the number of cable channels increases, the opportunity for effective and economical placement of a radio station message becomes even greater. Cable operators tend to be less expensive than on-the-air TV, so there can be some expense spared.

These are the drawbacks to cable TV:

1. Cable is not supported by any consistent ratings service; therefore, documentation of audience size is speculative. The number of subscribers to a cable system is only a measure of people who receive the service, but does not indicate which channels they are watching or whether they are watching at all. Cable subscription numbers are similar to newspaper circulation numbers in that generally neither can verify any actual usage of the product, much less any specific channel/section.

2. Only those homes wired for cable will get the message, and some areas are served by several different cable companies. Since many markets have more than one cable operator/system, making a market-wide advertising campaign can be difficult and costly. Often these operators compete with each other for subscribers, making cooperation difficult.

3. Even though a majority of homes may be wired for cable, most preferred programming still comes from networks who have a regular TV station affiliate. If your message isn't on those stations, then it won't be seen by the largest audience.

4. Cable systems have only a limited coverage area and therefore may not be available in areas where a station may otherwise have listener-growth opportunities.

The TV SPOT

Radio station call letters, dial positions, logos, or formats should be clearly defined so that they can be remembered and recalled. We discussed in the chapter on station identity how important it is to project a simple, positive, unique image to the public. By using TV advertising to carry the message further, a clear selection of the appropriate program selections is of utmost importance. Some simple research into the TV viewing habits of existing listeners may give a strong clue as to the proper placement of advertising to reach non-listeners with similar tastes. Therefore, in selecting a TV message, simplicity is even more important. Remember that most television production departments don't really know very much about how to effectively advertise or market radio. Since the bulk of television revenue comes from retail or service-type advertisers, commercials for those companies are the model most stations use. If your radio station has a good promotions director, he or she should have some working familiarity with producing a television commercial. Similarly, many stations use the services of an outside advertising agency to develop an advertising plan for the station's television campaign. They, too, can be victims of the lack of familiarity with radio and can create well-produced, expensive commercials that are totally ineffective for achieving the radio station's goals.

There are dozens of excellent television production companies out there, specializing exclusively in radio spot production. They not only can offer you a custom-made spot, they will work with you to put together a good, attractive message, using local locations, your own talent, custom music, and a wide selection of logos and graphics. These spots are expensive and unfortunately are out of financial reach of all but the largest markets. Today there are fewer owners of radio stations in the United States as a result of consolidation, and many stations in a market may be owned by a single company. Therefore the cost of making a "group deal" with television producers is more possible now than ever before.

Many of these companies will also offer a prerecorded spot that can be customized for your station. These spots have disadvantages and advantages.

The advantages of a prerecorded spot are:

1. High-quality production values, both video and audio. Up-to-date ideas and references to current events and music trends (for music stations).

2. Lower cost than a custom-produced spot, since many stations in different markets can use the same material, making the appropriate substitutions in each market for station name, call letters, logo, personalities, etc.

3. The production company often can provide research information that went into the development of the commercial initially. Most TV spots for radio were already researched on similar audiences, so there is a viable track record of where the commercial has been used and what its effect was.

4. Usually some evidence of effectiveness from prior users. Get in touch with stations in other markets to ask their opinions about the effectiveness of the commercial.

5. No involvement required with local producers and the advantage of working with companies who really know radio.

6. Works best with nonpersonality formats or "cookie cutter" formats. (You don't have to admit it, but you know who you are.)

The disadvantages of a prerecorded spot are:

1. May not reflect your community/market image. There's only so much flexibility the production company has to adapt the spot to your needs and wishes.

2. No (or very little) creative input from the station.

3. Cannot significantly alter the spot; you get it as-is.

4. You don't own it; renewal fees are required for reuse.

5. Risk of audience seeing same spot in other markets.

The alternative to these prerecorded spots is to have a TV commercial produced locally. This service is often provided as part of an advertising package purchased from a TV station or cable operator in the same way that the production of a radio spot is a part of a radio station package. It is recommended that the station approach the TV station or independent producer with some concept or ideas about the message. At the very least, have a mission statement of what the desired outcome is. Make that statement specific.

WRONG: We want more listeners.

RIGHT: We want females 25 to 44 to know we play soft rock.

If the radio station regularly works through an advertising agency, then tap into its resources to put together your spot. Many stations farm out their advertising to agencies just as a retail client might do. If this is the case, be sure that someone from the station is involved in the creative process. Too often, advertising agencies don't understand radio (or they would place more client advertising), much less what the station message needs to be. Many agencies are trying to win local commercial awards—but not with your station's money, thanks. Cleverness is not as important in winning a new audience for a radio station as are simplicity and consistency. In the event that you do not use an agency and need to do a home-grown spot, all is not lost. Simple graphics and artwork can be very effective in delivering a basic message.

Here is a list of basic spot ideas that can be effective:

1. Identifiable station personality on camera, direct appeal.
2. Spokesperson (someone *not* on the station), direct appeal.
3. Slice-of-life appeal by on camera spokesperson in your target demographic. He/she looks like a listener.
4. Music formats: List of core artists scrolling on camera while announcer lists features, benefits.
5. Music formats: Play identifiable artists or selections.
6. Person-on-the-street testimonials from people who look like target listeners.

If you decide to put together your own spot, here are some basic rules:

1. Show call letters and dial position on camera for at least 10 seconds of a 30-second spot and 5 seconds of a 10-second spot.
2. Call letters and dial position are always last on the screen.
3. If station has a logo, use it. If the logo is unclear on TV, use easy-to-read letters.
4. Use an identifier slogan (what you call yourself and report to Arbitron) at least once.
5. If the station uses a color scheme, use it on TV if a true representation of your station colors comes across on TV; otherwise, use basic colors.
6. Don't clutter the spot with too much copy. Just make two or three basic points.
7. Don't use station personnel as talent unless they are on-the-air personalities and appear as themselves.
8. Be sure the audio portion of your spot could stand alone as if it were a radio spot.
9. Be sure the video portion of your spot could stand alone without the audio.

   Note: For items 8 and 9, many people only hear a TV spot from the next room or while not gazing at the picture. Others periodically mute the sound (especially during commercial breaks). Think about it!

Cleverness and originality are important in any television advertising, especially for radio stations. Don't miss the point, however. The cleverness or originality must reinforce or direct viewer attention toward a benefit that is offered by the radio station. Too often, the commercials are remembered, but not the radio station. If the station is music-intensive, then showcase the music in a clever or original way. If personality dominates, give the TV commercial viewer something about your personalities to remember, likewise for news or talk formats. If your station is represented by a slogan, mascot, or character, reinforce those identities with the station. Hats and horns, bells and whistles are all fun and exciting and feed our egos to the degree that we may feel we are so brilliant to come up with such-and-such an idea, but does the audience share in our enthusiasm and get the message?

Using television to promote radio makes sense. But because television can be the costliest segment of your promotional budget, use it wisely and effectively. Television puts a face on your radio station and makes the invisible visible. Be very comfortable with the company who produced your spot and with the spot itself.

The TV Schedule

Taking a chapter from our own radio sales pitch, frequency is the key in television advertising as well. Talk to the television station sales representative about the schedule, with the knowledge that no viewer gets the complete message on a single showing of a commercial. Several research studies indicate that most television messages don't begin to achieve viewer recognition until they have been seen at least three or four times. Therefore, when selecting a schedule for television, try to reach the same audience—the target audience—at least three or four times during the advertising campaign.

Television viewers are creatures of habit and tend to watch the same programs from day to day and week to week. Take advantage of this captive audience and give them several opportunities to accurately understand your complete message. Program loyalty is important to television advertising. Once the advertising team has identified an audience for which the TV commercial can have the greatest impact, schedule the commercial so that the audience will see it on those programs several times.

As is the case with all advertising campaigns, media experts agree that advertising works best when there is a combined effort to use more than one source for presenting the message. Like outdoor advertising, television has the ability to place a visual identity on a normally invisible medium such as radio. Television advertising needs to be planned in advance and not rushed. Television and cable stations have fewer local opportunities to place commercials than radio does, and the prime programming is the first to go. Don't get caught with the leftovers. It may not always be possible to completely dominate television, due to cost and availability of commercial opportunities, so look for specific audiences, lifestyle groups, or key demographics, and dominate at least one of them.

The goals of TV advertising for radio are:

1. To have the TV spot represent a key benefit of the radio station
2. To give an accurate impression of what the station represents, formatically
3. To have the TV spot seen and understood in its entirety during the advertising schedule
4. To reinforce any other advertising/promotion identities used by the station
5. To make viewers into listeners by driving viewers to sample the radio station, turn it on, listen

While the station is involved in negotiations with a TV station with the intention of spending some money with it, the door is open for a discussion of how radio can benefit the television station in its next promotional campaign. Use that opportunity!

ADVERTISING: OUTDOOR

Outdoor advertising and radio have been a long-time partnership. Most media experts agree that advertising works best when there is a concerted effort to combine more than one advertising source to present a message. Outdoor advertising has the ability to give something normally invisible, such as a radio station, a visual identity. This type of advertising is largely a matter of the availability of board locations relative to the station's target audience. Most cities have more than one outdoor advertising company, so there is frequently a game of jockeying for position in selecting board locations and getting the best financial deal. Unlike newspapers and TV, outdoor advertising is usually less receptive to trade or barter arrangements, but it occasionally offers some attractive packages for radio stations to use unsold billboards. Incidentally, by outdoor, we generally mean roadside billboards, although technically any other outdoor media qualify, including bus benches, bus sides, cab tops, etc. A few words about those later in this chapter.

There is disagreement about billboards. Some experts advise the use of lots of white space, with a total of only seven or eight words. For a while, I thought this idea was valid, especially if I was whizzing by at 55 miles per hour and had only one chance to comprehend the message on the board. This billboard message philosophy might work well for a nationally known product where name recognition and logo are already familiar. However, for those motorists regularly stuck in traffic on the same road every day at the same time, there is clearly an opportunity for a more comprehensive message. Prime candidates to become your listeners might work locally, and have an opportunity to read your billboard 50 times a week. Since radio is a local medium, and out-of-town through traffic is not the target audience, doesn't it make more sense to cater to local commuters by spending some quality time with them via the billboard?

The opportunity to tell a radio station's story on a billboard is greatly understated by traditional theories of what is correct. A billboard should be neat and uncluttered, but lists of artists, personalities, features, sports, and other entries should be considered. Since billboards are seen by people in cars, a billboard should sell the advantages of listening to the station. Using terminology from the world of sales, it should "ask for the order." It should beckon the driver to turn on the radio now. Therefore, I suggest the most important message a billboard can convey is "Listen now!" Other than the radio station itself, only a billboard addresses a potential listener at whatever time, day or night, is convenient to his schedule and with a radio within easy reach. Outdoor advertising should be easily readable day or night with prominent placement of call letters and dial position. If you're going to ask someone to listen, this first question to answer is, "Where is it on the dial?"

Note: Every FM station from 88 to 108 has a numeric counterpart on AM (880 to 1080, especially 88 to 99) so if you use a rounded-off numerical dial position, specify AM or FM. Just the number 92 or 97 or 99 should always require FM or AM. I suggest AM or FM should be included on all billboards.

A billboard should tell a station's whole story and convey an immediate benefit to potential listeners. Take a look at some of the radio station billboards in nearby communities. How many just don't tell you what you need to know? How many ask more questions than they answer? Worse, how many assume you already know everything about the station?

Here are some poor messages:

All the hits. All the time. (What format?)

Turtleville's most familiar music. (To whom?)

Serving Turtleville since 1938. (Yawn!)

Best hits of the 60s, 70s, 80s, 90s. (Nothing like narrowing it down! What format?)

Greatest Hits of Yesterday. (The Monkees, Elvis, or Glenn Miller?)

All the News You Need. (Shouldn't I decide that?)

(Call letters) Turn it on! (Give me one good reason.)

(Call letters) (No dial position, AM or FM.)

The best music, the best news. (Let me decide.)

Home of Fighting Turtle Football. (Football season only.)

#1 in Turtleville. (Station ranking is no motivation.)

Turtleville's first station. (Now I know where to listen if I ever become a time traveler.)

Billboards can reinforce the overall image of a station all year. Another effective use of billboards on a shorter term is to reinforce a specific hot promotion or event that the station is supporting. Even so, include the station's basic story so that it works for you even if the promotion does not.

Other types of outdoor media include:

- Bus sides (or interior)
- Cab tops
- Bus benches/bus stops
- Subway/rail station boards

Many of these types of outdoor visibility are regulated by local ordinances. Some city transportation systems do not permit advertising on public conveyance vehicles. Station visibility cannot be overstated; just carefully select the placement. My personal worst place for radio station advertising is on the back of a bus. It certainly gets seen, but following in traffic right behind a bus is probably one of the least desirable spots on earth. Between limited visibility, slow progress, and gagging on diesel fumes, a highly negative impression is probable, no matter how otherwise effective the message might be. Frequently, the environment you experience while you are receiving an advertising message can affect your overall impression of the message, even though the environment and the message may be totally unrelated.

Despite what their promotion or sales departments say, these types of outdoor advertising are seen more by pedestrians than by drivers.

1. Bus benches cannot be seen at all by drivers when people are sitting on them. It's a bench first, an advertising medium second.
2. Bus stop boards cannot be seen when people are standing in front of them waiting for a bus.
3. The same applies to train station boards. There is some exposure to passengers on passing trains, but people on the platform still create an obstruction.
4. There is never a guarantee of a clear, unobstructed message, except by pedestrians who are the first to arrive. These same pedestrians eventually become an obstacle to new arrivals who cannot see the message.
5. One person standing directly in front of a bus stop/train station board can obscure the entire message.
6. Pedestrians cannot turn on the radio now as drivers can, so the immediacy of an action message is lost.

Bus stops, benches, and subway/train stations are largely neighborhood locations. Placement of this type of advertising should be determined more by the match between the neighborhood or area itself and the demographic/lifestyle target of the station. When creating an advertising plan for a radio station, one of the most important rules is to use your resources wisely. Although every radio can attract a widely divergent group of listeners, practically speaking, it makes sense to develop a stereotypical profile of a listener to use as a guide in making advertising decisions.

Examples of a stereotypical, rule-of-thumb listener profile might include the following list of considerations in placing subway/train/bus stop advertising:

Station Format	Neighborhood/Location
Urban	Black/Hispanic
Country	Blue collar/industrial
Easy Listening	Older/retirement/office
CHR	Yuppie/preppie (any age)
Hard Rock	High school
Oldies	Blue collar/middle class
MOR	Upper middle class/older
AC	Upper middle class/younger
News/Info	Business/financial
Dance	Gay or ethnic
Classical	Cultural/college/upper class
Jazz	College/black

Although this is an incomplete and imperfect list, it gives an idea of how to start thinking of your listeners in their natural habitats. When spending cash for advertising, make the most of it, eliminate all wasted effort, and aim at a target you have some possibility of hitting. Even if the station has no cash budget and needs to rely on trade for its advertising, go into the arrangement with a plan of what needs to be accomplished and try to achieve those goals.

ADVERTISING: DIRECT MAIL

One of the most effective techniques for reaching a specific audience (or potential audience) for radio is to literally "ask for the order" with a letter or advertising piece sent directly to listeners via the U.S. Postal Service. Although effective, in most cases, a direct mail piece from a radio station must avoid one devastating characteristic:

A direct mail piece must not look like junk mail.

A direct mail piece must not look like junk mail.

In addition to the overall appearance and attractiveness of the mail piece, the real secret to effective direct mail advertising is the accuracy of the mailing lists provided. Most mailing companies can offer very specific mailing areas (whole communities down to individual neighborhoods) or demographics. The direct mail advertising piece for radio stations should be specific to the needs and provide benefits for those selected to be a part of the mail target and who could realistically be converted to regular station listeners. Since most major retailers, publishers, and almost every other type of business have gotten on the direct mail bandwagon, Americans are getting more mail than ever before; the bulk postage alone amounts to roughly $60 billion annually. Due to the unprecedented demand for mail pieces, the costs have become quite reasonable. The only guaranteed hard cost for a direct mail piece is the fixed postal rate, and even that can be variable. Because direct mail is tailor-made for each station (or should be), each design and message is unique for each station. Information on direct mail is readily available from dozens of suppliers. After all, they do printing for a living, so it's only natural that they can provide you with countless examples of their work.

For the sake of clarification and definition, a direct mail piece is a letter or printed material sent directly to listeners through the mail for the purpose of increasing listenership. As in all sales transactions, nothing happens until you ask for the order. In this case, the radio station is asking the listener to sample the station. For this reason, the message should be specific, personal, and appealing. Furthermore, there should be some notification of a radio station feature that is an obvious benefit to the recipient. Just telling people about the station isn't good enough. You have to tell them about it in terms that reveal benefit. This benefit can be in the form of an opportunity to play and win a contest, or more casually, the opportunity to enjoy unique entertainment, information, and feature material available via your programming.

The kind of direct mail often used by radio stations falls into three basic categories:

1. An introduction/description of the radio station, including:
    a. Music format, including lists of songs or artists and a description of the general appeal of the music played, defining it as clearly as possible
    b. Information and credibility, including network affiliations, news personalities, weather/traffic services, special informational programming
    c. Personalities, show times, features, recognition, identity, community popularity
    d. Events of station participation including sports, parades, fund-raisers, etc.
    e. Schedule of personality dayparts, special programming
    f. Visuals, photos of station personnel, identifiable logos, vehicles, mascots, etc.
    g. Invitation to listen to the station including text designed to sell the idea of listening. The invitation can be in the form of an urgent message/call-to-action (e.g., listen now!) or a personal appeal from a named station individual (general manager or program director).

2. A contest piece, including:
    a. Game piece, ticket, or lottery-type individual number
    b. Rules of the contest, including eligibility and restrictions by age, multiple family members, station employees, time limits
    c. Listening and how it enhances winning opportunities
    d. Prizes, including options, values, number, purpose, descriptions

3. An advertising piece, including:
    a. Message about the radio station and an indication that the enclosed material is being provided by the station in the interest of its listeners
    b. Values or coupons/gift certificates from sponsors

Usually, an advertising piece is accompanied by a paid schedule on the station. This double-pronged approach lets radio sales access advertiser dollars budgeted for direct mail, not radio. There are many excellent direct mail companies from which a wide variety of mail pieces can be selected. There are even a few who actually come to your market and assist your Sales Department in selling advertising or sell independently to clients already using some sort of direct mail. As these are usually not radio advertising clients, there is no conflict of selling "against" yourself. Consult with any trade publication to see the number of direct mail companies offering their services, or call our office at MOR Media for some companies we use for our clients.

ADVERTISING: GUERRILLA

Even the most carefully thought-out marketing plans, TV spots, billboards, or newspaper ads offer no guarantee that the radio station will succeed in its efforts to gain listeners or recognition. Often the least likely promotional efforts are the most remembered because of their unusual nature or unique appeal. Sometimes, stations with no outside advertising budget resort to what I call "guerrilla advertising." There are no real rules for these promotions, although a sense of humor and fair play don't hurt. Timing is essential. Successful guerrilla opportunities occur by seizing the moment.

Assuming that the station has its back to the wall but needs to get the word out, there are countless ways to create visibility. Effective guerrilla advertising requires creativity and perception. Stations who use guerrilla tactics best are driven by highly creative (and usually humorous) program directors or promotion directors. As is the case with any other advertising approach, the goals and anticipated results should be mapped out in advance; in this case, however, advance may mean a few days or hours. The ability to size up a situation is imperative. Think of a military general ready to attack, going to the hilltop, seeing the enemy, knowing the terrain, assessing the weaponry, and anticipating the number of troops required to do battle.

One of radio's best advantages over other media is its ability to be immediate and portable. Radio can react instantly to any occasion. Therefore, radio should (in the guerrilla mode) be ready to seize on any opportunity that may occur and for which there can be a strategic benefit to the radio station in establishing market identity.

Since I'm one of those people who has always taken a positive outlook toward radio, I do not recommend the mean-spirited sort of intrusion and invasion that some radio personalities and companies have employed to promote themselves. As in all things relative to American law, my rights stop where someone else's begin. I don't mind competitive game-playing and one-upsmanship, but some radio promotions and the persons who approve them have bordered on criminal activity at worst and an invasion of privacy and intrusion at best. If a radio promotion brings humiliation, pain, inconvenience, or harm to a listener, you didn't read about it here.

Here are thought-provoking, low-cost guerrilla ideas. Can any of them be applied to your station?

Goal: To take over another station's event (concert, dance)

Weaponry: Buttons (I like station buttons, if only for these occasions), printed flyers with station information

Strategy: Get something into event attendees' hands to make them think of your station, particularly right after the event, or do things on the air to create the impression that your station's participating.

1. Pass out buttons or flyers about your station as people leave the other station's event.
2. Have your air talent, with name tags, outside the building, shaking hands and thanking listeners for coming.
3. Have station vehicle parked on the closest public parking next to the other station's event. Give away free coffee, soda, or other items of small value.
4. Put your flyers on parked cars, thanking them for attending and inviting them to tune to your station on the way home for a special contest, concert, etc.
5. Use station vehicle or public area, clearly identified with your station banner, as an entry-blank sign-up location after the event for an upcoming contest. Winner's name announced the following day on your morning show.
6. Host a post-event party at an area club; require event ticket stub to get in.
7. Have a "mystery" person attend the event (buy a ticket) and hand out money or merchandise (gift certificates) to selected attendees who wear your button at the event itself. Prepromotion on the air is required.
8. If it's a concert, have special featured music by the artist before and after the event.
9. Get live interview with artist before the event.

10. Give special traffic reports before and after the event.

11. Position station vehicle or air talent at parking lot exit.

12. Tell attendees to bring their ticket stubs to your station the following day for a free gift.

Goal: Get the word out about a new air talent.

Weaponry: Phone, newspaper, printing

Strategy: Start word of mouth, on and off the air.

1. Buy cheapest classified ads under a variety of headings:
   • For Sale: Morning show
   • For Rent: radio studio 6 AM to 10 AM
   • Business Opportunities: Commercials for sale
   • Personals: Lonely Evening Host wants calls.
   • New Morning Man craves affection.
   • Educated, bright, witty, charming, attractive guy seeks 10,000 women 25 to 34 years old to listen to his morning show.

2. Use entire staff, get phone book, call people personally, ask them to listen. He's new, he's a great guy, and we think you'll like him. Fifty to a hundred calls per day, minimum.

3. New personality personally calls 20 to 30 business numbers per day, introduces himself, asks them to listen.

4. Invite newspaper columnists, reporters to cover the story background of new personality.

5. Run single, tiny ads throughout newspapers with just a phone number and an invitation to call.

6. Set up a special phone number with message machine or voice mail with new personality introducing himself/herself and asking them to listen.

Goal: To increase format awareness

Weaponry: Printing, buttons

Strategy: To expose primary, identifiable artists with your station call letters

1. Print station logo on cocktail napkins/matchbooks and give free to any club or venue that features music from your format.

2. Be all over any concert appearance by any artist featured by your format. Give away commercials, donate blood, do whatever it takes! Don't let any other station have your artists.

3. Print program guides with personality lineups, programs, etc. Leave on seats or tables of concert venue.

4. Photo session with artist and station personalities with station call letters or logo in every picture.

5. Positioning on the air should include phrases like "When you hear Janet Jackson, you must be listening to KTUR."

6. Print flyers with artist lists (minimum 10 artists), such as:

   KTUR Plays. . . .

   Celene Dion, Clay Aiken, Mariah Carey, Jessica Simpson, Norah Jones, Counting Crows, Wilson Phillips, Matchbox Twenty, Avril Lavigne, Kimberly Locke, KTUR (logo) AM 1610

7. Order very inexpensive buttons, ten different colors and artist names on each, such as:

   Janet is on KTUR AM 1610

   Clay is on KTUR AM 1610

   Avril is on KTUR AM 1610

Distribute to listeners all station events. Create a collection set by introducing a different button each week. Station sales staff should wear a different one every day on client calls. Give to advertisers to wear or distribute in stores.

Goal: To announce or introduce a new format

Weaponry: Phone, printing

Strategy: Build anticipation, generate curiosity

1. Print cards that say, "Coming (date): A new radio station . . . KTUR AM 1610. . . Listen!" Pass out personally to businesses and individuals.

2. Pass out cards to businesses or in public places. Enlist a volunteer corps: students, senior citizens, social groups. Find volunteers in the correct demographic for your station. Attractive persons to deliver or hand out material can be hired at modeling schools, often in exchange for trade advertising. Station can "pay" its volunteers with CDs, gift certificates, event tickets, etc.

3. Ask retail clients to put flyer in all purchases and packages.

4. During final days of old format, have fun; count down the hours to new format.

5. Give phony sneak previews of new format by playing songs of *everything but* the music of the new format. If the new format details are still secret, confusion and anticipation will work in your favor.

6. Use special phone numbers for sales business, but let message machine answer all other incoming calls for last few days of old format. Message could say, "KTUR is getting ready for its new, exciting format starting at noon on Monday. Until then, we have suspended normal business operations."

7. Print tags announcing the new station, call letters, and dial position. Arrange to tag hundreds of radios (for a few days) at stereo stores, department stores, car radios at dealers, or any other place where a radio is sold. Offer promotional mentions or commercials on the air in exchange for the tagging promotion opportunities.

8. Make some physical change to the building so that passersby will detect a change.

9. Set up a "listener squad." Print cards with a special phone number and hand out in public locations to persons in the target demographic. Card explains when they should listen and why. Their opinions are valuable. The special phone number is to an answering machine that records comments about the new format. If the station has an interactive phone system, it can be set for gathering more specific information.

To summarize: The unpredictability of radio lends itself to dozens of creative ways to promote. Look around, perceive, study. Don't be afraid to break old habits. Assume nothing. Try some of these ideas. Build on them. Adapt them to your situation. The bottom line is: You must win.

Throw every effort, whether traditional or extraordinary, at the winning process. People always recall the unusual more easily than the routine. Observe other businesses in action. See how they get the word out about their services and products. Are there any tactics they use that you can adapt to promoting your radio station? Don't be afraid to fail. In baseball, having a .300 batting average is considered excellent. But a .300 success translates to a .700

failure rate. Most often, success is an event enjoyed by a minority of businesses, a minority of the time. Here's the familiar lesson:

- Extraordinary ideas come from great ideas.
- Great ideas come from good ideas.
- Good ideas come from failures.
- Nothing comes from no ideas.
- There can be neither success nor failure without an effort to try something.

PROMOTIONS

PROMOTIONS DESIGNED AROUND THE LISTENERS

I started as a listener and I think that most of the best broadcasters that I've ever worked with over many years have been people who started by being intent listeners to radio. They studied radio, they listened to radio stations, they had their favorite DJs, they went to station promotions, they played station contests, and they knew when the new music was coming out. Much like other kids may have collected model planes or toy soldiers or played Little League, many of us who got our early starts in radio started by being great listeners. So whatever impact radio has on people, primarily the listeners, is due to how effectively we can create a product for which they give us their time and expect something entertaining and important to listen to. If we don't give people something good to listen to, they won't listen. If they won't listen, their listening can't be effectively measured, and without the effective measurement of listening, there are no ratings, which translates into no advertising, which translates into no money, which translates into, "Where's my next job?"

In addition to giving people an overall view of how programming fits into the big picture of radio, let's try to keep an eye and an ear toward what the listeners might be thinking and put ourselves in their lifestyles from time to time. At many radio stations we get caught up in the day-to-day operations of what goes on behind the four walls or what goes on behind the microphone. We sit for hours staring at computer screens generating music logs and trying to do ratings analysis, and we spend too little time trying to understand the lifestyles of the actual people we are trying to reach.

The most effective radio stations have a sine wave of the station activities over the year that very closely parallel the same activity sine wave of the community in which they are licensed. The stations that most closely replicate the interests of the users, or the activities of the listeners, will be more closely identified with those listeners. The listeners will start to think of the radio station as having the same ups and downs that they do. They both celebrate the same great weather days, the same local sporting events, the same holidays, and the same feelings of excitement and of despair depending on the economic status of the community. A radio station can't do that if it only listens to what's going on behind its own four walls. Any opportunity that station personnel have to spend time with the listeners can only benefit the listeners and ultimately the station in the long run.

Another mysterious but often unexplored thing about listeners is that they are a valuable resource in the promotion and marketing end of the business. Most radio stations tend to want to compose stations promotions and giveaways with conventional premiums like bumper stickers, T-shirts, and things that promotional companies want us to purchase to give away to people. But what we fail to do is ask listeners what it is they would like to get from us; what are their needs? Many radio stations fail to assess the needs of the listeners accurately. They base their promotions and their premiums and their giveaways on things that come to them through the back door, either from record companies or from merchants with whom they have advertising relationships rather than trying to fulfill needs that the listeners actually have. That may be one of the great benefits of learning about your audience. Be the radio station in the community that more closely identifies with the listener in everything he or she does, not just the music, not just in the selection of news and information, not just in the attitude of the DJs. Also be a station that offers promotional opportunities that directly benefit an immediate need that the listeners have. In this regard, listeners can be a terrific resource in learning about the market and about how listeners feel and what people want. Many radio stations conduct research using listeners, but this is usually research based on music preferences. There doesn't seem to be any attention given to the other aspects of the radio station. If more research companies and more radio stations decided to ask more difficult and more probing questions of their listeners apart from what songs they like and dislike, they might find a lot of other things the station can be doing to serve the listeners and to gain their allegiance and therefore gain greater listenership.

HOW TO PROMOTE A RADIO STATION WITH SOMEONE ELSE'S MONEY

Some of the best kinds of promotions are those that pay for themselves by participation of other business interests within the promotion. A promotion that requires a prize, entry blanks, signs, newspaper ads, etc. can be effectively developed into a self-paying opportunity by the mutual participation of several parties other than the radio station.

For example, approach a local newspaper and ask if it would like to be a sponsor of the promotion or the event along with the radio station. With its consent and participation, the radio station automatically has access to the newspaper's readership and has taken care of the newspaper advertising portion of the promotion.

Similarly, entry blanks, signs, or posters can be obtained by enlisting the services of a printer. In exchange, the printer gets acknowledgment on the radio station as a cosponsor as well as having its logo or name appear with the station in promotional advertising. If the station enlists the resources of cosponsors like a car dealer, restaurant, or retail store, let the new partners print any necessary materials using their existing printing budgets. Remember to provide them with the station logo and, by all means, retain the right of approval before going to press. Prizes can be obtained from one of the cosponsors (to reinforce a product line) or from other participating sponsors who provide supplemental prizes in exchange for promotional mentions on the radio station. It's not necessary for the items being given away to be promoted if they are not significant parts of the prize. Sometimes the provider wants to promote something else at a later date.

Other self-liquidating promotions involve station merchandise where the station has enough audience popularity to invest in its own promotional items (T-shirts, caps, jackets, etc.) that are sold at commercial locations. The station can benefit enormously from these items, since people want to pay the station for free advertising. Promotional merchandise must be compatible with the station image, demographic, and format. Distribute self-liquidating station merchandise items through the participation of a retailer, preferably a clothing store, where station merchandise can be sold as an exclusive item. A regular schedule of commercial announcements on the station proclaims the store as the exclusive outlet for station items, providing additional foot traffic to the merchant's location. In exchange is the commitment to display and sell station merchandise. This method of selling station items also provides easy sale procedures, since most stores are set up to accept checks and credit cards, whereas the station itself may not be.

Occasionally, but not regularly, it may be possible for a participating cosponsor to have some visibility on station merchandise items. I recommend this only in exceptional cases. Too many logos or conflicting promotional messages clutter a piece of apparel or other item. Work out the financial matters in advance and contractually agree on the price for each item, the division of the revenue, and the accounting and/or accountability.

Take advantage of the self-liquidating sale of merchandise through mail order. Listeners write and request items, pay by check, and receive the item by return mail. Provide a small display case at the station for promotional items and sell them there. If the station does this, be in compliance with state and local laws that may require collection of taxes, licensing, or permits. Should the station wish to set up a small retail operation, the opportunity for additional revenue is considerable; just keep the operation under control and on the books. Avoid potential problems by not selling items via a cigar box full of cash at the receptionist's desk. Selling merchandise directly eliminates the middle person and can indeed become another revenue center for the station. For another approach, a portion of the profit of the sale of each item can go to a designated charity, adding a positive dimension to the popularity of the item and enhancing the community image of the station. The merchandise can be available at the charities' other public events, too.

In setting up promotions, it's crucial to draw up a game plan of exactly what you want the promotion to accomplish. Then, run through a list of potential participants. Approach the participants individually to assess their willingness to become involved. Set up a list of potential participants based on the function they are to perform within the promotion. If food is required, look for five or six food sources (restaurants, supermarkets, caterers). If the promotion requires equipment or supplies, establish a list of businesses that specialize in those items. If the station feels the promotion can be significantly enhanced by additional promotion from outside media, establish a list of potential alternative media participants, such as cable, newspaper, weekly publications, TV, or outdoor (billboards). If you need a location, then shop around for that, too.

Having broken the event into its various potential participants and elements, direct different station personnel, with their varying degrees of experience and influence, to approach potential participants with the opportunity to join forces with the station on this event. Chapter 4 on public service announcements (PSAs) also suggests opportunities to tie in charity or nonprofit organizations for mutual benefit. The chapter on meetings sets up a structure for any type of productive meeting format.

Once the station has found a willing participant for each of the elements required for a successful promotion, get everyone together for a planning meeting, mapping out the goals and expectations for the promotion so each is clear about his or her contribution. The initial organizational meeting is critical for establishing duties and accountability. At that meeting, outline specifically who is accountable for what and by when. Most important, establish the radio station generally (and one person specifically) as the chairperson for the event. In most cases, this person would be the station promotions manager, but it could also be the program director or often the PSA director in the event of a community-involved promotion. It is important to establish a person in charge, station and participant accountability, and a clear operating framework for a successful promotion. Explain from the beginning what is expected of each participant in dollars and cents, labor and merchandise, as well as the obligation to promote the event and participate in its success. As payback, the station should be sensitive to what each participant wants in return from the station in exchange for involvement.

Putting together promotions of this sort should become routine. An active, promotionally viable radio station should put together several promotions a year based on this pattern. Promotion must be done regularly for a radio station to continue to project its identity effectively. As long as the system is in place for setting up and operating successful self-liquidating promotions, why dismantle it? Hopscotch right into the next promotion, often using the same participants, or others on the original lists. Businesses not included in one promotion are often eager to participate in the next because of its visibility and former involvement of a competitor. Those likely sponsors on the lists will, one hopes, have perceived something positive from the successful promotion and will not miss the opportunity to be involved next time.

If a promotion is really successful, get the same sponsors participating on a regular basis. It's always great to sign up sponsors if you don't have any, but don't get painted into a corner and exclude other potential sponsors from future promotions. Don't lock someone out, or the sponsor might take a previously pitched promotional idea to a competing radio station and launch a promotion. This could result in losing touch with that client and running the risk that a competing station will have a more successful promotion.

Some final thoughts on promotions:

A. It's always advisable to get everything in writing. (Remember, a verbal contract isn't worth the paper it's written on.)

   1. Outline and explain the details and responsibilities.

   2. Make sure all parties are copied on all correspondence.

B. Since timing is everything in promotion, time-bind every expectation at every level of the event and each participant to a firm schedule of completion and reporting.

C. Since many promotions are also considered contests, specific rules and regulations containing all the necessary legal language required by your state and/or legal advisors should be established and available to the public for inspection.

D. Did anything actually get promoted?

TIME TARGETS

One of the pivotal characteristics of all radio is its perpetual association with time. Being a 24-hour, 7-day-a-week industry, radio stations are like giant clocks that mark off the seconds, minutes, and hours of the day. It's the only industry that comes to mind that actually establishes procedures and mechanics for telling time. You don't walk through an insurance company, bookshop, restaurant, or department store and hear an employee announcing the time of day every 3 minutes. The very essence of programming revolves around correctly timed hours of music—hour after hour after hour. To accommodate the need for correct timing, radio also places specific time restrictions on other programming elements within those hours (e.g., commercial breaks, newscasts, weather, phone calls).

An important and valuable number in ratings surveys is the Time Spent Listening (TSL). TSL measurements relate how many hours and minutes of each day listeners spend with each station. The TSL is also broken down into each individual daypart. Because time is of the essence in all radio, it's important to understand how radio programmers can make time work to the station's advantage and when it can prove harmful. In Chapter 5, I touched on the subject of time targets and how they can affect listening. A time target is just what its name implies, a target for accomplishing something on the air in the time allowed. Time targets make up an important part of our daily life, whether or not we know it. We all have them:

• Having to be at work at 8:30 AM

• Meeting someone for lunch at 12:15 PM

• Picking up the dry cleaning at 4:00 PM

• Simmering the spaghetti sauce for 90 minutes

• Getting to the theater for the 8:00 PM performance

We leapfrog our life schedules, going from one time target to the next and then on to the next. Problems arise when time targets conflict or coincide. On the air at radio stations, time targets work in somewhat the same way. Of course, there is a more direct purpose, and it does not necessarily follow a 24-hour rhythm, as life does. A housefly lives 4 days; some trees live four centuries; a radio show lives about 4 hours. Each accomplishes certain things while getting from start to finish. At the radio station, if you know listening patterns throughout the day, it can be a valuable tool in developing time targets that will work. Radio survives and sells itself through on-the-air promotion of itself and its programming elements.

Ever heard these expressions on the air before?

- "Another chance to win coming up next hour."
- "It's Bob and Company tomorrow morning at 6."
- "Paul Harvey News at noon today."
- "I have a toll-free number for tax tips right after this."
- "Tonight at 7:30 it's the Mets and the Cardinals."
- "Something new from Michael Jackson after Captain Katie takes a look at traffic."
- "Major fire may disrupt your phone service; details in 10 minutes on KTUR News."

We've all heard them. But few programmers really know how to use time targets realistically. The secret of effectively using time targets is to make them realistic and specific. Make them correspond to how long you really believe a listener will wait for what you promise. Imagine just how long you yourself would wait for the same thing. Here are some unrealistic time targets, why they are no good, and how to improve them:

Example 1: Music is one of the most promotable items on a radio station if the station positions itself as a music leader.

Announcer: "Next hour, something from the 'Garth Brooks: Live in Central Park' concert CD."

What's wrong? No specific target. No matter how big a Garth fan I am, I gotta get to work. Next hour I'm gone. Imagine someone circling the parking lot waiting for this tune.

Fix it: "At exactly 9:15 this morning, I've got a classic from the 'Garth in Central Park' concert. Plan to be near a radio at work and turn it up."

Example 2: Contests, by their very purpose, are designed to augment radio listenership. Few radio stations give prizes to be nice guys. There should be a design and a purpose to each contest. It's amazing how many stations give thousands of dollars in contest prizes but fail to attain the goal of increased audience.

Announcer: "More chances to win throughout the day here on Turtle-98."

What's wrong? Even though listeners may need the money desperately, the motivation simply isn't there to sit by the radio all day.

Fix it: "Next time to win on Turtle-98 will be between 2:00 and 2:30 this afternoon, so if you have to be away from the radio for a while, go ahead, but be back in time to win." This really makes them think they have a shot at winning.

Example 3: Next to the music and contests, the artists who make up the format are very promotable, if the promotion is done correctly.

Announcer: "It's 3:10 in the afternoon at Turtle-98. Later this hour, I'll have Madonna, Celene Dion, Sting, and Suzy Sweet."

What's wrong? It's too general. Also promotes an unknown: Suzy who?

Fix it: "It's 3:10 . . . . The best song the Madonna ever had, Sting, and Celene Dion's top selling song of all time between now and 3:30 on Turtle-98." Note: Promote only heavy hitters and make it a short wait. Give the station a feeling of playing only bombastic music by constantly reinforcing it with reminders, and play it!

Example 4: The station's personalities can benefit from time target promoting. A little preparation helps.

Announcer: "Listen later this afternoon for Steve Warren here on Turtle-98."

What's wrong? Too general. No motivation to listen; what's the benefit to the listener?

Fix it: "This afternoon between 4:15 and 4:30, Steve Warren will tell you the truth behind the Little Bo Peep legend in another chapter of his 'Mother Goose Uncovered' series."

Note: In case you're curious, the sheep in the Bo Peep legend are an obvious symbol for Bo Peep's many suitors, including Jack Spratt and Humpty Dumpty. Peep, through carelessness, alienated her suitors, but they will come back "wagging their tails behind them"—that is, still faithful and happy to court her.

Another note: Know what the personalities are famous for and what their daily features and bits are. Reinforce them throughout other dayparts, but be specific. Rotate several regular items that give an overall picture of the other air talent. If the listeners cannot listen to the other personalities, give them an idea of what they are missing.

WHAT PAYS THE BILLS?

We cannot close out the topic of time targets without a discussion of commercial copy. The actual copy, as well as the presentation format of that copy, must be treated with the utmost respect. That's what pays the bills. We'll also see how critical the awareness of timing is to commercial ads.

Although some new technology allows for commercial copy to be shown to the announcer on a computer monitor, most stations still rely on some form of simple paper copy. Some stations have gone to great lengths to reproduce vast numbers of the same commercials so that each hour of the day has all the copy necessary hour by hour, without having to flip back and forth in an alphabetical file book. Aside from being wasteful of paper, the sheer volume of paper can be cumbersome. I still suggest a simple alphabetical ring-binder type of copy book with durable (plastic) alphabetical tabs that won't wear out with heavy use. A small clamp to mark upcoming copy will suffice for turning quickly to the next piece of copy required. I've even seen a station very effectively use a clamp-type laundry clothespin for this purpose. Copy books should be a bit lower than eye height and angled to avoid glare from overhead lighting. Adequate space should be allotted to the commercial copy book when designing the announcer's environment. It should not be required to be put away and taken out when needed. A commercial copy book is a permanent part of the radio studio, as important as the microphone and other technical equipment. Reading is still the primary task of an announcer, and commercial copy is the most important reading an announcer will ever do. All commercial copy should be only an arm's length away from the announcer at all times. Commercial copy should never be kept in a file drawer or hanging file, requiring a separate function to access the copy and refile it. This is no more than an interruption of the announcer's thought process and is mere busywork that interferes with the quality of the announcer's performance.

On recorded commercials, careful attention should be given to exactly what a commercial says, particularly dated material. Nothing destroys the credibility of a station's commercial integrity than running out-of-date commercial copy. All written copy should have clear end dates indicated. The same is true for commercial tape cartridges or any other media used for commercials. Another problem with some commercial copywriters is their desire to make one piece of copy suffice for a multidated event.

For example:

> Everyone is invited this weekend to the big tent sale at Angus Al's Cattle Auction. On Friday, Angus Al will kick off the event with a fireworks display at 9 PM, then all day Saturday, there will be pony rides for the kids, free hot dogs and balloons, and a trick-riding demonstration at 6 PM. Then Sunday, it'll be live Country music from 2 PM to 5 PM with Ronny and the Ragweeds and a big finale chili supper at 6. That's all the fun you'll have this weekend at Angus Al's Cattle Auction on County Road 23, just past where the old church used to be.

This might be an exciting piece of copy to run all week in advance of the event, but how many stations would actually run it through the conclusion of the event? Experience taught me. Too many!

There are critically important rules for anyone writing, scheduling, or producing radio commercials:

It's important to remember that as each day passes during an event, there is mention of things past, thereby wasting the advertiser's ad time. We've all heard them. Particularly vulnerable are weekend promotions, festivals, and sales with a schedule of special events, concerts, shows, giveaways, and presentations for each day. By Saturday, Friday's events have ended. By Sunday, Saturday's fun is history. Haven't you ever heard a commercial on Sunday afternoon promoting a concert from the night before or a commercial containing a lineup of entertainment and appearances which happened yesterday? Holidays are other bad times for running outdated commercials. I'm amazed at how much advertising money is wasted on commercials promoting events that have already occurred or sales that are over. We all hear this wasteful and ineffective advertising all the time. As programmers, we must direct the advertising-related departments within the station with mandatory policies that control putting anything on the air. Three or four variations of the commercial copy presented here would have been sufficient to correct the problem. Incidentally, advertising agencies are sometimes equally guilty of producing this kind of copy, so make sure your station policies are not compromised and the advertiser's money is not wasted. Remember, listeners hold the radio station responsible for everything they hear, so regardless of where the errors originate, it's your job to correct them before they affect your listeners. There should never be one outdated second wasted on any radio commercial or promo.

LINER CARDS

One of the facts of life in any radio studio is "thought starters" or *liner cards*. With all that goes on around the station, it's always convenient to have a set of announcer reminder cards for events or activities. Use 4 × 6 inch cards rather than 3 × 5 inch cards so that each card can contain more information and larger typeface for easier reading. Although most radio studios are equipped with computer screens that provide promotional liners and other copy for announcers to read, the simple piece of paper or file card may be a part of radio forever. So whether we use a computer or cards, the principle is the same. We need different kinds of cards for different reasons and some structure to control their usage on the air.

All office supply stores sell multicolored, inexpensive quantities of file cards, so let's start by selecting the lightest tint of four colors of unlined cards including yellow, blue, salmon (orange), and white. Invest in several hundred of each color, especially white, since you will constantly be updating, changing, and replacing them. This simple, efficient system will help the air staff stay organized and the station sound consistent. Ratings services, particularly Arbitron, require regular usage of slogans for identifying purposes. Most of the items on these "C" promo cards will be automatic. But sometimes, even the best professionals overlook the obvious. In this case, these items are really reminders of key programming slogans. It's easy to get lazy and forget the basics, especially because they are so repetitive, but radio works by repetition and mandates their regular and frequent usage.

Here are the definitions and features of the four types of cards:

1. Orange "A" PROMOS: The hottest top promotions or next main event:
   - Current contest
   - Concert or station co-promote event
   - Tease special event or start of something "coming" to the station
   - New air staff member, program, contest, feature
   - Make these your next event only.
   - Life span on each card should be only a few days.
   - Replace often for variety.
   - Never more than two items to promote at a time and never more than two cards (different copy) each.
   - Read one per hour in the first break; paraphrase another version 20 to 40 minutes later.

Using the warm color orange is a reminder that these few cards represent the biggest thing happening at the station. This is top priority. It's hot! It's the next main event the audience can anticipate or participate in. This is front-page stuff!

2. Yellow "B" PROMOS: Secondary promotions, programming, and cross-plugs:
   - A card for every announcer shift (put the actual air-shift hours of each announcer)
   - When plugging, refer generally to daypart (Steve Warren, mornings; Jim Shew, evenings)
   - Incidental contests and games (Jim Shew has more circus tickets to win on tonight's trivia contest)
   - Weekend or special program promotion (e.g., countdowns, artist specials, holiday features)
   - Commercial or sales promotional announcements, remote appearances (You'll have a logged schedule of commercial remote plugs, but programming can run some, too; play up the programming benefits and play down the commercial. Save that for the paid spots.)
   - News, public affairs, and informational promos, including weather, traffic, sports, etc.
   - This category may contain as many as 10 to 15 items.
   - Read one hourly during the second commercial break.

3. Blue "C" PROMOS: Station slogans, positioning liners:
   - Call letters and dial position reminders
   - Arbitron slogan file liners
   - Station catchphrases
   - Technical phrases (most powerful, Stereo Digital, HD radio, surround sound, etc.)
   - Music or information positioning
   - Community positioning (oldest, first, involved, recognized, etc.)
   - Read one hourly as a drop-in, no fixed position. Since these items are phrases rather than promos, they should be used at the rate of at least one per hour as drop-ins anywhere convenient in the flow of programming. Make them a part of regular conver-

sation rather than as stand-alone remarks. For best response, select six to eight different phrases, one per card. Double up (two cards) on a key phrase so it comes up more often.

4. White PSA ITEMS (More on these in Chapter 4.)

Now that you have the cards typed and sorted with selected phrases, promos, contests, etc., here's the operation of the card file system:

1. Build a special, clear plastic box to hold the liner cards so that the announcer on duty can look through the plastic to see what's next. You can order one directly from our company, MOR Media International (see our website, www.radiothebook.com). Mount it at eye level so that it's never out of sight. Off-to-the-side file boxes or copy books are too cumbersome and don't serve as constant reminders to the announcer about the station's positioning and activities.

2. Place the cards in the box from left to right: A, B, C, PSA. Orange-Yellow-Blue-White.

3. After you have explained the formatics of the contest or promotion to the air staff, both personally *and* in writing, ask them to help write some liner card promos themselves for variety. This lets the air staff take part in the promotion and also frequently unearths some misunderstandings regarding the instructions or the concepts. Promos can be scheduled by the traffic department on the program log, or they can be a part of the hourly format as indicated on the Format Clock. In the latter case, a tracking system is necessary to avoid repetition and ensure maximum exposure. We suggest a small rubber stamp of blank boxes to be stamped on each card, so that the times can be recorded. This rubber stamp is particularly important in tracking PSAs, so there are more details and an example in our chapter on PSAs.

Here are the four basic liner card groups:

A. Orange promotional liners:

Define, describe, reinforce the station's hot promotion. The primary and singular promotional thrust you want listeners to keep top of mind.

"Your $100 a day radio station!"

"Your Mick Jagger, Michael Jackson, Barbra Streisand World Tour ticket station!"

B. Yellow plug liners:

Sell yourself! Cross promote all other programming elements from weekend special programming to announcer shifts.

"Big Al takes your requests tonight starting at 8."

"Another Seventies Sunday Morning this weekend at Turtle 98!"

"Bob and Company with special guest, Bart Simpson, again tomorrow morning at 6!"

C. Blue image liners:

ARB slogan file liners or slogans and station image material:

"The home of eleven in a row!"

"Your Station to Dance to, Turtle 98!"

"The great 98!"

D. White public service liners (now Public Involvement)

Civic and community announcements emphasize station involvement.

"Diabetes tests Saturday at the Small Mall Health Fair only $5.00, free if you mention Turtle 98!"

"Tonight at 7:30, the Turtle Truck will be at the high school, collecting canned food for Food Share."

A little planning and organization in constructing and updating liner cards will remind the air staff to execute basics and to repeat and reinforce key elements, benefiting the radio station with regularity and consistency. Make your card verbiage short and concise, so that it triggers your announcer to create a unique way to say the message each time it comes up, rather than to read the liners, promos, and PSAs verbatim.

HOW TO PROMOTE A RADIO STATION (WITHOUT MONEY)!

I have yet to encounter a radio station that had enough money to accomplish a promotion it wanted to execute. It seems that promotion, to many station owners, is a bottomless pit, constantly sucking cash from the bottom line with, too frequently, no evidence of having accomplished anything. Certainly money is very helpful when it comes to promoting a radio station, but let's take a look at a few ways a station can be promoted without using cash (or very little). If any funding does become available, it can be used to augment these techniques for even greater effectiveness.

1. Use the radio station itself.

A successful radio station is always talking about itself. Several times each hour, radio personalities, around the clock, need to be reinforcing in listeners' minds about all the promotable aspects of the radio station, whether they are programming features, outside promotions, contests, or services that the station performs. Sometimes, unfortunately, station promotions take only the position of promoting through outside-medium newspapers, billboards, or television spots, and neglect to use their own radio stations to promote themselves. Saturate with self-promotion.

Although radio works by repetition, too frequent repetition of station promotional material can become very tiring to the audience and produce listener fatigue. Therefore, station promotional announcements should be frequently updated, using new copy, different announcers, different production music—some fast, some slow—short, long, detailed, or brief. But never let up on the constant selling of the radio station. Run promotional announcements during the day just like normal commercials. Stations usually have promo positions in their broadcast hours in addition to their commercial time. Most radio audiences don't understand the difference, or see any difference at all, between a promotional announcement and a commercial announcement. A station promo will be just another commercial to them. Rather than develop individual promo locations each hour, schedule station promos in unsold commercial slots that are available, even if this means the occasional expense of bumping a commercial spot. This will happen from time to time (mostly in drive time), but the programming integrity of the music and entertainment image of the station should not be encroached upon by an excessive number of interruptions, whether they are commercial or promotional.

Take a lesson from the radio station sales department manual and use radio sales as they should be used. "Buy" some time on the station itself during prime broadcasting hours to get the message across. If this approach is supposed to work for paying advertisers, then it should work for the station itself. Station promotional announcements are thought of as free, but there is nothing free about them. They could be the most expensive and the most valuable chunks of time on the air.

2. Piggyback station activities with events that are already going to happen.

For example, if a major charity is going to throw a major fund-raising event, like a show or a chili cook-off, get to the organizers far enough in advance to throw complete support behind their event. The charity then will use the station exclusively in promoting its event. Ask for permission from the event sponsor to have station signs or banners at the event itself. Have the station logo or call letters included in the sponsor's print material. Be a part of its press releases to the newspapers and television stations, perhaps on the posters, or even on the letterhead. This costs nothing other than the time of the staff person who takes the responsibility to work out the details and spearhead the station's participation.

A good, aggressive radio station can find some significant public affairs event every month of the year and can make many of these events appear to be its own promotions, with the total expense nearly zero. In putting together a promotional event that is connected to a charity, it is often much easier to go to the businesses with whom a commercial relationship already exists and get it to contribute materials such as printing or food that will be used at the event itself. After all, the businesses are doing it for the ultimate success of the fund-raising event itself, the charity, and then, vicariously, for the radio station involved.

Promotion and positioning the station within the community for public affairs events is an excellent way to gain free and positive publicity. In mentioning positive publicity, there are some causes or charitable organizations that, for one reason or another, tend to polarize certain members of the population. Therefore, it is always a good idea to double-check an involvement with some nonprofit organizations to be sure that they represent the same ideals that the station represents. Some examples of these are social organizations or non-profit organizations that deal with health issues, sexual issues, educational issues, and political alliances (some organizations may have affiliations that would alienate a portion of the audience, while gratifying another portion of it). Select promotional opportunities that can affect the largest number of people and, in as many cases as possible, try to associate with community events where large numbers of people are involved and where the potential for large crowds and maximum station exposure exists.

3. Be at the right place at the right time. Among the right places and right times are these:

   a. If the station has a vehicle, make sure it is painted front, back, and sides so that, no matter which direction the vehicle is pointing and no matter where it is parked, the call letters are obvious. It's a good idea to paint call letters on the roof of the car just as police cars sometimes print their numbers on their roofs so they can be visible from the air. If there's an airport with planes coming in and out, people are going to remember a car they see with call letters on the roof.

   b. Never let the news department staff go out of the building without call letters on their microphones. Microphone flags are inexpensive but worth their weight in gold when seen on nightly television at news conferences or the front page of the daily paper.

   c. Make sure all station personnel are identified in public. For a few dollars apiece, an attractive name tag can be fashioned for each member of the radio station staff. Include office personnel who participate in promotions. Nobody should have to ask if someone works at the station. Make name tags consistent with colors selected for station identity. Be consistent with call letters (lettering) and the logo, too.

d. A popular way for radio stations to get publicity without having to pay (cash) for it is through barter or trade agreements with other businesses. By using unsold inventory on the air in exchange for other businesses' goods and services, the station can access everything from sign painters, printers, balloon manufacturers, and sky-writers to billboards, newspapers, and television.

e. Frequently, television, newspaper, and billboard trade agreements are expensive and may involve annual commitments. In many cases they require (or are enhanced by) cash commitment along with the trade agreement. In dealing with smaller merchants at a lower level, items that normally cost just a few hundred dollars can very easily be traded. Every radio station function should have its own custom-made paper cups and plates, balloons, posters, name tags, banners, and whatever signs may be appropriate for station events.

f. Use printed materials. Place table tents in restaurants or nightclubs where the station may be appearing. Leave flyers on tables and chairs and seats; distribute them at remote locations, outlining the station's programming activities or containing coupons or entry blanks for contests. These materials can almost always be traded through a local printer. Any opportunity you have to place the station logo plus some additional information about the station itself in front of a crowd is excellent for reinforcing the station identity.

g. Look for opportunities to exchange program space with community theaters, school or community theaters, sporting events, public functions, or concerts where advertising space is available in the material that is passed out to those attending. When done right, none of this costs anything. You are just exchanging services. That's what barter is all about. It's an underused opportunity, especially for small- and medium-market stations.

h. At functions like movie openings, concerts, or shows where there has been no actual ticket used, it is easy for a radio station to print its own, making sure that every station event has a ticket that is distributed in advance of the event. This reminds the listener of the upcoming event and, because there is a tangible representation of the event in the form of a ticket, the event is less likely to be forgotten. This usually ensures greater participation.

i. Use (favorably exploit) air talent. Radio personalities accept this fact: If you're going to be a public person, then wherever you go, you represent the radio station. It just goes with the territory. This is not a 9-to-5 job for anyone in the business, and any member of the air staff known to the audience by ear should be similarly known to the audience when seen in public. The opportunities for members of the air staff to participate in public events as individuals representing the station are considerable. I would encourage each announcer, including (if not especially including) evening, overnight, and weekend personalities, to be available to volunteer for telethons, to judge any type of celebrity event that may be occurring in the city, to work as a telephone operator for a fund-raising pledge drive, and to volunteer for any type of charitable function where he or she can possibly gain notice through another medium and certainly be recognized by the public. This also includes speaking engagements for those members of the staff who are comfortable addressing luncheons or dinner meetings.

j. If the air staff is blessed with persons talented in other areas, by all means, promote such appearances. Consider that their experience as musicians, actors in community theater, magicians, cooks, athletes, or whatever other areas of expertise they may possess can have a favorable impact on their associations with the radio station.

4. Commercial opportunities.

Advertising clients sometimes like to run station promotions as part of their own promotion. The station participates with them in exchange for some advertising dollars. Frequently, radio stations will be asked to participate in promotions by motion picture companies or by national marketing groups that are looking for some kind of exposure in the market. They may be travel agents, hotel chains, airlines that serve the community, restaurant groups that are doing grand openings, or other businesses that are coming to town and are looking to augment their promotional budgets by bringing a radio station on board as a partner.

5. The promotion must promote the radio station.

It doesn't matter what form it takes or who else participates (within reason). In some cases, no promotion is better than a poor promotion or a promotion that is not targeted toward the type of listener the station wants. Be careful when selecting promotions, whether they are paid or whether they are free, that the opportunity to present the promotion is compatible with the image of the radio station. Is it something the station can live with before, during, and after the promotion?

MY FAVORITE PROMOTIONS

As a radio listener, I heard many promotions, mostly on-the-air contests, while growing up during the 1950s and 1960s and listening to the Louisville, Kentucky, area radio stations around my hometown. Many of the promotions on WAKY and WKLO had to do with calling the station to win a record or some sort of gift certificate or food coupon. I didn't really become aware of the inner workings of radio promotions until I moved to Indianapolis in 1965 for my job at WIRE Radio, which at the time was an NBC radio affiliate that carried several weekend NBC network programs. During the week, WIRE played current music mixed with adult standards. The format was professionally referred to as Chicken 40, because it featured contemporary music, but none of the hard rock stuff (i.e., it was "chickening out"). However, the station did have an enormous presence in the community, mostly because it had a large news department, and those news department vehicles were on the street all the time. They were veritable rolling billboards for the radio station. Later WIRE became the flagship station for the Indiana Pacers basketball team, which offered a bounty of other promotional opportunities, including my ability to attend many basketball games and get considerable visibility in front of the audience. Still, however, most of my experience in promotions was more behind the scenes, as I was only a part-time person for WIRE, initially. When finally making it to full-time status, I was getting the hang of the execution and planning for station promotional events.

At about the same time, a new Top 40 station, WIFE AM 1310 "Lucky 13" came on the air in Indianapolis and quickly became the big #1 Top 40 station. Because Top 40 radio was hot everywhere, promotions really went into high gear, with many group owners executing similar promotion at all their stations and many companies stealing ideas from one market to the next. WIFE was an intensely promotionally oriented radio station, owned by radio legend Don Burden, who owned a group of stations called the Star Stations. WIFE was doing something promotional just about every single week. There was always some sort of an on-the-air giveaway or promotion, but the one thing that I remember the most were the WIFE "Good Guys" events. WIFE actually took the "Good Guys" concept from WMCA in New York, as did many other radio stations around the United States in the 1960s. WIFE had a "Good Guys" basketball team composed of the DJs and newsmen, and occasionally some people from the station back office or sales department.

Following my 3 years at WIRE, I joined WIFE as a newsman. Our radio station basketball team, the Good Guys, would play a full schedule of games. Just about every single weekend there would be a game at a high school gymnasium somewhere in the greater Indianapolis area, taking on the faculty of the local high school. Needless to say, these games had incredible attendance by the student body who came out not only to see their teachers play, but also to meet the WIFE Good Guys. We usually would do some sort of a record sock dance after the basketball game and give away some prizes to contest winners.

For someone who comes from Indiana who has played basketball since he was old enough to hold one, it was a lot of fun to be a part of the WIFE Good Guys basketball team and see what it's like to be a member of a radio station and the sort of reception that one can get. When you're associated with a popular radio station, the kind of respect and admiration that you can get from your audience is remarkable.

After WIFE, I worked at several other radio stations around the Indianapolis area, one of which was WGEE. WGEE was owned by a broadcast group known as Rollins Broadcasting, headquartered in Wilmington, Delaware. It, too, owned several radio stations in major markets, including WDEE in Detroit, WBEE in Chicago, and, as mentioned, WGEE in Indianapolis. My time at WGEE was less than a year. I was the production director for the radio station and I did afternoon drive on the air. However, the reason I joined Rollins Broadcasting was not to work in Indianapolis but because I wanted to move east. Knowing that Rollins did own some radio stations in the eastern United States, it would be my logical opportunity to be transferred to one of its properties. This is exactly what happened, so in 1970, I was transferred from WGEE to Rollins's flagship station, WAMS, in Wilmington, Delaware. WAMS was a terrific Top 40 radio station, very promotionally oriented, with the difficult job of fighting off the incoming signals of the nearby Philadelphia radio stations. Delaware listeners were very loyal. Most resisted the Philly stations in favor of hometown WAMS, keeping the integrity of a local Top 40 station going for the Wilmington, Delaware, market. One of the more notable promotions I remember from WAMS was the "Wamathon Wakathon."

The Wamathon Wakathon was literally a stay-awake marathon, the radio version of *They Shoot Horses Don't They*. I was not only the program director of the station, but as the afternoon drive announcer, was given the opportunity to do a live broadcast from the window of a local music store called The Drum Shop in downtown Wilmington. A studio was set up inside the store window with turntables, a full set of records, commercials, and tape players. It was also set up with regular furniture and a living space, because I was going to be on the air nonstop until I couldn't take it anymore.

We started the broadcast on a Thursday afternoon and after I went on the air, I stayed on the air for at least 24 hours. Then I kept going on through Friday and on into Saturday. I loved this and all it cost was some sleep. On Sunday, the station management decided to cut back my live segments to just two or three breaks per hour while most of the music programming would then originate at the WAMS studios. Even so, I was still awake in the window at The Drum Shop. My endurance contest lasted for 110 hours. On Monday morning, school buses with "We're with you Steve; hang in there" detoured past The Drum Shop on the way to local schools. By Monday night, however, I was really starting to feel the effects of no sleep, and we decided that we had done what we wanted to do, so I was escorted out of The Drum Shop to a cheering crowd, into a station-provided limo, and driven home. We had thousands of people in and out of the store over the weekend, including musicians late at night or even after midnight if they had band jobs earlier in the evening. They would jam with some of the store employees and I'd kick in a few licks on the drums or keyboards. Since they were frequent customers of The Drum Shop anyway, it was a natural hangout and a great environment with nice music.

During the weekend, most of the sponsors at WAMS participated. I got a massage from a massage therapist who advertised on the radio station; I got clothing provided by one of the clothing stores; I even had a custom-made hairpiece (even though I didn't need one, thankfully, at the time) made for me while I was in the window. What we wouldn't do for sales! At the conclusion of the Wamathon Wakathon, I slept for about 12 hours straight and went back to work for my Tuesday afternoon show. The sleep deprivation left me none the worse for wear, or so I have hoped all these years. That will ultimately be for others to decide. Two weeks later, there was a challenge to my 110-hour record taken up by one of the other DJs at the radio station, Bob Wood, except instead of The Drum Shop, they put Bob in a dry cleaning store—no music, just hangers, polyethylene bags, and cleaning fluid. Let me tell you, the dynamic wasn't the same and my record still stands.

After WAMS, I went to WKIP in Poughkeepsie, New York. WKIP had adopted a new format called "The Fun One." The Fun One format was a very humor-oriented format with a lot of specialty programming to get people to laugh. We had some syndicated programming called "The Story Lady" and many comedy bits produced by Hollywood voice legends like Gary Owens and Jesse White or people who did cartoon voices for popular cartoons, like June Foray and Mel Blanc. With talent like that doing all our promotional announcements and liners, I remember that the WKIP years were the most fun for being on the air because we were very, very unpredictable. That's where I had the opportunity to work with Edd Neilson again, formerly my General Manager at WGEE, Indianapolis. I have acknowledged Edd elsewhere in this book, and many of the creative ideas that were part of that relationship are things that I try to pass on to new broadcasters. Promotionally, we did most of our things on the air.

The heavy demand on humor, writing, and doing the actual daily shows was time consuming, but we made people listen. Edd used the name Jack Daniels on the air. Other DJs included names like Johnny Walker, Bud Wiser, Jim Beam, and J.W. Dant. Our studios were located in a reclaimed city landfill that we referred to on the air as beautiful Mt. Dump. The theater-of-the-mind was fully employed in promoting WKIP.

After WKIP, in 1971 I went to New York City, and I worked at WPAT, which was a beautiful music/easy listening station. For the most part it did very few promotions other than that we, too, had a basketball team and a softball team. And our WPAT softball team participated in the Summer League that played in Central Park and included other radio and media outlets. It also included modeling agencies and talent agencies in the New York area. I can remember playing several games against companies like Ford Models, which had the most visible stable of well-known models in the United States at the time. Everyone playing every position looked absolutely perfect. When we played the Ford models, there was not a lot of sliding or diving into bases head-first. The team was all male, but the Ford cheering section looked like a year's worth of Vogue covers.

After WPAT, I was appointed music director at WHN in New York. WHN was New York's first country station, and country obviously has a lot of promotional opportunities. We took advantage of many of them. At WHN, we had a basketball team as well, and we also had a softball team, which we called the WHN Bumpkins. We played against various fire companies, police departments, and civic organizations. We scheduled an aggressive season of games for several years. In addition, at WHN, we frequently made public appearances at concert venues around the New York area where country artists would appear. A favorite hangout was O'Lunneys on Second Avenue, which was a small Irish bar most of the time, but a country music venue on weekend evenings. Most cities have such a place, and if it reflects the music and life group of your listeners, your station should be involved in some participation. At O'Lunneys, many famous country artists stopped by if they were heading toward New York. Johnny Rodriguez, Gary Stewart, Crystal Gayle, Larry Gatlin all made it to the O'Lunney's stage at some point during the early 1970s. Each evening, one of the announcers from WHN would be obliged to be the MC for the evening to host the show.

After WHN, I went to WNBC, New York. WNBC was a huge 50,000-watt AM giant with an abridged Top 40 music format that usually ran in second place to WABC's Top 40 format in the ratings. But we were not without our own audience and our own promotional opportunities. WNBC also had a softball team and we played police companies and fire companies throughout the greater metropolitan New York area. If you see a trend developing here, it's because the ability to get out into the public and play at sporting events as a softball player and as a basketball player is an extremely important way to get to know what your audience looks like and what its tastes are. It's a great equalizer to be on the playing field of a sporting event with the people to whom you talk every day on the air. I strongly advise every company that has the staff to do it, to try to do as many promotions as possible that put its on-the-air talent and its on-the-street salespeople in front of its audience using as many opportunities as it possibly can.

I've mentioned the team concept a few times. Shortly before I arrived, WNBC spent a fortune on huge billboards all over town with a group photo of all the DJs; these were scheduled to run for several months. I like the team idea, and think that seeing the gang all together is a wonderful idea. However, one of the announcers left the station shortly after the billboards went up, so the station was promoting someone who wasn't there and unable to promote the new replacement guy, which was yours truly. So pick the time and place to promote, keeping in mind that short-term promotions need short-term media exposure, while longer-term station institutional images may survive a longer run.

Following the adventure at WNBC, culminating with the dismissal of the entire announcer staff in 1977, I went to Florida and worked at WDAE in Tampa. At WDAE we had a terrific Adult Contemporary format and I had the honor of being the morning host there. In addition to our WDAE dances and concerts and promotions, we also were the flagship station for the Tampa Bay Buccaneers, which gave us an opportunity to have a presence at most of the Buccaneers' home games. We hosted tailgate parties, barbecues, and "I love you Tampa Bay" parties, which we held at various venues around town as cheerleading events for the Buccaneers. If you have a sports franchise affiliated with your radio station, don't fail to take full advantage of the promotional opportunities that it offers.

Smaller markets are often stuck with carrying a sports franchise on an otherwise all music station, but sports franchises can make money and can offer unique opportunities for listeners to sample your station at times other than when the games are on. You have to be extremely promotion-minded to even think about bringing a sports franchise onto your station, because you actually become two stations, the station when the games are on and another station when they are not.

After WDAE in Tampa Bay, I came back to New York and worked at a new country FM station, WKHK ("Kick FM"), and although we did very few promotions at Kick FM, we did have some posters and billboards that people still remember. One was the Empire

State Building with King Kong climbing up the side of the building wearing cowboy boots. The other poster received some criticism when it hit the streets; it was a likeness of the Statue of Liberty with cowboy boots coming out from under Liberty's robes. This was deemed a sacrilege by some people, but it took advantage of a local icon to reinforce the station's image. The promotion showed that even two icons like the Statue of Liberty and King Kong could be a little bit country and WKHK was there if they needed us.

After Kick FM, my career attentions turned to being a full-time program director, and for that opportunity, I went to another 50,000-watt AM giant, WPTR in Albany. The station had formerly been a huge Top 40 station serving most of the northeastern United States, especially New England and southern Canada. But Top 40 AM stations had fallen on hard times as Top 40 listeners gravitated to FM stations that had adopted the format. Our job at WPTR was to flip the station to country, then tell the audience, including the listeners who had grown up with the station, about the new format. One of our most fun recurring events at WPTR was the "I Love You Country" parties. We took over a nightclub for the evening, offered a very inexpensive draft beer price, brought in a local band, invited the audience to come eat and drink on us for an hour or two, and then turned the venue back to its owner to keep the audience there partying for the rest of the evening. We were able to involve a lot of sponsorships, and the "I Love You Country" parties were great successes. It was a success that we carried with us through the next several years at WPTR in Albany and it won the station the #1 spot in the market.

The other promotion in which I take personal pride was our adoption of the Cohoes Music Hall, a 100-year-old music hall in Cohoes, N.Y., a former textile mill town and a suburb of Albany. Once the heart of the artistic lives of the mill workers, the landmark music hall had a series of theater troupes and concert performances over the years, but was falling into disrepair and infrequent usage. I first became aware of the place at a local production of *The Fantasticks* early after my arrival in Albany. It definitely had possibilities, but the hall was regularly strapped for funding for needed repairs, building code upgrades, and operating expenses. Discussions between WPTR and the music hall management set up a series of country music concerts to run weekly for several months. We took over the hall and made it look like a miniature version of the Ryman Auditorium in Nashville, the legendary home of the Grand Ol' Opry. We put "On The Air" signs on stage, read live commercials from a side box, let people come down front to take pictures of the performers, and everything was broadcast live on WPTR. We served hot dogs, popcorn, beer, and soda, had door prizes, and just had a great time. (We didn't advertise Goo-Goo candy bars.) The music hall kept the admission money and the concessions, while WPTR profited by selling sponsorships on the broadcast. I had the pleasure of being the MC of the show every week while the other announcers did the commercials and bantered with me on stage between acts. I wore my good luck blue suit for every performance. That blue suit could have done the show without me after a few weeks. The Cohoes Music Hall example was just a matter of finding the right community venue, making a long-term commitment, giving listeners something fun to do, and allowing them to get inside the hall to see what we were there to preserve. Almost every town with a radio station has such a venue, whether theater, rail station, old library, or historic home. Getting behind events that not only raise money but also bring listeners face-to-face with the venue reinforces the reasoning behind the effort.

Our poster from the Cohoes Music Hall country music concerts on WPTR in 1984.

WPTR

AM 1540 · YOUR COUNTRY FRIEND

presents

COUNTRY MUSIC LIVE!

HELD OVER from **COHOES Music Hall** **THREE MORE WEEKS!**

58 Remsen St. Cohoes

ALL SHOWS BROADCAST **LIVE** ON WPTR at 8 P.M.!

General Admission $3.00
Senior Citizen $2.00
Pre-Adult (under 12) $1.00

Our Very Special Guests:

July 7 — **Gloria Curtis & the Country Classic and Southbound**

July 14 — **Aged in the Hills**

July 21 — **Ramblin' Fever and Badge**

July 28 — **Seeds 'n' Stems**

Tickets Conveniently Available At:

★ WPTR 9 A.M.-5 P.M. Monday-Friday. Phone 456-1144.

★Cohoes Music Hall Box Office from 12 noon to 5 P.M. Monday thru Friday. Phone 235-7969.

★ Hilton Music Stores
13 3rd St., Troy
900 Central Ave., Albany

Telephone Res. accepted at either location

Now more than ever. . .
YOUR Country Radio Station!

24 Hr. Country Contact Line 456-1540

WPTR

17

After a few years at WPTR, I interviewed for and was offered an opportunity to take my country program director skills to Texas. I'd publicly like to thank Bill Rohde, the former general manager of KKYX, San Antonio, for having the courage to bring someone from New York in to program a major country radio station in Texas. The station was another 50,000-watt AM station with a signal covering about 110 Texas counties and northern Mexico. Although the station had a few regular promotions, it was fun to reinvent some of the ideas and try some new ones over the next few years. The country parties concept resurfaced at KKYX as did more live broadcasts (I love live broadcasts), two of which were the Great Country River Festival when the downtown Riverwalk area of San Antonio, including the Arneson River Theater, was taken over by country performers for the better part of three days, as were a number of indoor performance venues. KKYX was very influ-

On stage at the Cohoes Music Hall live broadcasts in 1984. Note "Applause" sign flashing for audience response at appropriate moments.

ential in record sales and artist promotion, so we enjoyed an excellent reputation and rapport with many artists and record companies. Long time KKYX announcer Jerry King (now in the Country DJ Hall of Fame) is credited with launching the career of George Strait, among others.

KKYX signed up every single country artist who could hitchhike, bicycle, truck, bus, or walk into San Antonio to come in and perform. It was a much sought-after publicity event for most of the artists, so we had some of the biggest artists of the day, including Gary Morris, George Strait, Johnny Rodriguez, Moe Bandy, Kathy Mattea, and Reba McEntyre. All came in for virtually nothing to perform at the Great Country River Festival. Since the performance areas were filled to capacity, the only other opportunity to make the event bigger was to broadcast it live, which we did during my years with KKYX.

The Arneson River Theatre stage in San Antonio for the KKYX Great Country River Festival, with local favorite Billy Mata performing in 1986.

The other annual event at KKYX was the KKYX Great Country Chili Cookoff. Chili cookoffs are not uncommon in Texas; they happen a lot. This was a huge chili cookoff. It was sanctioned, which means it actually fell under the auspices of, and was governed by, the board of official Chili Cookoff people that do that sort of thing in the state of Texas. We regularly attracted hundreds and hundreds of fans who set up camp and cooked chili from scratch from morning till night. Also on the stage was a full day of entertainment provided by the radio station. All of the DJs and employees at KKYX fully participated in this event. A chili cookoff or a cooking contest of any sort is a fine way to relate to your audience, particularly if it reflects a regional food favorite, which could be everything from hot dogs to steaks to chili to nachos to baked potatoes to liver and onions to whatever happens to be hot in your neck of the woods. At the cookoff, we outfitted the stage area and several golf carts with remote broadcasting equipment to carry a full day of activities and entertainment for KKYX listeners. Of course, not only did we get a lot of publicity by broadcasting the event, but also every participant had the station on at his or her cookoff campsite—and thereafter on the way home and the next day and the next day, etc.

The author tasting a long line of chili samples at the KKYX Chili Cookoff in 1986.

After KKYX, I went to Dayton, Ohio, at WING, which was an oldies format. The station had been there for many, many years, and it owned a large GMC van, which we referred to as "The Legend." Imagine a Mr. Softee truck on steroids. It was painted with the station logo, it had DJ studio equipment inside the vehicle, and we took it everywhere. There wasn't a parade that went by or a civic function anywhere within the Dayton listening area where The Legend was not present. One of the most fun events we had each year at WING with our Legend truck was to go Christmas caroling. Members of the staff would ride in the truck from one neighborhood to the other, and we would get out and be met by a group of listeners. We served hot chocolate and doughnuts and sang Christmas carols. Then we jumped back into the truck and moved on to the next neighborhood. Although your radio station may not have the proceeds to purchase a vehicle during the holiday season or at any other time of the year when having a vehicle would be to your advantage, there are many car and truck dealers eager to trade or lend a vehicle for promotional consideration. Therefore, it becomes very easy to have some portable signage made that you can put on a variety of vehicles over the course of a year depending on your needs and your budget. (Magnetic signs are especially good.)

As a WING program director and personality, there were other opportunities to get involved in regular community events. We did live broadcasts from the annual Dayton Days (great bratwurst!) and attended countless car shows and drive-in cruisin' parties with cars from the 50s and 60s era paralleling the era of WING music. I do remember one event with some fondness, the Dayton Oyster Eat Off, featuring contestants eating raw oysters. Always looking for station publicity, I entered the so-called celebrity division that included local DJs, TV personalities, newspaper people, and politicians. I love oysters and I ate a lot of them, enough said? Sometimes the events need to reflect the community. When *you* think "oyster," do you think "Dayton"?

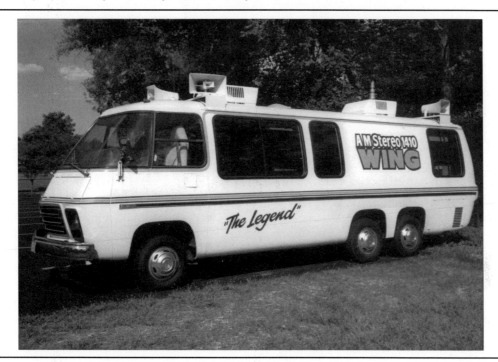

Our oldies cruiser, The Legend, at WING in Dayton, 1987.

After WING, I went back to San Antonio to another AM station, KTSA, which had had very bad luck over the past years in its Top 40 format, since FM stations were getting most of the Top 40 ratings at that point. As mentioned, AM Top 40 stations were dwindling across the country. It was determined that we would take KTSA into an adult standards format, something that was not happening in San Antonio. They did not have an adult standards station, so we put on a format my company, MOR Media International, developed called the "Great Entertainers." We kicked off the Great Entertainers format with a beautiful evening at the Josephine Theater in downtown San Antonio. All the members of the disk jockey and announcer staff at KTSA were dressed up in tuxedos; we had local entertainers including singing groups, local performers, actors, and a small orchestra. We invited listeners as well as the media to come to the kickoff party for the Great Entertainers, which went on the air at exactly the same time the kickoff party started so that when people left the building that night, they could turn on their radios and hear our new format. This is the sort of event that I would strongly recommend for any station

The author, representing WING in 1987 (seated, white shirt, left), prepares to attack a plate of raw oysters in the annual Dayton Oyster Eat Off while morning DJ Steve Kirk MC's (standing with mic).

considering changing its music format. Nothing draws more attention to a format change than as many outside activities as you can muster. Having an event built around the format, in this case playing Broadway show music and standards at an elegant private party, was the best way to convey the elegant standards/Broadway image that we went on to follow up with our broadcasts on KTSA. Although KTSA was ultimately sold by its owner and, prior to its sale, went through another format change to talk radio (taking advantage of the great opportunities afforded talk radio as the 1990s began), I am pleased that at present the adult standards listening audience in San Antonio is as great as it has ever been. I would like to thank the staff of KTSA and the people of San Antonio for proving that that format, attracting older listeners, was viable enough so that it remains a significant player on the radio landscape to this day.

One of our KTSA Great Entertainers printed "invitations", required for admission to our regular Sunday Afternoon Tea Dances with live orchestra, 1988.

KTSA 550 AM

Classic Songs. Great Entertainers.

presents

Sunday Afternoon Tea Dance

with Jack Melick, his Piano & Orchestra . . .

featuring the Moon Maids + 1

Sunday, April 9th   5 pm - 9 pm

Alzafar Shrine Temple

$10 per person   Semi-formal

After KTSA, I came back to New York City to devote full time to station consulting. I had, at that point, 30 years' experience and enjoyed sharing my experience with radio stations—and charging them for it. However, that axiom of "never give up the mic" bit me, and I shuffled over to WYNY, which was the New York country station at that time, and in 1994 started hosting the Sunday Night Country Oldies Show. I eventually syndicated the show and it's still on across the United States and in several foreign countries. WYNY was involved greatly in promotions as the New York country station, hosting many country events as country artists came into the city. During that time we hosted country music performances by the Oak Ridge Boys, Crystal Gayle, and Willie Nelson at venues such as the Westbury Music Fair on Long Island, as well as Radio City Music Hall, where I had the opportunity to be the Master of Ceremonies for John Denver's final concert in New York City before his death. I also had the wonderful opportunity to be the Master of Ceremonies at the final Johnny Cash concert at Carnegie Hall in New York. I know that it is typically the job of local radio announcers to host events, and many of these events (if you look back on them in your career) turn out to be much, much bigger and much more important than they seemed to be at the time. Therefore, what I thought was a routine MC job at a venue in New York turned out to be a pivotal moment in my career. No one knew that Johnny Cash would not make another appearance at Carnegie Hall and that John Denver would not make another appearance at Radio City. So those were singular moments and I treasure them. Anyone who has an opportunity to host or MC entertainment events shouldn't miss the chance. Please don't be afraid to meet the artists and spend a few moments with them.

I also strongly suggest that if you are an announcer or representative of a radio station and have access to artists, do not ask them for an autograph. It's a professional courtesy and it's always been my opinion that when you have access to people that the public doesn't have, you should not take advantage of your position. Therefore, although I've met hundreds of personalities over the dozens of years I've been working in radio, I do not have one autograph. That is not to say that there are not cameras clicking, because third parties off in the corner somewhere do that. You clearly have your picture taken many times but you have no control over that. So meet the artists, enjoy the artists, be a fan of the artists, and praise their work, but stop short of asking for their autograph.

At WYNY in addition to those concerts, the radio station was involved in a St. Jude's Children's Hospital campaign drive every year as are country stations throughout the United States. On a number of occasions, WYNY set up St. Jude's weekend radiothon broadcasts at several shopping malls around the greater New York area. The radiothon raised millions of dollars, which is a remarkable feat for any market, particularly a country music market in New York where country clearly would not be the most popular format available. One thing we did do at WYNY at one of the St. Jude's events was to hold an all-day fair, where we not only had live broadcasts and live entertainment, but also took advantage of members of the staff who had other interests, qualities, and characteristics. I was interested in teaching broadcasting at that time and it was about the same time that the first edition of this book had come out. So I held seminars on what it's like to be in broadcasting. Fortunately, a classroom full of people attended my talks each of the days of the WYNY festival. Chances are you have many people at your radio station who do everything from painting to clay modeling to gardening; they could provide a great service at some sort of a job fair or career event and could show that your radio station is composed of people with interests similar to those of the audience. That's why it's important to know the depth of your own staff at your radio station and look beyond what they bring to their day-to-day, 9-to-5 responsibilities, and to see how these talents can best be applied in other capacities throughout the year for your station's publicity.

Promotion. You have to do it, but rather than just buy bumper stickers and other things to give away, look for the opportunities that make people remember you. Look for the events in people's lives that you can get involved with so that they can remember your radio station on their terms rather than trying to impose on them the radio station's terms.

Get out! Have fun! Make sense!

THE STATION'S PERSONNEL

MEETINGS

"He can't take your call right now. He's in a meeting."

"I'm in a meeting; can I call you right back?"

"Gotta run; I'm late for a meeting."

"Every time I try to reach you at the radio station, you're in a meeting."

The word *meeting* has taken on new meaning in recent years. The term is now an all-inclusive excuse for not doing things. Someone appearing in your office unexpectedly is not a meeting. A water-cooler chat with the music director is not a meeting. Sitting on the edge of a salesperson's desk discussing a promotion is not a meeting. We've redefined *meeting* as any time two or more people assemble to talk about anything. Don't confuse (or let a receptionist or secretary confuse) conversations and meetings. To people outside radio, who hear us utter these quotes regularly, it seems like we must live in a terrible professional environment, trudging from one office to another, meeting all the time.

Let's get this under control. Radio is a medium of communication, but, as a business, we are often guilty of not communicating effectively enough internally to run the business properly. Radio stations can deliver a message across town or halfway across a state, but have difficulty getting a message correctly interpreted from one office to another within their own four walls. Meetings are necessary, especially in a business that runs 24 hours a day, as most radio stations do. It is imperative that the air staff and all programming persons assemble on a regular basis to coordinate the many activities of the radio station that depend on them for success. This is why scheduling regular staff meetings at radio stations is a very important function, and one that can be made into a more positive experience for all concerned.

My favorite staff meetings combined some degree of pleasure with exchange of radio station information. In New York City at WHN, Program Director Ruth Meyer's secretary called each air staff member in the morning to remind us of the announcer meeting that day at noon and to take our lunch order. When we arrived in the conference room, our lunches were waiting at our conference table. The ice was broken from not having seen each other for a week. Then we could get to the business of listening to music and exchanging ideas about the station. In some major markets, announcer union regulations place restrictions on how frequently management can call in staff members for meetings without additional compensation, but in other instances, regular meetings are a built-in part of the announcer contract. In either case, there is still a need for internal communication.

Radio station meetings should follow these rules:

Warning: Meeting up ahead!

1. Meetings should be scheduled at the same hour every time. That is to say, every Tuesday at 1 PM or every payday at 2 PM. (Payday is an excellent time to have a meeting because staff members usually come to the station to pick up their checks that day, anyway.) These days with direct deposit, picking up a paycheck isn't as ceremonial as it once was, but it is still generally done on the same days of the month, so it remains an easy date to remember for meetings.

2. Meetings should be of fixed length; 30 to 45 minutes should be ample time to discuss most radio station business. For every minute past this length of time, the meeting becomes less and less productive. Staff members want to be elsewhere, taking care of business, and not sitting in a meeting. There's a law of time-related diminishing returns here. This isn't to say that some of the employees may have other business with one another, but they can take care of that later without involving other staff members. Taking a cue from "computerese," they can do it offline.

3. Meetings must start on time. The best way to get meetings to start on time and to have people show up to attend them on time is to start them on time yourself, whether or not everybody is there. You will notice the attendance level will pick up and the meetings will start on time once you have established your intention to start on time regardless of a few missing staff members. You cannot let the least disciplined person on your staff dictate the use of the valuable time of other staff members and the program director. Coming in late to a meeting that's already started offers its own form of negative reinforcement for everyone but the most insensitive. I mean, when the train leaves the station . . . .

4. A meeting should have a fixed agenda. It should not be a "let's all get together and talk about anything that comes up" session. Write five or six major topics on a prepared sheet and distribute it to all persons attending the meeting so that they may review the topics for discussion, have a chance to think about them, and be able to respond during the meeting. Then, stick to the agenda. All sorts of distractions and side trips and diversions usually come up, but it's up to the chair of the meeting to keep discussions strictly on target. Divergent thinking is valuable in its place, such as in a brainstorming session, but it slows down an agenda where specific decisions must be made or actionable items put forward. There will be some divergent thinkers in the group—there always are—and they'll probably resent being reined in. Reining them in requires subtlety and tact, but if the meeting is to end on time, it must be done.

5. In planning the meeting, make sure the agenda includes only those items intended for the whole staff. Don't waste some staff members' time on particular items that deal only with a few specific individuals. Smaller meetings in your office or even a one-on-one get-together can accomplish this better than using the time of the whole staff. And in the meeting, when something is decided that will involve only part of the staff, don't waste the time of the others by discussing it at length. Arrange to meet with the staff members who will actually do whatever it is to be done. You'll be tempted to include everyone, thinking that it's good communication for everyone to know everything about what others are doing. In some sense it is, but not if it wastes time. Besides, sooner or later everyone knows what everyone else is doing anyway.

6. Stick to the point. The person running the meeting should avoid the temptation to allow staff members to ramble on subjects unrelated to the topics at hand. In every meeting there are certain roles that are assumed by staff members present.

There's always the Eager Beaver, the one who volunteers to do everything and seems sincere and enthusiastic about doing whatever it is. It's easy to give it to him or her, but be sure he or she is the best person for the job. Sometimes the Eager Beaver isn't very good at following through, and sometimes the Eager Beaver has bitten off more than he or she can masticate.

There's always the "Yes, but . . ." obstructionist person, who has a million reasons why something is a bad idea, won't work, is too time-consuming, or not worthwhile. This person is cautious by nature and timid about testing new waters. It's not always that the person is just negative by nature, but often it's someone who is reluctant to jump into the pool, but who, once in, enjoys the swim completely. It's a useful role because it causes others to stop and think about possible unintended consequences.

Another type is the Innocent, who wants everything explained in detail and who isn't sure that he or she fully understands. This role can potentially waste everyone's time. The way to handle this is to say, "Meet with me after the meeting and I'll explain."

Then there's the Show Off. This person's agenda is to display wit and information by being more knowledgeable about everything and funnier than everybody else. This person can add humor and often really does know it all—at least about the subject under discussion. The trick is to steer things back to the agenda item and allow the show-off a time-limited audience. Sometimes this person is bucking for promotion or needs the reassurance of applause, but the meeting can't be subverted to meet his or her needs.

Then there's the Martyr. This person has never had a burden that was reasonable or just. He cries out against further responsibilities and seeks pity from others, while also seeking recognition of the extra time and work he or she puts in.

Finally, there's the Passive Resister. This person says little. Instead, the resister focuses attention on doodling, counting the ceiling tiles, or concentrating on looking just interested enough to avoid reprimand but not interested enough to be fully convincing.

The ideal leader of a meeting says little but listens well. This person makes sure notes or minutes are taken. The ideal leader is a timekeeper, a moderator, and a person who suffers fools gladly—but not when they're wasting everyone's time. The ideal leader has an unshakeable determination to keep the meeting on track and end it on time. Some leaders want meetings only to hear themselves think aloud. Other people at the meeting soon sense this and relapse into sullen passive resistance.

A word should be said about what a meeting—a committee or a group—can do and what it can't do. What it can't do is actual creative work. I say work, not thinking. A group can build on an idea, which must always come from one individual, but once the edifice is built in words, some one person or persons must do the work. The group came up with a great idea, but it's only hot air until it's written down or put into practice. If the leader always dumps the work back on the person who made the suggestion, then suggestions are soon likely to dry up. And some leaders are guilty of not making specific assignments for things decided in the meeting. "We'll" do thus and thus means only that someone else will do it. It's important to say to a specific person or persons, "Will you take care of that by Friday?" The time limitation is an important part of the assignment. Be sure that it's recorded in the notes or minutes.

7. There are other roles that are sometimes assumed by attendees at a meeting. These could include Wicked Witch, Cynic, Seer, Bah-Humbugger, and so on, but radio stations' meetings often become contests for the role of Comedian. Meetings can be fun, but they often turn into cleverness contests between staff members to see who can get the most laughs. Once you establish a meeting as a business function and not a game of verbal one-upmanship, you can get more accomplished for the business needs of the station.

You might think of a meeting as improvisational theater. All of the same elements are there: plot, character, theme, drama, comedy, pathos, slapstick, tragedy, and role-playing. The better you know the people at the meeting, the better you can understand why they react as they do. During the meeting, character is being revealed to the audience (other people at the meeting), plots are being hatched, and underlying themes played out.

There's the meeting agenda, and then there's everyone's personal agenda. Your agenda may be to plan for a new promotion in connection with the shopping mall's big sale, but Alice is worried about her son Norbert's recital coming up and that lump she felt in a private spot this morning. Also, she thinks Bill is a sexist pig and is looking for revenge for some sexist remarks he made last week. George, who is African American, is wondering if Tom's mention of writing on a blackboard could be a racist remark. Meanwhile, Tom is worried about his wife's finding out that he really didn't have to work late last night. George took Bill to the cleaners at their Friday night poker game and wasn't a good sport about it. He'll pay for that. Susan's promotion is being considered and she's trying to make a good impression at this meeting. Jim's résumé is out to the station in the bigger market, and he got a phone call about it that morning. No one knows yet. Susan is really irritated that Tom keeps tipping back in his chair, and she thinks that Bill's habit of chewing gum is disgusting. Alice is trying keep her shoes under the table; she forgot to change into her work shoes this morning and the canvas numbers are pretty shabby.

So there's a lot going on. The plot you want to develop—the shopping center promotion—carries with it a number of personal subplots that may or may not interfere with progress.

Sometimes in a meeting the nay-sayers and the yea-sayers will abruptly change roles. The reason is that the operative dynamic is conflict within cooperation, and one way of pulling off a surprise attack is to abruptly change positions.

No one can afford to appear incompetent, so to supply meaningful input, people resort to opposition even when it's not called for. And speaking of input, be careful about asking for it when you don't need it. Everyone will feel called on, when asked, to offer advice, comfort, or counsel; and it may not be motivated by anything more than an effort to keep up appearances. A Chinese proverb says, "Don't build a bridge where there is no river." Some things are good enough as they are, and involving too many cooks, well . . . .

8. At the conclusion of the meeting, the meeting leader needs to summarize what has been discussed, particularly reminding those who have taken on tasks or been assigned them just what those specific things are and when, and especially when they are to be completed.

9. Someone other than the person running the meeting should keep an accurate set of minutes.

A brief meeting *outline* taken from the minutes (not the minutes themselves) should be distributed to staff members no later than 1 day after the meeting has taken place to reinforce what was discussed and what the intentions were in having a meeting in the first place. Promptness is very important here, along with brevity. Have you ever gotten five pages of minutes from a meeting that was weeks ago? How much attention did you give it?

Since radio air staff members are always dealing with time in their studio work, it can sometimes be beneficial to devise a clock face similar to the in-studio hot clock with the meeting elements placed on it. An example of a meeting hot clock is shown on page 148.

Going by these guidelines, meeting participants can see that there are, in fact, deadlines for getting things accomplished at the meetings just as there are on the air. Believe it or not, this does help move a meeting along. Not all radio station meetings need to be formal, conference room meetings. I have found that social gatherings are excellent ways to exchange ideas in a less formal setting. Save the actual business, station discipline, and format-related meetings for the radio station, but brainstorming sessions and meetings for the exchange of artistic and creative ideas are best done away from the radio station.

For this purpose, I have often used my home as a meeting place where I can provide a relaxed atmosphere, food, and beverages and where there are few time constraints. It's also nice, occasionally, to meet at location away from the radio station, such as a restaurant, where the station may trade for the cost of a lunch, dinner, or refreshments for an informal dinner party/meeting.

Even at informal meetings, it's necessary to have an agenda highlighting specific topics, but in the less formal setting, you may permit greater latitude in rambling away from the central subject. There can be an inclination to invite too many people to a meeting. I have found myself guilty of inviting the promotion director, the news director, members of the news department, members of the sales department, or members of any other department who would like to be a part of the meeting, all in the interest of establishing teamwork and camaraderie at the radio station. This interdepartmental meeting scenario tends to become a contest for each department's advocating its own special interests, with very little getting accomplished. I suggest that, perhaps once a month, a general staff meeting be held, including members of other departments. This meeting may be handled by the general manager of the station and include individual presentations by the various department heads. In this case, the several departments can share general information, and little participation by other attending staff members is required or encouraged, other than to be informed and to pay attention to the items on the agenda. Although it's impossible to share all programming staff information with the rest of the departments, it is not impossible to share the minutes of your meeting. Copies of the minutes should also be directed to other department heads, including the sales manager and the general manager. When writing minutes, highlight areas of particular interest to other departments on their copies. This opens the door for programming to gain access to information being exchanged at meetings conducted by other departments.

One final note on scheduling. The best time to schedule a staff meeting is generally somewhere between 11 AM and 1 PM. Obviously the overnight employees will have to get a short sleep period on those meeting days, but it ultimately is the best policy to have consistent meeting times. Now, with so many radio stations automated or voice-tracked overnight, this is even less of an issue, but it still exists in many markets. It especially helps to reinforce the regular meeting time, which cuts down on poor attendance. The person on the air needs to prerecord, if possible, that portion of the program in order to attend the meeting. Bring in a part-timer or board operator at his or her regular hourly wage to operate the station during the meeting. Meetings in the 11 AM to 1 PM time frame are the least taxing to most staff members, and they inconvenience the fewest people. Because the meeting occurs during regular office hours, often during lunch, there are fewer members of the station's business and sales staff in the building, affording your department more comfortable access to the conference room and station facilities. Meetings held over the lunch hour also are less subject to interruptions. After all, there are fewer people in the building to need your time and fewer people to claim your time with telephone calls because most of them are at lunch, too.

In preparation for outside-the-station promotions that require the attendance of a majority of the air staff, have a small 10- to 15-minute business orientation meeting prior to the event at the location of the promotion. The purpose is to coordinate the operation of the event and to make clear any details or obstacles that may be encountered during the promotion. This short prepromotional event meeting is an invaluable tool for making the function run smoothly and efficiently. It also demonstrates to the clients and nonstation employees that you conduct yourself in a businesslike manner and that you have established a routine. That makes them feel more comfortable about their association with the station, since you at least appear to be organized and, in most cases, probably are.

If you would like a more in-depth treatment of meetings and business organization in general, I recommend R. Alec Mackenzie's *The Time Trap* (McGraw-Hill, 1972). It is a useful handbook for managing yourself and your affairs.

Finally, in this era of telecommuting and doing everything by e-mail and computer, the need for actual face-to-face meetings may seem to be passé. But as someone who feels the need to meet listeners face-to-face, I cannot pass on the even more important opportunity to see each other face-to-face. We're all in this together and, traditionally, stations that perform well in a team environment make a more cohesive and effective impact on their listeners and the marketplace. Thinking of the legendary radio stations that made a huge impact on listeners and the radio landscape, we recall the WMCA Good Guys in New York or the KHJ Boss Jocks in L.A., as well as all the other stations around the country that mimicked them. Coming together occasionally at a meeting of the minds can only enhance and reinforce the impact of the station.

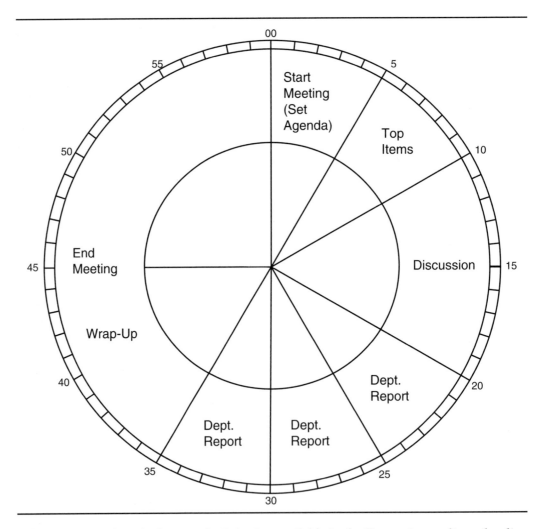

Now, here's that hot clock example. It is also available in the Forms Appendix and online at www.radiothebook.com.

STUDIO MANNERS

A radio studio is a small, cramped, claustrophobic, stuffy, ill-lighted, poorly ventilated, underdecorated room from which much creativity and excellence is expected to emerge. It is occupied 24 hours every day, 7 days every week, all months, every year, forever. It's the plane that never lands. I'm pleased to see that more attention seems to be paid to studio decor and comfort than in previous years. Part of this is due to the miniaturization of electronic studio equipment. Computer screens and compact mixing consoles have replaced stacks of cart machines, reel-to-reel decks, and turntables. Many broadcasting companies, especially the ones who have acquired multiple stations in a single market, are moving into new studio/office operations. With many departments combining into smaller, more efficient operations, the air studios for each station seem to have become less impersonal and more closely reflect the personality of the format and the staff that uses them.

Glaring fluorescent lights seem to be giving way to area lighting, to be adjusted by the person on the air. Old-style fiber soundproofing seems to be yielding to carpeted walls. If you are still working in a shabby, cluttered air studio, let me suggest that it is very likely affecting your performance and the performances of every other staff member. With a little effort, maybe some towels and cleaning supplies, a trip to the local home center, and suggestions from all staff members, you just might make a big difference in the degree of performance your station exhibits and the attitude of each staff member.

In spite of the physical facility itself, there are a few general rules for program directors and announcers to observe regarding the studio. Studios are much like automobiles. All the parts are there, but the arrangement of the parts may not be the same. In putting together the following long list, I've tried to include my personal preferences but also those preferences that have been expressed to me by others over the years. I know we can't always have everything, and building a radio station is a symphony of compromise, but I do believe it is beneficial to articulate as many different possibilities and options as possible to include different points of view. Also there's no particular priority in the way these items are arranged here since most people who work in radio studios have to accept the final decisions as dealt. But review this list, anyway, just in case some day someone asks for your opinion. You never get what you don't ask for.

1. Sitting down is better than standing. The theory that our voices sound better while we stand is something someone invented after seeing pictures of old dramatic radio actors standing around microphones holding their scripts at arm's length. With today's finely processed equipment and limited pick-up microphones, voices sound like voices, sitting or standing. The thing stand-up operations do enhance vocally is how tired and distracted an announcer can become in such a studio. Even in studios where an option exists to stand or sit, the sitting position should be comfortable. Standing or sitting uncomfortably for a long period can increase fatigue on your back and certainly on your feet.

In the old photos where you see Jack Benny, Mary Livingston, Dennis Day, and Don Wilson standing closely around a stand-up CBS mike, they're standing there because they have to be very close to the microphone and so that each can walk away when his or her bit is done. They dropped the pages of their scripts to the floor, and the microphones couldn't pick up the rustles of those particular falling leaves. On the other hand, when we see old-time newsman Walter Winchell in old photos, he's seated at a desk with a very large microphone in front of him. He had that luxury because his was a solo performance. Actually, there may have been more to it than the mechanics. Interactions among standing people tend to be a little different from interactions among seated people. Standing exchanges tend to be more performance-oriented and seated ones more intimate. In modern radio, on-site interviews tend to be standing, something that makes them more dramatic, but the seated air talent person speaking directly to the listeners may have a better chance of creating a sense of intimacy. It depends on what you want.

2. Sit-down studios are also more comfortable for creative people because the studio equipment isn't spread over a larger area. Rather than being at arm's reach, as in a well-designed sit-down studio, things are only a few steps away in a stand-up operation.

3. If your studio is a stand-up operation, be prepared to accommodate present and future employees who may be very tall, very short, or very uncomfortable with their legs dangling from a tall stool.

4. The studio is not a social gathering spot. Meetings with other staff members, sales, news, or whomever should not be conducted during an air shift in the studio. You can be one-on-one with only one person at a time. When you're on the air, always remember, it's listeners first!

5. Rule 4 also applies to other announcers before or after their shifts. Get in the studio about 15 minutes before airtime to get stuff together. Then, clear out completely a few minutes after the shift. It's someone else's turn to be magnificent.

6. Starting or ending a shift is a crucial time for either establishing or wrapping up that day's relationship with the listeners. That is when distractions can do the most damage. The first few minutes of a shift are usually a bit shaky, anyway. No one needs company in the studio to complicate matters.

7. Smoking. Don't! I know this sounds simple. I absolutely cannot justify how or why anyone who is seeking to use his or her voice professionally and who deals with other people on a daily basis or shares a close working space with other people can be a smoker. I am very pleased that most large radio groups in the United States operate in a nonsmoking environment. I'm even more gratified that many company health plans cover the costs of quit-smoking plans.

These days, many state and local regulations determine the smoking or nonsmoking regulations within office buildings and places of public accommodation. Further, since employee health insurance is company paid, many insurance carriers offer greater benefits to companies with nonsmoking environments. Whatever the company policy may be, it should be respected and observed by everyone as a condition of employment.

As someone who has dealt with radio engineers for many years, it is rare to find one who smokes. All radio equipment, especially studio equipment, is subject to a continuous electronic charge that attracts airborne matter. Ever notice how your TV or computer screen gets dirtier than any piece of furniture? It's actually attracting matter the same as air cleaners using ion charges. For this reason, internal electrical contacts inside mixing boards, CD players, and tape decks can produce poor performance by the buildup of such matter, of which smoke is the most dense. Such is also the case in any environment where many computers are at use, which seems to be everywhere. In this case we're talking about the physics of smoke on electronic equipment, not the political rights of smokers vs nonsmokers. Have your station engineer run a cotton swab along the internal contacts of a mixing board in a studio and then, if possible, in a location that may have been subject to smoking to check this physical characteristic. Additionally, most studio microphones are covered by a wind shield to protect against "popping of p's." Usually these are no more than a casing of foam rubber but also pick up any bacteria, or exhalant of each user, including smokers. They should be regularly washed with antibacterial soap and may be the most unsanitary object in the studio.

Attitudes about this matter tend to be polarizing, but then that's what makes us individuals. Abide by company regulations, respect the rights of others, and be mindful of common work spaces, whether it's smoking, dirty cups, waste paper, or heavy perfume. It would not be productive for the success of the radio station to make a political issue out of everyone's individual choices.

8. Phone calls. Again . . . listeners first. The time during an air shift is not the time to review domestic plans, argue with creditors, patch up relationships, etc. Talk to as many listeners as time allows, briefly. Listen to what they have to say, but establish a personal policy of being brief. If a caller has something more in depth that's interesting, then have the listener call back when you're off the air.

9. Avoid clutter. A simple, prominently placed bulletin board listing only current information is necessary.

10. Staff lists, technical or discrepancy forms, policy books, etc. can best be assigned to specific, out-of-the-way locations.

11. Avoid using tape to stick things up for the announcer to read. Use metal or plastic clips. They're movable so that each announcer can adjust them.

12. If there are studio windows to the lobby, hallway, other studio, etc., keep them clear of notes or taped-up messages.

13. Keep windows clean so you can see through them and let in light. That's why they're there.

14. The best time to paint or carpet a studio is simultaneously with a new programming strategy, policy, or promotion. A different work environment reinforces something new and different to the employees. An obvious physical change in the air studio serves as a constant reminder about the changes. In the case of a major format change, repaint or redecorate, even if it's not necessary. It enhances the new attitudes.

15. Keep personal items (cups, snacks, earphones, supplies) in a separate location, away from the studio. If there is an announcers' lounge area, locking file drawers are preferred. Even small half-lockers, like those in a health club or spa, work very nicely.

16. Every radio studio in America has a roll of toilet tissue in it. Rather than have it sitting out, buy a regular bathroom roll dispenser and mount it conveniently under the counter or table.

17. The on-air studio is probably the only room occupied 24 hours, whereas regular office space functions on a more routine 8-hour day. For this reason, the studio will get dirty, need cleaning, and suffer wear-and-tear three times over. Adding to an already claustrophobic environment, overflowing trash cans and excessive foot traffic can create a very unhealthy workspace. I advise a system of more frequent maintenance service, including more frequent carpet vacuuming and shampooing. Most stations have at least one maintenance or utility person whose job it should be to keep a watchful eye on the air studio.

18. The control room on-air microphone may be the most germ-ridden device at the radio station. Protective foam-rubber windscreens should always be used. They should be removable and washable, regularly sanitized with disinfectant.

19. Wooden cotton swabs for tapehead cleaning are good for cleaning ears. Similarly, single-edge tape-editing razor blades do wonders for fingernail/cuticle annoyances. Only kidding! Be careful. Occasionally, I need to see if you're paying attention! Remember, this is a fun programming manual.

20. Finally, and let's get serious here. Personal hygiene and good grooming manners are always appreciated. A spare deodorant, mouthwash, and toothbrush in your desk drawer can come in very handy.

21. I almost forgot. This is a new one: Easy on the cologne or perfume. It lingers long after you leave the studio. After all, whom are you trying to impress? The listeners, right? They can't smell it.

TITLES

It has often been said that one gets titles rather than raises. Obviously, you can't take a title to the bank, but in many cases, eventually you can. Titles may be conferred upon deserving employees and may include a salary increase for the new duties and responsibilities. However, sometimes the titles come without the money. But though they might not put any money in the pocket at the moment, titles tend to be the sort of thing that look good on a résumé and play well on the ears of the banks, stores, and the public. If there are actual duties and responsibilities that accompany the title, the opportunity to learn another area of radio station operations can actually become a big advantage.

Over the years of handing out (and receiving) titles in lieu of raises, I've found there are a few titles that fit almost every radio station. In building the team concept at a station, it's always a good idea to distribute significant responsibility so that every member of the staff has a stake in its success. Giving a staff member, especially someone on the air, a title also solves the problem of what to print on business cards under his/her name. "Disc Jockey" never did it for me, although some stations use "Air Personality" or "Announcer." These titles sound sort of silly to the general public or at a cocktail party where business cards are being handed out with titles like "Consulting Engineer," "Attorney at Law," or "Osteopathic Physician." Creative titles that actually do indicate responsibilities and duties assigned to staff members may open doors for them and the station. It makes the staff member feel more significant and important in the eyes of those in the community with whom the staff member will conduct station business. In conferring titles, take it seriously. Although it may be the best you can do in lieu of offering a raise, attach importance and responsibility to the appointment. Print business cards. Issue a congratulatory memo. Shake hands. Buy drinks.

When hiring, it's perfectly legal (and desirable) to recruit applicants for a titled position; this may bring forth a more talented, experienced, and in-depth individual for what might formerly have been an air-shift position. It is better to set up a series of potential duties and responsibilities for an employee and give that position a title than to hire an announcer and then pile on a bunch of surprise extra responsibilities. Now that consolidation has swept the United States, there is a variety of new titles, primarily on the management and sales side. Titles such as Market Manager and Regional Sales Manager didn't exist a few years ago. On the programming side, a few program directors and operations managers have more sets of call letters under their names on their business cards, but most of the internal programming day-to-day responsibilities are the same. Here are a few of the titles and some of the job descriptions that go along with them.

- *Promotions Director.* If the station does not have a promotion department as such, this can be a perfect job title and responsibility for the member of the staff who is most likely to be assisting in the station's promotional operations. This title can also go to someone outgoing and aggressive toward promoting station events, in general. Look for someone who is detail-oriented and can follow through. There also may occasionally be some physical activity involved with this position, so assign it accordingly. Because this title literally says "promotion," this person must be able to represent the radio station professionally and effectively to other businesses and to listeners.

- *Production Director.* Some stations double an announcer position as the production director, but someone must be assigned the responsibility for commercial production, the production studio, systems, and standards. Even if all air-staff members share production responsibilities on a pick-up basis, it's still advisable to name one person to oversee the department (or to make it into a department). As technology has advanced the audio-production arts, this job has taken on a new, highly technical, computer-literate characteristic. Good production directors, well experienced with digital editing, sampling, and recording techniques, are in demand. This is one job title then can definitely be a stepping-stone to a better job and more money in the future, if not at the present station. Two of the often overlooked qualities of a good production director are speed and efficiency. With today's commercial loads increasing and the demand for quality production at an all-time high, it simply is impossible to agonize meticulously over producing a single commercial. Production shortcuts that won't compromise quality and the application of experience from repetitive, efficient procedures will always be required of good production directors.

- *Director of Special Programs.* I like this one. It's a title given to an announcer, usually the all-night or evening person (often even a part-timer). This person is responsible for the incoming weekend and special programs that arrive at the station by mail, UPS, satellite, etc. Weekend countdowns, music specials, interviews, special-events programs, public affairs, religious, ethnic—you name it. Let this person handle the arrangements with the network and syndicators who supply this programming. Let him/her check in the discs, mail back the tapes, fill out the affidavits, and take care of the multitude of other minor matters requiring regular attention. This position is very helpful around holidays, when there is an abundance of special programs, all of which need to be organized. A good director of special programs can clear up a lot of time for the program director to work on matters that are more profitable. This is not a public job and can be ideal for an employee who may not be as comfortable in public as others on the staff. Neatness, organization, and good phone skills are imperative.

- *Music Director.* This title that in many cases fairly belongs on the shoulders of one of the air staff members is most influential with adding and removing music from the play list. This director needs to be someone who can work with the music and the record companies in a fair and responsible manner. Depending on the format, the size of the music library, or the management's music policy, a music director can be completely responsible for the operation of the station's music programming. The job may also involve scheduling, computer entry, adding new songs, assembling weekly charts, or cataloging the storage library. At stations where music programming is very competitive and intense, the music director may be a full-time position and exercise considerable artistic control of music selection. Some of the best people with whom I've worked have been music directors particularly when they were not frustrated would-be program directors.

- *Director of Special Projects.* A catch-all title that falls under the classification of "utility infielder." This person can be pressed into service in a number of areas, such as promotions, driving the station vehicle, setting up a remote, running errands, or any other responsibilities requiring him or her to deal with listeners and the business community. More than a delivery person or "go-fer," the director of special projects title adds importance to even the smallest jobs at the station because it binds them together in an ongoing effort toward station success. Many station activities are seasonal and don't require year-round attention. When holidays, the chili cook-off, and opening day at the ballpark roll around, it's nice to have someone there to depend on for those occasions.

- *Public Service Director.* Rarely is this a full-time position at any radio station, but it is an excellent position and title to give to the member of the air staff selected to be a liaison with public service and community organizations. This person can be very helpful in working with the program director on public service promotions and contests, as well as providing visibility by attending public relations and public affairs events. The public service director represents the radio station on the front line, interfacing with the community. This person can carry a tape recorder and microphone as an appendage to the news department via access to events and people in the community. This person enjoys exposure and doesn't mind an occasional free lunch or ribbon-cutting ceremony. It may not require being a full-time member of the air staff (or someone from another area of the station, not on the air at all) but is an excellent position for someone who likes the visibility and appearance of being a station personality.

Occasionally, the public service director title is given to a member of the news staff. Since most stations already have a news director and perhaps even an assistant news director, the third position in the newsroom can be the public service director. The newsroom is, by definition, already aware of what is going on in the community and receives press releases from various organizations. Thus, it is already equipped to handle interviews and news-oriented items that deal with public affairs issues.

Delegation, Delegation, Delegation

There are six significant areas of delegation that can be subdivided, mixed, matched, or combined. Whether or not to give titles to staff members is a personal and/or company choice. However, here are some of the job responsibilities that can be (and should be) delegated to members of the air staff:

Description #1: Coordinate, develop, and produce promos for remotes, special events, listener comments, and contests.

Description #2: Collect, write, and file public service information and provide an events list for the staff. Keep a running calendar of scheduled public service and public affairs events where the station enjoys participation.

Description #3: Audience research. A liaison with area media, theater, civic groups, and sports franchises. Locate and list events for participation in terms of opportunities for onsite audience research or to represent the station at potential research opportunity events.

Description #4: Produce the daily music list or schedule. Edit music computer, delete, update, add songs in music library. Fix discrepancies, run music reports. Generally assist in all aspects of station music operations.

Description #5: Preferably an evening air staff member who can do some audience research, coordinate contest winners, and coordinate the operation of contests. This is a good job for an evening person since most contests run in the daytime. The contest activities will have ended for the day and can be updated by this person, who can also prepare for the next day's activities.

Description #6: Weekend/special programming check-in. Make sure promos are recorded and in-studio for specials. Send in affidavits from syndication companies. Keep records and schedules of upcoming programs. This person can also assist in adding music and in training new employees.

STATION RESOURCES

In Chapter 5, I address the importance of formal research, as presented by institutional research organizations. Turning away from the research company approach long enough to see what the station itself has to offer is sometimes a difficult task. It is common for radio station management to overlook the talent and capabilities available on its own payroll completely in order to accept information coming from an outside source or research company. It would be my hope that most modern radio operations have the good sense to exploit positively what is already theirs. Many radio stations have enormous, untapped resources at their fingertips. Without involving a research company, it is not unusual for great radio stations to use their listeners to find needed music, for determining the types of promotions that best work effectively, by determining what type of programming is needed at certain times of the day, and by providing the station some measure of its success in sales and promotional matters.

This is not a long section, but it states a valuable principle that is often overlooked. Radio stations, above and beyond all else, need to hire talented and skilled programming management people, equip them with the best tools possible, and let them use their own creativity, imaginations, and originality. Mistakes will be made, but great ideas come from good ideas, which come from bad ideas, which may have originally resulted in failure. This is how the process works. Give talented people the opportunity, even the opportunity to fail now and then, and they will create a product that is unlike any other in the market. Station management that repeatedly bypasses its own staff to import data and information from the outside is doing it and its ownership a great disservice.

While it is worthwhile to get a fresh view of the operation from an outside source, such an audit cannot and should not be considered a substitute for the inestimably valuable insights into a market that staff members possess by virtue of their daily participation in the process of executing the format. After all, it is the waiter and the bartender who are the restaurant, not the owner. It is the sales help and checkout clerk who are the store, not the shareholders. It is the front-line, customer-interface people who hear all the suggestions, all the complaints, and all the congratulatory comments. Without even knowing it, the staff of a radio station has a market awareness that no outside consultant can match with structured, formal, time-restricted interviews or demographics. Unless really drastic (read format change) measures are contemplated, it is simply a waste of talent to leave in-house staff out of discussions that relate to listeners and listeners' attitudes.

A radio station speaks with a big voice in the community it serves. Unlike any other form of business, it can attract resources to its doors that can in turn be used successfully. This is the business of communication, and communication is the exchange of ideas. Not only should a radio station be defined by its own format and staff, but every one of its listeners is also a part of the composite radio station identity. Communication with those listeners is a daily external process. Therefore, a business built on the exchange of ideas can actually be very successful, but not if it fails to exchange ideas among its own staff. To facilitate this internal exchange of ideas, hold frequent "brainstorming" sessions with the station staff. Start by setting up a list of topics, including proposed topics, promotions, and needs that may occur within several months. Each person at the session is given a sheet of paper with 10 blank lines and a blank topic heading, which is filled in at the direction of the leader. Then, open the topic and have everyone write as many ideas as possible about the subject on the blank lines. The three basic rules for the session are:

- Rule 1: There are to be no negative ideas or discussions of why any idea won't work.
- Rule 2: We are just looking for ideas; nothing about the ideas is actually discussed in detail. That comes later when the ideas have all been collected and arranged by project.
- Rule 3: There are no bad ideas, so write down every thought about a topic. Often what may appear to be a bad or poorly developed idea may yield a better idea that would not have occurred without the original bad idea.

Radio stations attract all kinds of talented, diverse people. Brainstorming sessions should include persons from outside the programming realm but who work in other departments at the station. The perspective they bring by being slightly away from the intimate day-to-day programming team can bring fresh insight. Key nonprogramming people may include the reception person who meets your listeners face-to-face daily, or someone from a demographic inside or outside the format target. Let someone from the sales or technical side of your operation be a participant once in a while. People from these areas not only have ideas to contribute, but become aware of how the creative process works by being a part of it. Watching creative people create is like watching salespeople sell. There's a time to appreciate what the other person does and how he or she does it.

A good brainstorming session should last exactly an hour. Making the session a time-bound event forces thinking and speeds up the process of getting the maximum number of ideas written down. In the weeks following the brainstorming session, when there is time to actually review and organize each of the projects, you'll have a stack of ideas, contributed by the entire staff, from which to choose the direction and methods of execution of the plan. As you execute the new ideas, the members of your staff will recognize where they came from and acknowledge the person contributing. Brainstorming is not new. There are books in the library and at bookstores dealing with enhancing the creative process in some form of structured thinking process. Refine your brainstorming sessions with new ideas from other authors in advertising, marketing, business, technology, and commerce. Apply the good ones to your sessions. Let participants make suggestions on how to better exercise future brainstorming sessions or let them hold sessions of their own for solutions and ideas within areas of their particular expertise (e.g., a promotions brainstorm, a production brainstorm, a remote-broadcast brainstorm). Ultimately, there's no bad way to come up with a good idea (although the invention of the parachute may be an exception).

TAKE A BREAK

Even though this section is found here, I actually wrote it last. I saved a spot right here because that's where it belongs, no matter when it was written. As the weeks turned into months and the months into years, this section remained "To Be Announced" on my table of contents. Finally, as I was within weeks of submitting the final version to the publisher, there was the empty section with just a title staring me in the face. Before throwing in the towel by just renumbering the other sections and discarding "To Be Announced," I decided it would be wise if I took a break and just thought about what to do.

Then it happened! While taking a break, I realized how important it is: Take a break! We are a business where workaholics abound. We create enormous workloads for ourselves and are so in touch with every aspect of our radio stations that we begin to feel that the station simply cannot function without us. We come in earlier each day and we stay later each evening. We come back to the station at nights and on weekends. Ever taken an official day off only to find yourself stopping by the station just to check on things? I knew a guy once who stopped by the station on his way to the airport for vacation, only to miss his flight by spending too long checking phone messages.

The timeliness and intensity of most station activities require an enormous degree of focus. That's good! But the downside is that, by definition, focus requires restricting one's attention toward a single point. This often occurs to the exclusion of everything else. For a better perspective, do yourself a favor and take a break. You'll actually be surprised at how much more creative you can be when you put something aside for just a little while, then get back to it with a slightly different frame of mind.

We all have individual ways of taking breaks. It's an acquired skill, however. There are many young program directors who really don't know how to relax. They're smothering themselves with office work that follows them to lunch and then home at night. The key to effective break-taking is delegation. It is not important that a program director consider his or her skills secrets. Occasionally, the paranoia of thinking that others can do the job better keeps many talented people closed off from sharing things with staff. By failing to delegate (which can be interpreted as a failure to trust), an opposite impression can be developed at the radio station—that you are power hungry and possessive, which are definitely characteristics of candidates for eventual replacement.

Day-to-day operations can be boring and time-consuming. The best characteristic of a good program director is creativity. Mundane chores rarely feed creativity. As long as the program director is accountable to the station manager, and the work gets done, few managers really care who does the hands-on tasks. By passing along several of your key operations duties to others, three important things begin to happen.

1. The others feel that they have a greater responsibility because you trust them.

2. You have more time available.

3. You can move into a more creative state of mind.

As for the paranoiacs, good program directors win by staying ahead of the pack, not by keeping up with it. The sooner I can delegate a function to a deserving staff member, the sooner I can move farther ahead of the pack. As soon as I teach someone a new skill, I can stay ahead by developing a new skill for myself. Don't find yourself so caught up in being singularly possessive of every aspect of station activity that someone else on staff has the time to be more creative than you are.

See next Signpost.

Learn to delegate. As soon as you complete this section, give every member of your staff one of your secrets and make that duty part of their day-to-day job description. Then, take a good look at your own work schedule for the day, month, and year ahead. Start thinking about all the time you'd like to reclaim in order to get your creative process going again. Remember that creativity does not mean just daydreaming. You can develop strategies or tactics. You can put yourself in another place physically and benefit from all you see and hear.

Most good managers know the importance of taking breaks, so your station manager can be supportive of the practice. Notice how the station manager or other key managerial personnel at the station take their breaks, and follow their lead. Once you can delegate and once you can put a task aside and clear your calendar, then take a break. Taking a break really means getting your mind away from the taxing issues that seem to consume too much thought and time. Just getting up and walking around the office can be stimulating. Have you ever tried to think of someone's name for hours, then the minute you get distracted and think about something else, that name pops into your head? It's almost as if our bodies and brains are sending us a signal that it's time to shift gears because the current processing has bogged down.

Learn to delegate.

In former decades, program directors were not spending all day at computers, tethered to a few feet of the same desk and chair for most of an entire day. Maybe in former decades program directors were more creative, too. Perhaps the lack of creative stimulation has narrowed our range of possibilities to those which can be accomplished with a keyboard and mouse. Before the widespread use of the personal computer, there seemed to be more interaction among staff members. The slowness of the typewriter somehow allowed us a few more minutes to think between the sentences of the letters or promos we were writing.

A break can be a day, an afternoon, an hour, or a few minutes. On the next page is a list of potential break opportunities.

Are there some breaks here you should be considering to enhance your job performance?

1. Take every vacation day coming to you. Don't sell them back or forfeit them, ever.

2. Holidays should be enjoyed away from the station. If you've worked your way into a management position that allows you to be off on holidays, take advantage of it.

3. Spend weekends away from the station. If an air shift is required, then negotiate alternating weekends off.

4. Lunch! Never eat at your desk! Get away from the station. Take a full hour. Eat outdoors in fair weather. Bringing a lunch from home may be economical and convenient, but seeing you eating at your desk creates the opposite impression from the one you want. Your message is that you are so busy you can't even get away for a minute to eat. The message received is that you are doing something that's possibly messy and unsanitary in a place of work. Even if you have a private office, other people will drop in, and there's something a little distasteful about seeing other people eat unless it's in a place reserved for that purpose. So, if you must bring your lunch, or get something and carry it back to the station, at least eat it in the lounge and not at your desk. Maybe this is a place for a word about that refrigerator that management has thoughtfully provided for staff. It's best to set up a rotating schedule for everyone who uses it to share in the responsibility for cleaning it out—every week. Anything left in there, name on it or not, is to be thrown out on cleanup day and the interior swabbed out thoroughly. In some places I've been, there are ancient artifacts in the station refrigerator that could easily have been recovered from tombs in the Valley of the Kings.

5. Your home time is anything routinely outside of office hours.

6. Mid-morning or mid-afternoon, take a short walk outside the station.

7. Get coffee or soda down the street rather than in the staff lounge.

8. Close your office door, turn off the lights. Rest your eyes or lie on the floor.

9. Work occasional half-days during the week.

10. Listen to air checks during office hours at home rather than at the station.

11. Take a long lunch.

12. Do physical exercise (go to the health club, shoot some baskets, hit the driving range, etc.).

13. Celebrate employee birthdays at the station with cakes and candles, and get everybody to take a break from their jobs for a few minutes.

14. Sit in the lobby for a few minutes. Chat with the receptionist or listeners who stop by.

15. Ask other employees to take a break with you. Spend time walking around the block or having a snack.

16. Go into an empty studio by yourself. Listen to some favorite songs (not from your format).

17. Give those who work for you a break. If you respect the concept, then you respect what it can do for everyone else, too.

18. Sometimes, issues and projects require everyone involved to take a break. Be the leader and volunteer the idea that everyone needs to take a collective break.

19. By now, you should get the idea!

20. So, stop reading *Radio: The Book* for a few minutes and take a break (because the author will turn off the computer and pour a glass of pinot noir).

VACATION POLICIES

Most broadcasting companies establish vacation policies at the corporate level. Unfortunately, because of the peculiar 24-hour nature of the air staff, vacation policies for other employees are often difficult to apply. For station managers—owners as well as program directors—I've devoted a few pages to the subject of vacations. Realizing full well that company policy sometimes seems inflexible, it is still important to reevaluate vacation policy in light of the peculiar nature of the radio business. In Europe and other parts of the world, many working people start their jobs with 4 weeks' vacation annually. In the United States, most companies consider only 1 week for the first few years on the job, building to 2 weeks after a few years and 3 weeks after 5 or 10 years on the job. It's easy to see how job burnout is a common employee crisis in many companies. My buddies in corporate radio are probably not willing to rewrite the book on vacation policy, but we can take a more realistic approach to the subject.

Here is a list of items to consider for establishing vacation policy:

1. Have two different policies in effect (and in writing) as part of company procedures, one for the air staff and another for other employees. This helps enormously in reconciling the diverse functions each performs and defining vacation procedures accordingly.

2. Since ratings services now operate all year, there really isn't any ratings downtime for vacations. Develop a creative schedule when air talent absence will be less noticeable. Summer is still regarded as the best vacation time. Less importance is usually placed on summer ratings for sales purposes.

3. At the beginning of each year, post a notice asking for proposed vacation requests. No obligation, just some proposed dates from each air staff member, utilizing all of the vacation time they have accrued. This gives you, at least, a starting point for planning around their requests.

4. Pencil these dates on a planning calendar and post it in some conspicuous place so that everyone can visually see the schedule unfold. Watch for overlaps and notify persons with conflicting dates.

5. Use seniority (if you have to) in settling conflicts. Vacation policy is one of the few remaining benefits of longevity with the company.

6. When hiring a new employee, especially a key player on the team, consider having the employee's proposed and preferred vacation dates included contractually in the work agreement.

7. Suggest to employees that they take their vacation from mid-week to mid-week. This leaves them on the air for a portion of 2 weeks and reduces their absence. Rather than being away a whole week (bracketed by two weekends), they're only away one weekend. This frequently can help the employee take advantage of better airfares and hotel rates.

8. Reconsider any policy of taking only whole weeks. Permit vacations to be taken in 3- or 4-day increments rather than weeks. Most air talent seem to prefer more frequent, shorter breaks, like 3- or 4-day weekends. Taking a break from being on the air is an ongoing need, not completely satisfied by 2- or 3-week vacations.

9. Vacation time is cherished by air staff members. But usually, so is their work and devotion to their performance. Since their absence from the station is more obvious than that of other staff members, there seems to be an unwritten obligation for air talent to have generally good attendance records. Recognize this characteristic in the staff, but

encourage them to take vacations for the mutual benefit of the station, as well as the individual.

10. Use bonus vacation days as incentive or rewards for exceptional performance. For example:
    a. ratings achievement
    b. performing a particularly impressive civic function
    c. working on a holiday
    d. completing an assigned station project
    e. as rewards for personal appearances (see section on personal appearance)

Leisure time becomes more important to employees who are consistently required to perform under pressure on an ongoing basis. Being on the air is like being on stage for 4 or more hours, often solo, and without a full script. Consider that a single corporate vacation policy is probably not very realistic in a creative industry such as radio. Respect the different duties throughout the whole radio station and establish a vacation policy accordingly. It is also extremely practical to ask new employees what their vacation preferences might be, so that you can build it into the employment agreement.

There are also occasions when you might reward an employee with a working vacation, by attending an out-of-town station event (concert, theme park, sports event) at station expense, but does interviews or phone reports back to the station. The station has a presence at the event, it sounds great, and gives the employee a break from the daily routine. I once gave my assistant program director (Rob Ellis) at WING in Dayton, Ohio, a trip to Florida to cover an oldies beach party featuring some rock stars of the 1950s and 1960s. Turns out it was his very first airline flight. He liked it so much, I later fixed him up with a hot-air balloon trip. On both occasions, he filed entertaining live reports back to the station, while enjoying the event at station expense.

HEALTH TIPS

Working on the air at a radio station is generally clean and easy work with no heavy lifting and no likelihood of being subjected to any health dangers. Yet there are a few maladies that recur among radio station employees. A common ailment of announcers is a sore throat. Sometimes an announcer just becomes exhausted vocally, and the sore throat is not symptomatic of any greater illness. When the sore throat is serious and is diagnosed as such, get professional medical treatment. However, the simple irritated sore throat that many of us suffer because we spend hours on the air or at some public function can be easily corrected.

Sore Throat. This homemade concoction is the best potion I ever tried:

    1/4 cup Listerine or similar oral antiseptic
    Juice from 1 lemon
    Two tablespoons of table salt
    Four pulverized aspirins
    1/4 cup hot water

Dissolve the aspirin in the hot water, and then add all the other ingredients until you have a liquid containing the antiseptic, lemon juice, table salt, aspirin, and hot water. Gargle with this combination hourly for 1 to 2 minutes each time, especially before going to bed and overnight (should you arise during the evening for other purposes). This gargle mixture has gotten me through dozens of minor sore throat irritations over the years. It doesn't taste *terrible*, but you wouldn't want to swallow much of it, either.

Backache. The next common ailment seems to be miscellaneous back discomfort. Particularly for men, I have found a simple remedy for occasional back discomfort by going right to the source.

The wallet in the rear pocket.

Sitting on a wallet that is a half-inch thick or more is the same as sitting on a block of wood of the same size. It places an undue pressure on the nerves on the hip and causes you to sit slightly off center. Believe it or not, when I first changed my behavior and began removing my wallet from my trousers prior to sitting down for doing an air shift, I found that my backache and subsequent headaches stopped almost instantly.

OTHER RADIO MEDIA

SYNDICATED PROGRAMMING

Radio programming can originate from a variety of sources. If we assume that the basic radio station begins as a 100% live operation, then let's see where some additional programming can come from and how to deal with it. Although many stations now engage in virtual programming, where the operation is almost automated, we'll limit this chapter to programming from real outside sources like syndicators and networks. Satellite programming has become very popular these days, whether as one of the many full-time programming formats now available or as a distribution system for special programming. Not too many years ago, almost all outside programming came into the station either on tape or disk. Both of these delivery systems require a tangible element with built-in cost factors, including the cost of the tape itself, producing the recording, pressing the record, and delivery. Regardless of the delivery system, most stations continue to carry one or more syndicated programs on a regular basis.

Syndicated programs should fulfill several objectives in the overall programming profile of the radio station. They are as follows:

1. To provide information and entertainment not readily available locally
2. To enhance sales opportunities by offering a specific program rather than the general spot sales otherwise offered via the regular format
3. To offer some staff relief by providing programming for dayparts where announcers may not be required
4. To maintain/establish relationships between the station and program suppliers

Since syndicators have the resources to put together high-quality programs, the station benefits from professional sound and in-depth information that may not otherwise be available locally.

Syndicated material is usually in one of three forms:

1. Long-form format: A complete format, delivered hour by hour, around the clock, usually by satellite.
2. Long-form program: Usually from 30 minutes to 3 to 4 hours long. Specific subject, music emphasis, or topic. For example: weekly countdown shows, artist salutes, special holiday programming, concert specials
3. Short-form program (or feature): Hourly, daily, or weekly feature dealing with an item or topic of specific interest, usually 2 to 5 minutes long. For example: financial news, artist profiles, consumer tips, health information.

Most syndicated programs are provided on a barter basis, meaning that within each program are commercials provided by the syndicator to national advertisers. Opportunities for local sale are available for local commercials in the show as well. Syndicators make their money by selling national advertising, then guaranteeing to those advertisers that their message will be heard on so many station's in so many markets. It is vitally important for syndicators to be on the air with their programs in as many different markets as possible. It is also important that the station carrying the program have a significant, measurable audience in the demographics sought by the advertiser. Although we programmers look at what we do as artistic, the purpose of all programming (especially syndicated) is to provide a means to guarantee placement of advertising dollars on radio. For this reason, most syndicators also require either an affidavit or proof of performance document to verify that the show actually ran, including the commercials. Also, if there was ever anything that got lost in the mail, it's the affidavit forms from syndicators. A form is either included with each program or mailed from the syndicator monthly. In any case, make a copy of each completed form for your records. You'll probably be asked for it again a few times per year. Keeping track of all those forms from every station carrying the program is a major chore for the syndicator, but very necessary for it to verify that commercials were carried.

Frequently, a syndicator will allow a station to run a syndicated program more than once. As long as the initial commercial obligation is met, the show can run again, eliminating all the network commercials and either containing all local spots or as a commercial-free program. Usually, syndicators ask for program clearance between 6 AM and 12 midnight. However, on programs of 3 to 4 hours, you can usually ask for and get permission to expand that by a few hours from 5 AM to 1 AM. My syndicator friends usually don't want to hear this, but if you have a strong weekend program (a countdown, concert, or featured artist type program), run it as-is Sunday morning 5 AM to 9 AM, then run a commercial-free version Sunday night (or the Saturday night before in prime time), when a greater listenership is available. To my ear, most syndicated shows, especially those from major networks, are vastly overly commercial, running up to 12 spots per hour, every hour, often repeating products. I understand this from a business point of view, but I just don't think it sounds good, especially when the network spots are to be followed by the local spots. In most cases, syndicators also will permit the show to be run commercial-free if the commercials themselves are played at a different time from the program, but within the allowable time frame for broadcast.

Many stations with production talent available get the incoming program, strip the commercials out of it, run the commercials spread out over the whole weekend, and run the program itself commercial-free or with local sponsorship only. As long as the station owns up to the commercial commitment agreed to with the syndicator, it can run the program where it will do the most good and in the most listenable form.

Most syndicated programs, especially long form, have opportunities within the program to insert local identifiers and/or promos. Even though the program is coming from an outside source and the audience is reasonably sure the show is not locally produced, make the extra effort to make the program sound as much like your station as possible. Having been the host of *The Country Oldies Show* for the past several years, I have the opportunity to talk with our affiliated stations on a regular basis, so here are the basics for effective localization of syndicated shows:

1. Have the show's host record local breaks and promos. Even though the show is not trying to sound locally produced, the link between local station and host is imperative.
2. Promote the program during other dayparts. If it is on your program schedule, you should talk about it.
3. Use frequent I.D.s during the show. Even your syndicated programs should sound like your radio station.
4. Use recorded promos within the program to promote the next event on the air (e.g., another program or air talent).
5. When available, obtain advance information about upcoming program content to promote specifics each week.
6. Use station jingles during the program.

Many syndicators want the programs returned, but most specify that the program be destroyed or kept by the station. In some cases (check with the syndicator for permission), try running a mail-in contest within the program each week and award the program itself (if on cassette or CD) to the winner, announced within the following week's program. Generally, stations don't do enough to use syndicated programming to its greatest advantage and thereby cheat themselves of potential ratings opportunities by not making the best effort possible to be consistent and entertaining whether live or syndicated. Our show, *The Country Oldies Show*, has always had a policy of unlimited air play after the initial air date, and it's worked very well for gaining additional exposure for the show itself and the artists we feature.

For short features, the older the audience, the better the acceptance. Stopping the music for a few minutes to provide informative and entertaining material is not a serious blow to the programming. Most research shows that the older listeners get, the more they seek relaxation and information.

Before putting any feature on the air, do a little homework and make a careful assessment of the compatibility to mainstream programming. The number of 3- to 5-minute weekly or daily features available is astonishing. Of course, they all want to run in drive time.

Here's a good way to use features as a secret weapon for improving a usually dead daypart. Most syndicates, especially the small, independent guys, would rather be on the air at any time available than not in a market at all. Offer them placement on the all-night show. Accept their programs on a nonbinding month-to-month basis, offering them the opportunity to drop your station if they get a better affiliate (which they won't, so you're safe). Work with your all-night personality to schedule a different feature each hour all night. Let him/her take care of the incoming shows and affidavits. The features on money, gardening, safety, consumer news, pet care, etc. can transform an otherwise music-intensive, all-night show into almost a magazine and provide a good, informative lead-in to the morning drive shift. Few stations effectively sell overnight, but these specific features, which may be attractive to specific sponsors (at a not-to-be-believed rate), can generate some easy money from an otherwise unprofitable daypart. Statistics show that 65% of your total cume will listen to a portion of your all-night show every week. Work with that.

As technology has advanced faster and faster, distribution of programming has become commonplace. Satellite became the medium of choice for syndicators because it requires no investment in tape or CD, postage, packaging, or duplicating. Therefore, the resources of local stations are required to record the program from satellite if it is not carried live. Satellite distributed features or programs will increase only as distribution becomes less expensive and as syndicators look for more variety in opportunities to sell advertising to a wider spectrum of demographics that cover a broad range of subject matter.

Now, with the proliferation of high-quality audio on the Internet, there are still more methods for inexpensive diffusion of programming. As mentioned very early in this book, the minute I start talking about technology, the book starts to age very quickly. Regardless of what distribution technology is used, it's still all about the listener. No matter how much syndicated programming you may decide to carry, your radio station is still supported by listeners and must retain its own identity throughout all programming, regardless of origin.

Funny how things seem to develop circularly. In the days of the AM giants, almost all their programming was live and national. Then there was a shift to local with prerecorded music and commercials. Now, with virtual programming and satellite distribution, there's a shift back to national, even if not live. When radio shifted from network to local, it achieved an immediacy and vitality that made it unique and locally valued. It looks like, in some places, we're in danger of losing that, and my fear is that if we do, we may lose a great many of our listeners. The main idea of this section on syndicated shows is that we need to work to tie them into our local community of listeners as much as we can.

SATELLITE RADIO

In 1990, a proposal was put forth to develop a satellite radio technology to deliver programming from satellites directly to the consumer. Up to this point satellite radio delivery had been used generally to provide programming to radio stations that would relay the programming over to their regular listeners. This was the first opportunity for listeners to get material directly from satellite. To do this, some technology needed to be perfected that would accommodate that sort of activity. So the founders of Sirius Satellite Radio, Mr. David Margolese, a Canadian entrepreneur who had the lion's share of the Canadian cellular telephone system called CanTel, and Mr. Rob Briskman, a NASA scientist who had been involved in President Kennedy's quest to put a man on the moon, got together and decided to market a consumer-to-satellite technology. They developed labs that went about the business of perfecting not only the receivers but the necessary satellites and uplink/download/downlink technologies. Having done so, they took this information back to the federal government with a request to reallocate some secure existing satellite radio frequencies used by the military.

Eventually, those frequencies were released for this public satellite broadcasting process. But the fight wasn't over. The Federal Communications Commission (FCC), the organization that licenses radio stations, came into play at this point and developed a series of radio licenses for satellite broadcasters. Subsequently, the opportunity to bid on the frequencies went out for auction to determine if there were any corporate interests wanting to participate. Sirius Satellite Radio, which at the time was known as CD Radio, had actually to go back to the FCC and submit a bid to use the technology that it had perfected and patented. But such is government red tape. The company eventually did get one of the satellite broadcasting licenses secured in its name. Another company, which became XM Radio, received another one of the licenses. There was a third license that was also available and was held by a third company for a brief time and then returned to the FCC, as the company that held it did not really intend to act upon it, leaving the two major players in satellite radio as XM and CD Radio.

In 1999, CD Radio evolved into Sirius. The company had already been marketing CD radio to the public to a minor degree, although not having launched any satellites at that point, and not yet having any receivers in the market, there was still some buzz on Wall Street and among the investment community about this technology. CD Radio, however, decided that the name of the company was not what it wanted because the technology of compact discs was almost peaking at this point. Being on the horizon of new types of audio delivery, the company didn't want to be identified with an old technology. At a big party in New York City at the Beacon Theater, starring the artist Sting, a big relaunch party was held, inviting all the media. It was allegedly a press party for people to come and listen to Sting perform. CD Radio was going to be the sponsor with some sales pitch about satellite radio. Midway through the party, however, the entire series of logos, the marquee on the theater, all of the apparel being worn by all the staff and the waiters and waitresses and the employees of Sirius were changed within a matter of moments to read "Sirius." Sirius is named after the dog star in the constellation Orion. From that point forward, Sirius Satellite Radio was born.

I had the pleasure of working with Sirius, first as a consultant and then as a program manager for its country formats, so I became intimately involved in not only the technology at Sirius and the satellite radio pitch, but also in our major competitor, XM Satellite Radio. XM satellites were built by the Boeing Corporation and its satellites are in a geostationary orbit over the equator. The XM satellites, two of them (named Rock and Roll), hang directly over the equator in a stationary position requiring the satellite receivers at the consumer end to be aimed at the equator or to have adequate exposure to the Southern Hemisphere. XM and Sirius also built a series of land-based repeater transmitters to fill in geographic areas not effectively covered by their satellite signals. At this writing Sirius has about 130, but XM requires about 800 to supplement the satellite signal.

Sirius has three satellites that are geosynchronous. Geosynchronous satellites actually move in the sky. They move in a pattern from North to South America so two of the three Sirius satellites are always on and over North America while the third satellite is set in the south and recharges its batteries, gets its telemetry updates, and then returns to the Northern Hemisphere when one of the other two will then go back to the south. So two of Sirius's three satellites are always moving and offering virtually an unlimited view of the sky. Either system, XM or Sirius, requires purchasing a special satellite receiver, either an after-market model or built into a new car system. Having worked at Sirius, I had an opportunity to test the satellite receivers in many different states at many different locations and found the performance to be extremely robust and quite good.

Why satellite radio came to be was actually the fault of AM and FM radio. Sirius/CD Radio conducted some research by the Yankee Group in the early 1990s and determined at that point that the audience was finding some fault with radio. Among the things audiences didn't like were the lack of variety of programming on the air and the lack of variety of stations in their particular markets. Listeners were becoming more and more aware of too many commercials on the air and were finding them to be a great nuisance (this is at variance with Arbitron's findings mentioned in Chapter 5). There were also some indications that listeners were not happy with certain signal problems. While driving long distances, it was difficult to continue to receive standard radio stations, necessitating a lot of dial punching from one station to another as one traveled from town to town. Based upon those early objections to radio, the founders of the satellite radio movement were strengthened by the fact that there was apparently a significant market for their product because people who were told about this product reacted favorably to the Yankee Group questions. XM and Sirius took this and other information as the green light they needed to launch the satellites and to continue raising funds in the public sector. Both public companies, XM and Sirius/CD Radio, have had great success raising money and finding investors with either corporate partners or investment companies and the general public. The great advantage that satellite radio offers is the terrific variety of programming with at least 50 channels of talk, 50 channels of music, and more channels being added all the time. There isn't any radio market in the country that offers that type of variety, particularly on the music side. Sirius began and continues to be completely noncommercial on all of its music channels. XM Satellite Radio started with minimal commercials on a few of its channels, but in February 2004 it decided to follow Sirius's lead and become totally noncommercial on its music side. So now we have both players in the satellite industry with noncommercial music and some limited commercials on the talk and sports and nonmusic programming.

Many of the existing programs on Sirius and XM have come through alliances with conventional networks, program suppliers, and syndication companies. Sports franchises have been early to sign up, with NASCAR coverage going to XM and Sirius following with major league baseball, the NHL, the NFL, and the NBA. Sports, because of its huge fan base, is a natural for satellite. No matter what city your favorite team calls home and no matter where you live, you now have virtual access to all play-by-play of your hometown team wherever you are in the country.

As far as music is concerned, many music formats that would not be viable on the local level and certain niche formats have become popular as part of the Sirius and XM lineups. There wouldn't be enough audience in any specific local market to attain critical mass for commercial success, but taken as a national product, these same niche formats can amass a significant amount of listenership, and because both XM and Sirius depend on subscribers, the people who enjoy this niche programming only have to subscribe to the service on a monthly basis to have the programming they could never get on commercial radio. The niche formats offered by both systems are numerous, including two or more selections in many different areas. Popular music—whether adult contemporary, dance music, country, adult standards, urban, hip-hop, rap, or jazz—all have more than one variety available on each of XM's and Sirius's lineups. So if you are a jazz fan in a particular market, you may have only one local jazz radio station or perhaps only one jazz program only a few hours a week on a single station. With XM or Sirius you have 24 hours 7 days a week of jazz, and perhaps two or three different choices of jazz among them. The "getting to market" award for satellite radio goes to XM, who got its receivers at retail locations in the market ahead of Sirius. Sirius had some early developmental and manufacturing issues regarding the electronic chips required to make the receivers efficient. Although Sirius was not so quick to get into the marketplace, it has since made up a lot of that ground with multiple types of receivers. Satellite radio technology and different types of receivers that are being offered, as well as the programming lineup, are going to be changing almost daily, so it is difficult at this time to give a status report on either of those two companies' lineups. You should visit the companies' web sites for current marketing materials.

I can say, however, that because satellite radio is a subscription service, and because it requires the purchase of a specific receiver, there is no likelihood that any time in the near future there will be as many satellite radios available to the public as there are AM and FM radios. One study indicated that there were 6.2 AM/FM radio sets per household: boom boxes, kitchen radios, car radios, radios in the basement, or wherever. Do the math. It's not going to be anytime soon that a critical mass for satellite radio listening is going to be anywhere close to that of AM and FM. Because of that, the role that radio will play will not be altered very much by satellite radio.

I expect that because a lot of consumers will start listening to satellite radio, and because they will enjoy the commercial-free aspects of it and the niche format, one by one some radio stations may experience a dropping off of some of their core listenership, particularly if satellite radio is accepted as the best choice for automobile listening. Automobile listening accounts for a significant amount of the listenership of many radio stations, and that seems to be where satellite radio will gain its strongest foothold. I predict that any early indications of erosion of audience from conventional radio in favor of satellite radio will come from stations that depend on in-car listening. Having said that, Sirius or XM radios will not be in every car anytime soon. Both Sirius and XM spent an enormous amount of time and energy in their early days distributing their radio receivers by going for the after-market product. That is, they put a satellite radio receiver into an existing car, which required the potential subscriber to jump through quite a few hoops including purchase of a set and an antenna, installation and downtime for the vehicle, and then signing up for the subscription. However, both companies have secured successful car deals with new car manufacturers, with satellite radio equipment as standard equipment in most of the new models. It will take many, many, many years of people buying cars before we have 100% new model saturation on the highways. So it is still going to be decades before the saturation of satellite radio is anything resembling that of AM/FM, if ever, particularly if AM and FM continue a forward dynamic of interesting programming and contemporary technology.

Some lessons can be learned from satellite radio. I recommend that people at radio stations, including and especially the program director, take advantage of one of the satellite services and become a subscriber because there is going to be some programming available that you as a local programmer need to know about. At the top of the list will be your ability to use satellite radio to keep an eye on new music and new artists that your station may not be in a position to play or expose. It will give you a leg up if you are able to listen to and use the satellite music services as opportunities to audition music and artists that you might want to be aware of at some point in the future. So it could be a terrific research tool. Satellite radio, being national in reach and form, is going to attract major personalities as guests. These newsmakers may say things in interviews or be quoted or do a live performance on satellite radio, just as they may do a live performance on MTV or do an interview on NBC or CNN. If a major newsmaker does an exclusive interview for Sirius radio, then you should attribute it in your broadcast just like you would if the newsmaker had done the interview on CNN or NBC. Similarly, if there is an artist who does an exclusive live concert on Sirius or XM and it gets national attention, your announcers would be remiss in not saying that this particular event was on Sirius. Both XM and Sirius will be purchasing advertising on radio, and it will be your station's call as to whether it takes advantage of those opportunities. There will be some opportunities in the future to counterprogram to satellite, but for now I don't think it would be wise to go head-to-head against any satellite competitor. You're only giving Sirius and XM free publicity and acknowledging to your audience that they are a threat.

A satellite competitor's saturation in any given market for the near future is going to be quite small, considering that each satellite radio company has over 100 channels to listen to. Let's say, for example, there are 2 million people in a city and an amazingly high 5% have satellite radios. So that's 100,000 satellite subscribers spread out over two companies, XM and Sirius; each company has 50,000 subscribers. Then, each satellite company has 100 channels of programming, so the average satellite station, per company, has an average of 500 listeners—some more, some less. That's with 5% subscribers. Presently, the total subscribership of both companies is less than 1%, so we're talking about less than 100 listeners. The number continues to diminish with format, demographic, and regional date about the listener. Moreover, of those 100 listerners, some of their listening would still likely be shared with AM or FM stations in their local market.

The sky is not falling!

THE INTERNET AND INTERNET RADIO

The terms *Internet* and *radio* are not the same. You can't be both, by definition. Just because you eat popcorn at a movie doesn't make it dinner theater. Radio suggests transmission through the air by means of radio signals and antennae. Internet has evolved from a network of linked computers via phone or interconnection. Yes, some radio stations broadcast their programming by means of one of the audio components of the Internet. Other stations have been set up to program specifically to an Internet audio audience without being connected to a real radio station. The very essence of radio since its miniaturization and lack of dependence on a stationary power supply has been its portability. Since the 1930s in cars and the early 1940s, battery-operated portable radios, through the transistor years to the present, have been the "go anywhere, be anywhere" medium. The Internet's relationship with radio has been one of expansion. Internet listening is still done on a computer, which is generally a stationary device in a home or office, although wireless connections of up to about 100 feet are becoming more common. Additionally, few computers receiving Internet data can move easily from room to room, so the listener is tethered to the listening unit at reasonably close range. Real radio can still be bedside, in the bathroom, garage, and a variety of other places computers only dream about. Computers can still add, subtract, divide, send facsimiles, and write letters, so radio has a lot of catching up to do in that regard.

It is now possible to hear stations from out of town on your computer, so I suppose the curiosity factor of hearing the classical station in Seattle or the rock station from Los Angeles or Blue Danube Radio from Vienna has merit, things that used to be available only by short wave, and then only in a very limited way. I also suppose that you're prepared to do such listening by your computer and not in the same environment as you might with your favorite local radio stations. As computer audio has become vastly improved over recent years, so has the availability of various audio resources aside from radio stations. There are now download deliveries of new CDs, interviews, plays, news, comedy, and more. Some sophisticated audiophiles have run wires from their computer's audio outputs to their home stereo units to bring the Internet-obtained audio to every room of the house, of course while remaining on line. As of the writing of this book, I have not been convinced that the Internet has greatly enhanced radio listening, because that's just not what it does best.

What the Internet does best—better than anything thus far in recorded history—is exchange information. The absolute vastness of Internet resources (the combined resources of everyone on the Internet, worldwide) is nothing short of amazing. Everything is available on the Internet: theater seats to airline tickets; dinner reservations to recipes; weather and phone numbers to street maps; pornography to geography. In an earlier chapter, we explained that radio is a secondary medium. Listeners are almost always doing something else while listening to the radio. Perhaps this is true again as Internet radio listening has become the background while the listener is doing something else on the computer. Since you must be there, writing letters and balancing checkbooks, you might as well be listening to a radio station on the Internet. But Internet listening is not affecting radio to any measurable degree at this time and is not likely to do so in the near future. As mentioned, the best use of the Internet is as a resource for information.

It's tempting to dismiss Internet radio as a fad, but one must be careful about predicting what will be a fad and what will last. In the 1970s, the country was awash in 8-tracks, CB radios (Hey, good buddy!), and talk among audiophiles about quadraphonic sound, now all more or less marginalized—along with bell bottoms, wide ties, and hair "all the way down to where it stopped by itself." On the other hand, the telephone, color TV, and computers themselves had their detractors when they first appeared. There are still purists who collect vinyl LPs because of their "warm" sound and who use only old-style tube amps, similarly because they are "warm."

But speaking of the Internet, radio stations have finally answered the question about how to make the invisible, visible (and inexpensively).

Behold . . . the radio station website is born!

As a career radio personality and programmer, I would have killed to have had Internet technology 20 or 30 years ago. All the visual and informative things I wanted my past radio stations to project are now available to anyone with a computer and access to the Internet—pictures of the air staff, music play lists, newsletters, advertising as an extension of our radio advertisers' commitment, sports scores, weather. Let's go on: announcer schedules, weekend programs, team schedules, contests, promotional calendars, holiday greetings, listener club memberships. Every idea I ever had could have been embellished by the earlier discovery/invention of the Internet website. The website will not provide more listeners, nor will it put millions of dollars in the bank, but every opportunity you can exploit to develop a strong relationship with your listeners will make you more successful. E-mail communication alone has vastly increased the one-on-one communication between your staff and listeners. A website is very inexpensive and simple to keep and operate, and the job of web master can be built into one of your existing positions. Radio station websites are very easy to find. Usually the best place to start is the websites for trade publications (e.g., *Radio & Records*) that have developed a whole section of links to radio station websites, some with and some without audio or live programming.

Make your website totally reflective of your radio station. Put your colors, your logo, and your photos all over it. Make it shine and dazzle. If you don't put your whole programming lineup on your site's audio, at least include a jingle or welcome comment by your morning show. This is an opportunity to be a TV spot, billboard, bus side, flyer, program guide, photo album, and self-liquidating merchandise store all in one. Many good books out there can give you excellent advice for building a website. There's also ample opportunity to trade/barter for web hosting and building. So, take advantage of those situations and put a public face on your radio station.

Given the fact that Internet broadcasting has been available for several years already, I cannot predict any really bright future. The ramp-up for consumer acceptance of really exciting technology is usually very fast. CD players are still shy of complete home saturation. In fact, it's only about 58%. VCRs took off very quickly in the early 1970s but were somewhat hampered by the Beta vs VHS confusion. AM stereo, a good technology, just lay there. Mini-disk recorder/players are doing well, but may be eclipsed by the glut of CD recording devices and software on the market today but not when mini-disk made its debut. That the Internet, Internet audio, and Internet radio have already been around a few years suggests a less-than-stellar first wave of consumer acceptance. There's industry talk about receiving the Internet in your car, or from satellite, or cellular phone links, but those technologies will account only for a fraction of the already small consumer demand. Any technology that works in support of radio and that acknowledges our prime directive "It's All About the Listeners" works for me, but I'm not holding my breath waiting for Arbitron to show me an Internet radio station with numbers to sell.

WRAP-UP

10

BITS AND PIECES—COMMENTARY

So now we've gotten through the fourth edition of our book. A few years ago, when I was preparing the second edition, there were several issues I wanted to address, but they didn't seem to fit into any of the other chapters. In the interest of getting them down in writing and in being consistent with the expression of my feelings throughout this book, it became clear that I needed to establish a chapter just for them. So here it is, newly revised for the fourth edition. Let me just step up on this soapbox . . . now, where was I?

Don't Believe in Proverbs

Although we broadcasters often think of ourselves as great communicators, those skills often seem to go unused when there is a handy slogan, proverb, or epithet to rely on. Rather than give some serious thought to a subject worthy of consideration, we take no action based upon summing up the concept with a quick phrase. Ever heard these sayings used to stop the thought process dead in its tracks?

Don't believe in proverbs.

"If it isn't broken, don't fix it." This is a phrase commonly used to impede progress. It's the new version of leaving well enough alone. It implies mediocrity and status quo. We hear this phrase in relation to format changes or adjustments, staff changes, music policy shifts, etc. Radio isn't about being broken or getting fixed; it's about adapting and moving forward. Radio stations are works in progress, never finished products. Sometimes we need to dismantle a product to closely examine its working parts, so our revised version reads, "If it isn't broken, break it!" Failure to be continuously responsive to market needs and industry demands is to deny radio its primary qualities of flexibility and immediacy.

"Where there's smoke there's fire!" This is usually used as tacit confirmation of rumors or suspicions. Actually, a lot of times there's smoke when there's no sign of fire. And often the tiniest fire can create a huge volume of smoke. So, presume nothing. Better to suggest, "Where there's smoke there's smoke!" There's a logical fallacy here. Just because the pavements are wet, we can't conclude that it's been raining. Maybe there was a water leak in a nearby building.

"Blood is thicker than water." This is often used in defense of relatives who may also be in the industry and to whom favoritism is shown. Actually, a lot of people don't like some of their relatives. A strong friendship or professional relationship often is more powerful than family. Besides, talent runs in families. Maybe the family member is more talented than we suspect.

"When are you going to settle down and grow some roots?" This is very frequently the response to those of us in radio who have moved around a lot, much to the frustration of our friends and relatives who think life is all about staying in your hometown forever and working until retirement at the auto parts store. The reply is simply, "People don't have roots. Plants have roots. My parents wanted a houseplant, but got me." A lot of people have missed a lot of wonderful opportunities because they were unwilling to go to the places where the opportunities were. William James, in *The Principles of Psychology*, discusses habit formation and the security habits provide. Sometimes I read about unemployment in some areas of the country—the steel mill closed down—and opportunities in some other areas of the country—new auto plants in the South are hiring. Why is there such a reluctance to jump fences to reach greener pastures? Long ago when I lived in Indianapolis, I noticed that a lot of people were living in poor neighborhoods with dilapidated housing but paying more rent there than they would have in other, better areas. "Why don't they move?" I asked. "Familiar faces, familiar places," I was told. "They're comfortable where they are." "I see," I said.

So while living in Indianapolis, I lived in five apartments in 5 years. Following those 5 years I moved to Delaware, New Jersey, and New York, respectively, over the next 3 years, followed by California (twice), Ohio, Florida (twice), and New York (four times) over the next 30 years. What I learned is that my comfort zone was wherever I was and with whom I chose to associate. It was not geography dependent. Now, even though it's been many years since I've lived in some regions or have seen many friends who still live there, I can go back and enjoy a genuine sense of familiarity from having been a part of it once-upon-a-time.

Travel, even domestic, is knowledge, and the great enemy of prejudice. I just couldn't imagine my life without the experience of not only visiting but also living among so many different accents, foods, beliefs, ethnic origins, and political views, yet all singing the same national anthem together at the local ballpark. Subsequent travel and work in Europe only reinforced that feeling. As someone working in the communications industry, I have used the information I gathered about regions and colloquial language to get the message to the intended targets.

"Let's not reinvent the wheel." This old chestnut is a lazy man's way of saying that he'd rather recycle old ideas and old material than stretch himself to come up with something new. My response to this bromide is "Oh, let's do reinvent the wheel." The wheel, and by analogy everything else that has been created since time began, has been constantly reinvented ever since the first Neanderthal rolled a stone using a log for a roller. We are still reinventing the wheel, in the form of new gears and mechanisms based on the principle of the wheel. Not only that, we're constantly finding new applications for wheel technology. In radio, perhaps the most obvious examples are the compact disc, which is a kind of wheel, and the satellites that wheel so precisely through the night sky. So let's just chuck that old idea, and keep on reinventing and improving the wheel and everything else that the wheel stands for. Actually, reinventing the wheel is the key principle behind human progress.

Next time you work with someone (in any department) who sums up the conversation with a proverb, challenge it and be prepared to offer well-thought-out, fact-based discussion to move the subject beyond the proverb. As does anyone who enjoys public speaking, I like to use a lot of examples, parallels, and comparisons in my talks for clarifying an issue. Yet, it is easy to work at solving or resolving the example diligently, but leaving the problem. So, my advice is to deal with the actual problem, not examples or comparisons.

Business Advice

While I'm on my soapbox (and I'm starting to like it up here), I'm going to meander over into the area of business advice. I know this book is not sold in the Business section of the bookstore, but there's much about radio programming that relies on the good conduct of business values and procedures. There's a lot of bad business advice out there. For example, we are told to prioritize incoming tasks in order of importance. This is wrong for most purposes. Tasks should be prioritized in the order that they reach one's desk or one's attention. Obviously, tasks coming to us from our managers have been prioritized for us, as has the timeline for completion. In radio, we live and die by the clock, so broadcast deadlines and last-minute programming opportunities or news events need immediate action. Other than that, we have to know that each task, no matter how trivial, is important to someone or it wouldn't have come to us. The best way is to handle it immediately— the same day, if possible—by either doing it, delegating it, or destroying it. One of my favorite maxims is that "That which gets postponed often doesn't get done." This is actually a business technique employed by some: to postpone action for so long that the problem has dropped off the radar.

We have no right to prioritize tasks, with few exceptions, any more than the bank or the post office has a right to go down a line of waiting customers and pick out the most important people to serve first. Every task is important. One of the great advantages of not prioritizing is that we never get behind and then have to struggle with overtime and embarrassing explanations of why something wasn't done. You might even find that discharging a few items that have come in first provide an even greater clarity and insight on handling those other items deemed high priority by your managers.

Doing today's business today leaves you plenty of time to do a good job on tomorrow's business. Considering oneself as being caught up is not a sign that they're not giving you enough work; it's a sign that you're not working enough. There is no such thing as caught up and I don't have to tell you that. Time is called the fourth dimension and as such cannot be relegated to a two-dimensional piece of paper. A things-to-do list isn't a numbered page; it's a continuous scroll with the list of things to be accomplished fluctuating with how we hold the top and bottom of the scroll. Roll down a little bit on the bottom, wind up a little bit on the top.

Of those matters that come to us, let's look at the ones we do (as opposed to delegate or destroy). Note that postponement is not an option. Other elements out of our control may not be ready, and others involved in the same task may not be prepared, but resolution should be attempted. As mentioned, we actually may have more than one scroll working at a time, one with minor chores, another with project accomplishments, another with life-goals. We know it's possible to do more than one thing at a time. It's a common word these days called *multitasking*. The rhythm of accomplishing a project has an ebb and flow, allowing other smaller chores to be handled simultaneously, or permitting the construction of building blocks for larger tasks.

It's important to do tasks rapidly, because the next task may be waiting in line. It's important to do them correctly, because, if we don't, they're likely to come back and bite us where we don't want to be bitten. And it's important not to mess around with them. Too often I've heard, "Well, I couldn't do that because I didn't have. . . ." Get it, whatever it is, and get it right then. If you don't have time to do something *right*, when will you have time to do it *again*?

Business, whether in a small or large company, needs to be conducted in a set, structured, and efficient manner. Employees may be social friends at lunch or after work, but flying in formation while on the job is critical. Occasionally, I'll be called in to work with a radio station deemed by management to be underperforming. One stroll down the hallway on my initial visit tells me a lot. The way some day-to-day radio station business is conducted is the reason for the poor performance, not the format, the music, or the promotions. Someone comes into the office, gets a cup of coffee and chats for a bit about last night's game, goes to the desk and shuffles through some papers, but doesn't really dispose of any tasks. Then there's a long visit to the lobby and various other chats with co-workers there and back. Back at the desk, there may be a few phone calls piling up. After all, it's easier to make a phone call than it is to make a decision or do anything with the pile of tasks in the in-box. Then it's time for the meeting. Let's draw it out. It's easier after all, to discuss things than it is to actually do them. Then it's lunch, and so on through the day. At the end of the day, not much as been accomplished except that the pile in the in-box has grown a few inches taller.

A man is held up at gunpoint and pleads with his attacker, "Please don't kill me, I have things in my IN box."

More personal internal communication in an office should be done face to face. But external business is often done by telephone or by e-mail. It's much better to go to someone's desk, office, or cubicle and communicate personally with that person face to face. A friend of mine worked in a large government building with hundreds of offices. He habitually hiked all over the building to communicate with others face to face rather than by telephone or e-mail. It was amazing how much more he got done than others who were super-glued to their chairs. It's too easy to blow off telephone and e-mail messages, not so easy to ignore someone whose physical body is planted in your face and who won't go away until he/she gets what he/she needs. The farmer's shadow is the best fertilizer.

Do it now. Do it fast. Do it right. Don't mess around with it, and do it face to face. Taking time to prioritize takes time away from doing tasks.

To sum up my angle on business advice, I'd say:

Do it now. Do it fast. Do it right.

Don't mess around with it, and do it face to face.

Taking time to prioritize takes time away from doing tasks.

While we're on interpersonal communication and the in-box mentality, let me add a comment on the usage of e-mail. Sure, it's fast, it's convenient, it's inexpensive, but it is not a replacement for other communication conventions. Matters involving appointment scheduling, cancellation, and commitment of someone's time or resources should be confirmed by means other than e-mail. E-mail requires too much proactivity on behalf of the recipient. I, personally, have to stop what I'm doing to see if you are contacting me. Although some people sit at a computer all day and are alerted to incoming e-mail, there are far more people who do not. I can site two occasions as personal examples:

1. I enjoying preparing dinner parties for guests and friends. If I have a dinner planned, I usually go all out to buy the food, to make sure that my home is presentable, and to dedicate ample time to preparation. On one such evening, there was an 8:00 PM dinner planned for two personal and professional friends. By 7:45, I was home and feverishly getting everything ready. At 8:00, no guests, nor at 8:30 or 9:00. Table set, food fixed and holding, décor arranged, and beverages at the ready. Still no guests, so I called them. The reply, "We're sorry we cannot attend tonight; we sent you an e-mail at 6:00 to cancel." Here's a situation that could have saved a lot of time and wasted resources, in addition to the disappointment, by the courtesy of a personal phone call. Was it my fault that I failed to turn on the computer at home and check e-mails every few minutes to check on possible cancellation? I don't think so.

2. Another more commonplace example that has happened to me hundreds of times (and I am sure you share the experience) is the use of e-mail rather than memory. Have you ever met with someone, personally, and explained your project, answered questions, and interacted with the other party only to have the meeting conclude with the other party saying , "Shoot me an e-mail on all this and I'll get back to you." Wait a minute. That's why I came in here in the first place. Don't fear old-fashioned note taking or paying attention and don't expect a summary e-mail to take its place.

Finally, if anything has grown more rapidly than e-mail, it's cellular or mobile telephones. So we actually have more resources than ever to contact someone in person. Let's consider relegating e-mails to the status of casual note passing, but not as a substitute for interpersonal two-way communication or face-to-face conversation.

THE PHYSICAL PLANT

A radio station can be located anywhere from a house to office suite to an entire building. No two are alike. Because of the technical requirements of constructing a radio station, stations don't relocate too often. Moving to a new facility is always a wonderful experience, not only because the new place is exciting but also because the old place has been completely ignored in anticipation of the move. When the decision is made to move to a new facility, there are a few items that directly affect the programming department and that need stating. In most cases, a radio station is a 24-hour operation. The only department that makes it a 24-hour operation is the programming department. All other departments keep basic office hours and are not present evenings, overnight, and weekends. Therefore, specific needs and accommodations must be provided for the programming personnel, who may be singularly responsible for the operation of the radio station for extended periods of time, day or night, all by themselves.

The first accommodation is the toilet. I cannot imagine designing a new radio station without a toilet facility close to the main studio. If plumbing is not available in the part of the building where the studio is to be located, then redo the design or add additional plumbing to accommodate it. Never design a radio station that takes the primary operator away from the studio for longer than is absolutely necessary. Toilet facilities may have to be accessible in 2 or 3 minutes during a song. Having toilet facilities in close proximity to the studio is imperative. Also, put as few obstacles as possible between the toilet and the studio. Avoid locked doors requiring keys or codes to reenter. Many a dispirited announcer has, with great frustration, heard the final notes of his last song fading away on the monitors while he/she, having forgotten to take the key along, is locked out in the hallway, unable to reenter the studio. While we're addressing the needs of the air studio, announcers and program directors need to have some influence in the selection of the design and function of the announcers' environment. Frequently, studios are designed and built for the convenience of maintenance and repair, not for convenient day-to-day operation.

A kitchen or food preparation area should be required. Whenever possible, a full kitchen can accommodate a range of uses, from client parties to food preparation during inclement weather or other station events requiring a number of staff members for long hours, such as election coverage or bad weather (snow) emergencies. Include a dishwasher and real plates and dinnerware. It's more energy efficient, cleaner, and less likely to pile up. Care and responsibility of the kitchen should be given to an employee as part of his/her job duties. Usually, there actually is someone on staff who would take care of the eating area as a point of personal pride. Include studio access to windows or a view outside. There is something about being able to see the weather as it happens, or experience the seasons, that makes a studio more pleasant and stimulating. The studio may not have its own window, but maybe across the hall or through an open partition or glass door nearby, a peek at what's happening outside can translate into a more effective relationship between the listener and the announcer as they experience the climate and mood together.

Here is a checklist of items to be considered when designing an effective, efficient studio:

1. Location of audio equipment at arm's reach
2. Placement of copybook

3. Space for liner cards, weather, etc.

4. Counter space for writing (filling out logs, etc.)

5. Direct visibility to read CD or music labels when in machine (or computer screen)

6. Phone access, wires out of the way, easy-to-reach handset

7. Large, visible clock (both digital and analog)

8. Nonglare studio lighting, adjustable to each announcer

9. Nonheating studio lighting (spotlights look nice, but can make a studio an oven and really run up electricity usage)

10. Clearly marked control console

11. Comfortable standing surface, if stand-up operation

12. Smooth floor for rolling chair if sit-down operation

13. Individual heat/cool thermostat for studio, independent of the rest of the building

14. Durable, adjustable stool or chair. Regular office equipment, designed for an 8-hour day, 5-day week, will wear out four times faster in a 24-hour, 7-day studio. Prepare to replace it. Budget for several per year.

15. Adequate, convenient storage space for music, CDs, commercials, books, etc.

PROGRAMMING FOR SPECIAL DAYS AND HOLIDAYS

Many of us are accused of doing things in the eleventh hour—that is, waiting until the last minute to get something accomplished. Whether it was our weekend homework waiting for us to attack it late Sunday night or shopping for a birthday gift on the way to the party, we often have to confess that we are a society of people who generally put things off.

As broadcasters, we also fall victim to procrastination, particularly in the arena of preparing for holiday programming. I'm going to breeze over a few holidays worthy of attention, but you have my permission to mark your calendar for early November. Go ahead, do it now. Mark your calendar "Read Chapter 11." Think 11th month, 11th chapter, 11th hour Christmas stuff.

That noted, there are a few other special days worthy of some consideration. None, of course, has the complete set of music to accompany the holiday, but we've picked a few here. A technical note: Many music-scheduling software programs used by radio stations permit coding music with different themes or even song titles or lyrics with specific words. Knowing that, keep watching throughout the year for songs that might fit into a special holiday category.

Groundhog Day: This is one of my favorite holidays. Really. It's a symbol of optimism, the anticipation of spring. Radio stations should employ theater-of-the-ear and set this up a week in advance. Make Groundhog Day a big day. Plan a Groundhog Day party, if not really, at least on the air. Talk about all the Groundhog Day decorations festooning the radio station. Get listeners involved with a Groundhog Day Happy Hour after work at a local restaurant or bar, hosted by station personnel. Have the bartender concoct a special drink like a Groundhog Martini. Rename the bar food Groundhog Burgers, Groundhog Wings, or Groundhog Nuggets. Music for Groundhog Day? Use your imagination, but start with *I Feel the Earth Move*.

On the heels of Groundhog Day comes Valentine's Day. Your sales department may be way ahead of you on this, because it's a strong retail day. It should be attacking flower and candy and gift stores for advertising. Station programming of love songs or heart songs is the easiest to find in the entire music library. Solicit for listener phone calls proclaiming affection for a loved one on the air. Get Valentine's prizes (the same candy and flowers and gifts from the stores buying advertising) and invite listeners to be the tenth caller when they hear the kissing sound effect. Generating a basic Valentine's Day promotion is so natural and automatic that if you cannot come up with something, you should reevaluate your potential effectiveness as a program director.

National holidays (Memorial Day, 4th of July, Veterans Day) all share the same patriotic music. So every station should have a section of such songs. The past few years have generated a plethora of newly composed and performed patriotic music. If you know your community, then you'll know where they are with regard to their feeling about national holidays. A military community will enjoy military-based music like "Green Berets" or "Riding with Private Malone." General feel-good patriotism is expressed by "God Bless the USA" or "America the Beautiful." All communities large and small have celebrations and activities on national holidays. Make sure your radio station is a part of them. It's a feel-good inexpensive way to be with listeners in a positive environment. There's a whole library of patriotic music from the past, and it still plays well today. If listeners haven't heard Kate Smith sing "God Bless America" for a long time (or never), it's time they did. Patriotic holidays come with a built-in license to be sentimental. Local colleges and high schools all have good choirs or bands, and an aggressive station with some remote recording equipment could record their renditions of patriotic songs for playback on the air, adding more local interest and flavor.

Labor Day, also a national holiday, lets us salute working people. Music lyrics can reflect many occupations. Doing some creative brainstorming to connect known songs to the work theme is fun and challenging. Consider: "16 Tons" (miner), "Working My Way Back to You" (anything), "Come Rain or Come Shine" (weatherman), or "From This Moment On" (watchmaker). This can be a really fun and revealing brainstorming session, matching songs with jobs.

Halloween can be much of the same. Brainstorm and draw the connections. Have an on-air contest with creaking doors, howling wolves, hissing cats. I've always enjoyed having a (make-believe) station Halloween party all day long. Each member of the air staff wears a costume of some sort. It's up to them to make the audience *hear* the costume during the shift. By what they say and by comments from other employees stopping by the studio when the microphone is on, you can really make listeners believe in your costume. Think about how you can *hear* these costumes: The Tin Man, a ballerina (guy), or a football player with helmet (girl). My policy has always been to make the newest member of the staff wear the gorilla suit. Ever heard a gorilla suit?

Throughout the year, there are a handful of other regional and local holidays to celebrate or observe. By planning ahead and using some imagination, every day can be a holiday and particular holidays can give your station important listener recognition.

Make up holidays if none exists. A good comprehensive calendar, almanac, or on-this-date books or web site can reveal something happening every day of the year. Every program director should have one of these books. Stay about a month ahead and surprise everyone with how much you know about potential upcoming promotional opportunities. Share this information with your sales team and they have a new reason to contact advertisers about product or subject-specific promotions. Haven't you ever had a Millard E. Fillmore Birthday Celebration?

So, do you get the idea about holidays? Great. I'll see you back here in November to hang some tinsel on Christmas programming.

IN CONCLUSION

Language and learning often come from repetition. You may note that throughout the book, I may have explained a point in a few different ways. Radio commercials work most effectively by their repetition, so I learned long ago to restate my points in slightly different sets of expressions, even when I'm writing. It's not realistic or reasonable to ask you, the reader, to reread everything here, so I've made it convenient for you by restating a few important points.

There you have it! I'd like to say that this book is finished, but a book on radio can never be finished, because our medium is changing daily. As indicated by the fact that this is our fourth edition, there have been significant alterations in radio since our first book was published in 1992. Although radio's technology seems to move with the swiftest current, advances in equipment and facilities still remain only tools in the hands of those given the responsibility and authority to program radio stations. Rarely does technology contribute to radio station success. Creativity, persistence, and direction always do. The basics of programming a radio station haven't really changed very much. Internally, we still deal with personalities, systems, budgets, temperaments, and deadlines. Externally, we still have to sell our act to the audience in measurable numbers by paying attention to their needs and by persuasion or cleverness.

The radio industry is changing very rapidly. Now that deregulation and multiple ownerships are a reality, the old rules of five AM and five FM stations we lived by for decades seem antiquated and unbelievable. The rules are vastly different and the playing fields a bit less even now that a single company can own literally hundreds of radio stations. Throughout the book, I have referred to the changing face of the radio industry, not only in the United States, but worldwide. Commercial radio is becoming commonplace globally, with many countries finding their entrance into commercial broadcasting difficult and risky, while others reap vast success. Regardless of where radio is being broadcast, the undisputable truth remains:

IT'S ALL ABOUT THE LISTENER.

IT'S ALL ABOUT THE LISTENER

Wherever a radio station is on the evolutionary scale, the need to bond with the listeners is an imperative. While the rest of the broadcasting universe swirls around our heads in dizzying proportions, I'll stick by some very basic issues that deal with how and why programming will still be the primary device for the development of successful radio. When I first began to put my programming notes on paper in 1987, I started to see some trends developing as I worked on-site at a series of stations and as I consulted at dozens of others. Many of the same questions were asked as the problems and concerns seemed to repeat themselves from market to market. I never for a moment believed there would be any standard answers for every problem that came up, but I started to get the idea that, by having at hand some thought-provoking ideas, individual creativity would kick in and new solutions could be found.

By turning away momentarily from the problem and reviewing some solution options, whether by reading about them or talking to other programmers, I always felt more confident in developing a solution. My hope is that my work putting together this book will trigger some ideas from readers. Each solution, system, or idea, whether it is yours or mine, will become a new building block for those looking to us as examples. Those building blocks will also strengthen our own individual knowledge of our business and become a permanent part of our mental filing system.

The best application for this book is as a companion. Keep it in your office or close at hand. Don't try to memorize every subject. When a situation comes up, reach for it to see if somewhere within these pages is something that can assist your own creative style and intuition. You have the responsibility for solving the problems at your own radio station. So regardless of where the ideas come from, you'll get the credit for them if you are successful.

Now that you've finished this book, take a break, share it with a friend, let it sit on the desk for a week or so. Then each week, pick it up for a few minutes to see if there are some immediate applications for your current circumstances. Some of the gimmicks I use, like the liner card file box or the *A Christmas Carol* script, I have made available through our company. I'm always eager to hear your ideas, see your systems, and applaud your solutions. Last, and probably the most important thing to me, is to let this book serve as a way for me to meet you vicariously through these pages and perhaps in person some day. Now you know a lot more about me than I do about you, so make some waves, let me know you're out there. Make some great, new programming ideas breathe life. Resurrect some old ones with your own unique touch.

Welcome into my ever-growing circle of friends who share our exciting experiences in this business called:

CHRISTMAS PROGRAMMING 11

Welcome back! Thanks for marking your calendar and remembering to re-open the book and dive into our Chapter 11 on Christmas programming. This chapter was not written in the eleventh hour but is, in fact, the eleventh chapter because it deals with special holiday programming. I had earlier thought that a chapter on, say, Christmas programming should go with the other programming materials. Upon review, that would have been a virtual exit sign to put the book down and stop reading midway through. To think about or consider Christmas programming really requires being in the mood and up against a deadline. Therefore, Christmas programming has its very own chapter—Chapter 11 (as in 11th hour). So put on your Santa hat, draw up an egg nog, and read on.

One of the great mysteries of radio happens every holiday season. After spending thousands of dollars on music, advertising, talent, etc., most stations throw everything out the window at Christmas as they begin to infuse Christmas programming into their formats. Since it is virtually mandatory that every station participate in the holiday festivities (or risk being considered a Scrooge), we may as well make the best of it. There are only a limited number of Christmas song titles, but there are usually hundreds of versions of each title. Everybody in the record industry has a Christmas collection. Let's assume that the station will follow a typical pattern of gradually playing more Christmas selections during December, leading up to some sort of all-day Christmas Eve and Christmas Day extravaganza.

Here is a list of Christmas ideas and tactics that work:

CHRISTMAS MUSIC

1. Packet Christmas songs by title.
2. Select the artists that belong in the station music format or can be compatible with the music format.
3. Subdivide selections into religious and nonreligious titles. Save religious songs for later.
4. Classify songs by tempo, just like other music.
5. Play some Christmas songs the Friday, Saturday, and Sunday after Thanksgiving when the holiday mood really hits everyone.
6. Go with the spirit, announce the arrivals of Santa, kick off the mall promotions. Act as though the station is really ready to go for the holidays, then drop it Monday morning (for a few weeks).
7. The audience will survive on the inertia of the post-Thanksgiving thrust and be under Christmas siege from every store, mall, or restaurant it patronizes. The audience also will be exposed to promotional overkill by some competitors who will be trying to be the Christmas Station.
8. Let competitors burn their Christmas songs too soon, while you stay true to your established format. Hold off on Christmas music play until about December 15, ten days away from the holiday or two weekends' worth of shopping away from Christmas, depending upon what day of the week Christmas occurs. Since most

shopping is done on the last two weekends prior to the holiday, it makes sense to be in the swing of things on those days.

9. Probably more than half the commercial announcements will contain Christmas music or holiday messages, giving a de facto Christmas sound to programming anyway.

10. Create demand by holding off. It's like seeing lines in front of the theater. A short wait heightens the anticipation.

11. Play nonreligious songs, mostly up-tempo selections. Save Christmas ballads for nights. Suggested music programming schedules are on the following pages.

CHRISTMAS MUSIC PROGRAMMING CALENDAR

a.	December 15-18	One song every other hour
b.	December 18-19	One song every hour
c.	December 20	Two songs per hour (add ballads, down-tempo)
d.	December 21	Three songs per hour
e.	December 22	Four songs per hour (add religious)
f.	December 23	Six songs per hour to Dec. 24, 12 noon (add nonformat artists)
g.	December 24	12 Noon to 6 PM: All Christmas music
h.	December 24	6 PM to Christmas Day: Special programming
i.	December 25	Midnight, return to format, completely!

SPECIAL PROGRAMMING AND PROMOTIONS

1. Starting on December 15, call the station the "Official Christmas Station for (city)." If anyone asks who made the station the "Official Christmas Station," tell them the elves did it. That should be good enough or get a chuckle. Any Christmas sales packages or promotions should use the phrase "Official Christmas Station."

2. It's to be hoped that you have been propositioned by syndicated program suppliers to carry Christmas specials. You may even get a holiday version of a weekly special you already run. In any case, line up what Christmas programming you have to run from 6 PM Christmas Eve to midnight Christmas Day.

3. Open a Christmas store on the air an hour a day at noon. Listeners call for hard-to-find items and let other listeners or businesses reply with where to find them. This has proved to be a very fun and compelling program for my stations over the years. It is almost like a treasure hunt, unearthing really hard-to-find gifts and especially collectibles and provides a very sponsor-friendly holiday daily feature. You can usually run this from the Monday after Thanksgiving right up to Christmas Eve. Open the store every day with the sound effect from an old-fashioned bell that rings when a door opens, like the one in the movie *It's a Wonderful Life*.

4. Need Christmas jingles? Don't buy them. Use an existing jingle package by getting some sleigh bells (real or sound-effect record) and playing them over some slow cuts from your existing package. Since most jingle packages now come with multitrack editing or mixing, this is not as hard to do as it once was with a single-track mix. Let a few trail out with the jingle-bell sound effect (great for going into a Christmas song).

5. With so many events around the holiday, it's a good time to make the station very visible. Look for opportunities to participate in public gatherings. Seek the unusual. Christmas is a time of sensory overload for most people, so you need to do something very special to get noticed.

6. If you have a station vehicle, go caroling with the air staff at several locations. Use a public address system for singing from inside the vehicle to outdoors. Supermarket

parking lots are good locations in conjunction with food drives. If you don't have a vehicle, trade for usage of a motor home for a week and decorate it inside and out.

PROMO: "The KTUR Carolers will be out again tonight at the LOTTAFOOD Market. So look and listen for the Mel's Motor Homes-KTUR Christmas Cruiser in front of the store from 7 to 9 PM. While shopping, pick up a food item for our KTUR Salvation Army food barrel."

LOCALLY PRODUCED CHRISTMAS SPECIALS

Home-grown specials are a saleable and clever way to program for the holidays. So, assign each air talent the task of doing his or her own 1-hour special with guests and music.

Include other key station employees in the special lineup. I have heard some wonderful hour-long specials assembled by everyone from the morning DJ to the news director to the all-night DJ. Christmas is a special holiday and excellent opportunity for listeners to learn more about the air staff. Specials should be personal and include family, friends, written material, personal recollections, etc. Use regular formatics of 50 minutes of content, leaving time for news, weather, or commercials or go commercial-free or even sold to advertisers as full sponsorships.

PROMO: "The Steve Warren Christmas Special is being brought to you by the 8th National Bank, wishing you the happiest of holiday greetings."

PROMO: "Listen for the Steve Warren Christmas Special presented by the 8th National Bank Christmas Eve at 6 PM, and repeated Christmas Day at 7 AM and 4 PM."

A good first place to look for potential sponsors is at clients already identified with the air talent.

PROMO: "You've heard me talking every morning about how good the food is at the Rocket Cat Restaurant, so join me for my very own Christmas special Christmas Eve and again Christmas Day presented by our friends at the Rocket Cat, where you can put your head in your bowl if you want to."

Sell the sponsors and open/close and three 60-second positions within the program along with a promo schedule 5 to 7 days before Christmas. Really get them involved with the excitement of participating in Christmas programming. Put some signs in their stores advertising listening to the station and its sponsored special. Try to locally produce a minimum of six specials, mostly music, each of which can be repeated for maximum exposure from evening to daytime to overnight and scheduled around other syndicated specials. Schedule specials in the same chronology as the regular air staff lineup.

Invest in a one-time newspaper lineup of scheduled Christmas programming. Then call attention to it on the air. Invite listeners to clip it out and use it as their guide for holiday listening. Use every opportunity to talk about, promote, cross-plug, or tease the Christmas specials. Additionally, if you have received one 4-hour syndicated special and another 3-hour syndicated special from outside sources and six homegrown specials of 1 hour each, then here's a sample schedule:

Christmas Eve

6 PM	Morning Man Christmas Special
7 PM	Mid-day Lady Christmas Special
8 PM	Afternoon Team Christmas Special
9 PM	Evening Guy Christmas Special
10 PM	Overnight Person Christmas Special
11 PM	News Department Christmas Special

Christmas Day Morning

Midnight-4 AM	Syndicated Special #1
4 AM-7 AM	Syndicated Special #2
7 AM	Morning Man (corresponds with regular wake-up AM drive hour)
8 AM	Mid-day Lady
9 AM	Afternoon Team
10 AM	Evening Guy
11 AM	Overnight Person

Christmas Day Afternoon/Night

Noon-4 PM	Syndicated Special #1
4 PM	Morning
5 PM	Mid-day
6 PM	Afternoon (corresponds with regular PM drive-time shift)
7 PM	Evening (corresponds with regular evening shift)
8 PM	Overnight
9 PM-Midnight	Syndicated Special #2

Following the holiday, get back to business as usual as soon as possible. During Christmas specials, solicit for written comments about the holiday programming. Don't be surprised at the number of listeners who'll respond with their appreciation for the personal programming. Make a scrapbook of holiday activities to help plan next year. Put away the tinsel and lights until next year. Put all basic Christmas music on some form of permanent retrieval system. If you use a hard-disk system and don't want to take up storage space, consider making your own set of CDs or mini-disks just for your Christmas music, so you always have it ready from year to year. Programming this music should/can become almost automatic rather than the typical last-minute hassle. Determine which activities were the most popular and did the most for the station. Then develop an annual approach to the station's Christmas events. Nothing enhances a station's image more than having its name associated with a positive, visible, and effective annual charity event. Not only is it genuinely good for the community and the station from a public relations point of view, it also gives an exclusive event. Competing stations will most likely underperform at Christmas. They have to play defense by being compared to your event.

Be mindful that there are other seasonal holidays including Kwaanza, which sprang up relatively recently but is observed and, of course, Hanukkah. The dates for these holidays vary and may or may not coincide with Christmas. Although these holidays are celebrated primarily by specific segments of your audience, they should not be forgotten and overshadowed by Christmas. Allow some attention to them, in proportion.

Fa la-la, la-la. . . . . No other annual holiday is so captivating as Christmas, so make it work for the station with promotions, sales packages, appearances, and music that make sense to the listeners and are, compatible with the overall station position.

APPENDIX: FORMS

LIST OF FORMS

FOR THE WEEK OF: _____

TIME	MONDAY	TUESDAY	WEDNESDAY	THURSDAY	FRIDAY	SATURDAY	SUNDAY
12A-6A							
6A-10A							
10A-3P							
3P-7P							
7P-12A							

SPECIAL PROGRAMS

SPORTS _____
_____

REMOTES _____
_____

FEATURES _____
_____

AIR SHIFT SCHEDULE EXAMPLE

FOR THE WEEK OF: January 4, 1

TIME 8	MONDAY	TUESDAY	WEDNESDAY	THURSDAY	FRIDAY	SATURDAY	SUNDAY
12A–1 6A	BOB	BOB	BOB	BOB	BOB	SAM	GERT
6A–1 10A	STEVE	STEVE	STEVE	STEVE	STEVE	JEFF	SAM
10A–1 3A	CAROL	CAROL	CAROL	CAROL	CAROL	CAROL	JEFF
3P–1 1P	MARK	MARK	MARK	MARK	MARK	MARK	PETE
7P–1 12P	ROB	ROB	SAM**	SAM**	SAM**	PETE	BIFF

SPECIAL PROGRAMS

SPORTS Fleas vs. Bugs Sat 7:30pm

REMOTES Carol "House of Roofing" Sat 10-3

FEATURES New Years Resolution promotion all week

** ROB Vacation

LENGTH :60 _____ :30 _____ :10 _____

DATE: _____/_____ START **DATE:** _____/_____/_____ NEED **BY:** _____/_____/_____

ACCOUNT: _____ WRITER: _____

PRODUCTION	COPY
1.	
2.	
3.	
4.	
5.	
6.	
7.	
8.	
9.	
10.	
11.	
12.	
13.	
14.	
15.	
16.	
17.	
18.	
19.	
20.	

DATE: _7/22/92_   START **DATE:** _7/27/92_   NEED **BY:** _7/25/92_

ACCOUNT: _Tower of London_   WRITER: _5W_

PRODUCTION		COPY
SFX Pouring	1.	Ever wanted a great cup of tea in the middle of the afternoon, then you should go to the TOWER OF LONDON tea shop next time that tea thirst strikes.
Music "God save the Queen"	2.	
	3.	
SFX:Big Ben strikes three	4.	
	5.	So when it's tea time at your place, come on over to our place for a touch of Merry Old England at the TOWER OF LONDON Tea Shop.
	6.	
	7.	
	8.	Located in the Baker Street Mall in the food court.
	9.	
SFX: Plop plop	10.	One lump or two?
	11.	
	12.	
	13.	
	14.	
	15.	
	16.	
	17.	
	18.	
	19.	
	20.	

MUST BE COMPLETED: DAY _____ DATE _____ TIME _____

START DATE: , DAY _____ DATE _____ TIME _____

END **DATE**: DAY _____ DATE _____ TIME _____

NEW **SPOTS (S)** RE-DO AUTHORIZED BY _____

CLIENT/LABEL TITLE: _____

NUMBER OF SPOTS & LENGTH: _____ @ :60 _____ @ :30 _____ @ :10

NUMBER _____ NUMBERS _____

CUT/COPY INSTRUCTIONS

OTHER INFORMATION

MASTER NEEDED?

--YES-- **--NO--**

CO : NEEDED?

--YES-- **--NO--**

BOX LABEL INFORMATION

DUBS NEEDED FOR

_____

_____

_____

_____

_____

_____

VOICED BY _____ DATE _____

DATE COMPLETED _____ BY _____

MUSIC USED _____

COMMENTS _____

MUST BE COMPLETED: DAY ___Wed___ DATE ___7-22-04___ TIME ___9 AM___

START DATE: , DAY ___Fri___ DATE ___7-24-04___ TIME ___9 AM___

END DATE: DAY ___Fri___ DATE ___7-31-04___ TIME ___9 AM___

NEW SPORTS (S) (RE-DO) AUTHORIZED BY ___3W___

CLIENT/LABEL TITLE: ___Bob's Bait___

NUMBER OF SPOTS & LENGTH: ___20___ @ :60 _____ @ :30 _____ @ :10

NUMBER ___#526___ NUMBERS ___1, 7, 8___

CUT/COPY INSTRUCTIONS

412	Worms
413	Cheese
414	Hooks

OTHER INFORMATION

MASTER NEEDED?

--YES-- <-NO->

CO : NEEDED?

--YES-- <-NO->

BOX LABEL INFORMATION

DUBS NEEDED FOR

___KRM-FM___

___WTL-AM___

VOICED BY ___Steve___ DATE _____

DATE COMPLETED ___7-23-04___ BY ___Rob___

MUSIC USED ___La Mer___

COMMENTS ___Mid-Season Sale___

CONTEST DESCRIPTION:

GIVEAWAY DATE/TIME:

INSTRUCTIONS:

HOUR	NAME	ADDRESS CITY-STATE-ZIP	HOME & WORK NUMBERS	SS NUMBER	BIRTH DATE & AGE
			(H) (W)		
			(H) (W)		
			(H) (W)		
			(H) (W)		
			(H) (W)		
			(H) (W)		
			(H) (W)		
			(H) (W)		
			(H) (W)		
			(H) (W)		
			(H) (W)		
			(H) (W)		

VALUE OF PRELIMINARY PRIZE: $ _____   VALUE OF GRAND PRIZE: $ _____

CONTEST DESCRIPTION:	GIVEAWAY DATE/TIME:
Ring around the Hole **Donut** Shop 2 Dozen **Donuts** Giveaway	7-27-8/28

INSTRUCTIONS:

Listen for the sound of the dunking donut and be the 10th caller.

HOUR	NAME	ADDRESS CITY-STATE-ZIP	HOME & WORK NUMBERS	SS NUMBER	BIRTH DATE & AGE
6 am	Steve Warren	MOR Media	(H) 555-5111(W)	xxx-xxxx	98
			(H) (W)		
			(H) (W)		
			(H) (W)		
			(H) (W)		
			(H) (W)		
			(H) (W)		
			(H) (W)		
			(H) (W)		
			(H) (W)		
			(H) (W)		
			(H) (W)		

VALUE OF PRELIMINARY PRIZE: $ __5.00__   VALUE OF GRAND PRIZE: $ _____

DAY: _____   **DATE:** _____

TIME	ITEM	CLIENT/PROGRAM NAME	PROBLEM	ACTION	INITIAL

EMERGENCY PHONE NUMBERS

_____	Traffic Manager	_____ - _____
_____	Program Director	_____ - _____
_____	Production Director	_____ - _____
_____	General Manager	_____ - _____
_____	Sales Manager	_____ - _____
_____	Engineer	_____ - _____

DISCREPANCY REPORT EXAMPLE

DAY: _Tuesday_ DATE: _5 - 19 - 04_

TIME	ITEM	CLIENT/PROGRAM NAME	PROBLEM	ACTION	INITIAL
4 AM	"A"	May Memo	Missing	–	
6:26 AM	426	Big Al's	Outdated	Ran #427	
10:15 AM	512	Jeff's Jeeps	Not Received	Play of at 10:45	
10:55 A	"A"	May Powers	Still Missing	–	
2:32 AM	NET	News feed	Poor Quality	Told News	
415p	124	Pete's Eats Cafe	Machine ate cart	Re-dubbed Played 5:35	
7:40p	512	Jeffs Jeeps	Still Not cued Cart Bad	Re-dubbed after 12mi	
9 55pm	SONG-D-417	Big Samis Boogie	Runs slow Distortion	Gave to P.D	

EMERGENCY PHONE NUMBERS

_____	Traffic Manager	_____ - _____
_____	Program Director	_____ - _____
_____	Production Director	_____ - _____
_____	General Manager	_____ - _____
_____	Sales Manager	_____ - _____
_____	Engineer	_____ - _____

Name _____ Department _____ Year _____

Full Time Employment Date _____ Accumulated Vacation _____ Weeks

Used Absences:

Vacation Time Taken:

	1st week					
2nd week						
3rd week						
4th week						
5th week						

Date Of Absence	Half Day	Whole Day	Reason For Absence

From Date	To Date	Number Of Days

Tardy Date	Time Of Arrival	Reason Given

* Projected location dates for approval in advance then mark when taken in upper right hand Boxes

Name   Jim   **Shoe**   Department   **Programming**   Year 92

Full Time Employment Date   **2/14/87**   Accumulated Vacation & Weeks

Used Absences:

6/19	7/22				

Vacation Time Taken:

1st week	8/3	8/4	8/5	8/6	8/7	8/8
2nd week	11/4	11/5	11/6	11/7	11/8	11/9
3rd week	12/25	12/26	12/27	12/28	12/29	12/30
4th week						
5th week						

Date Of Absence	Half Day	Whole Day	Reason For Absence
6/19		X	Doctor
7/22		X	Wamgover

From Date	To Date	Number Of Days	
8/3	8/8	6	*
"A	11/9	6	
12/25	12/30	6	

None Left

Tardy Date	Time Of Arrival	Reason Given
4/13	9 AM	Overslept

* Projected vacation dates for approval in advance
  then mark when taken in upper right hand Boxes.

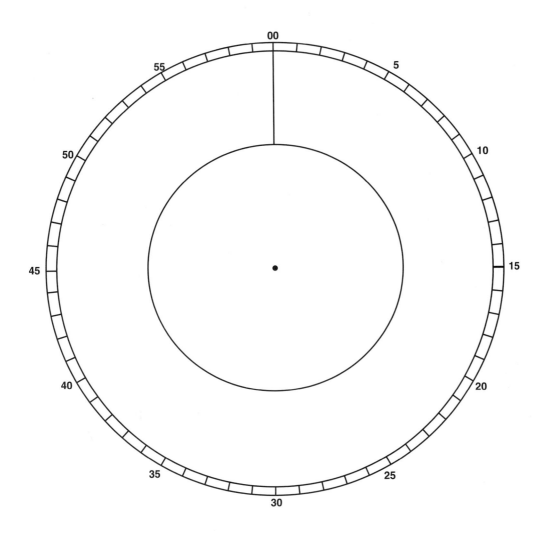

Even Days 10AM – 3PM M-F

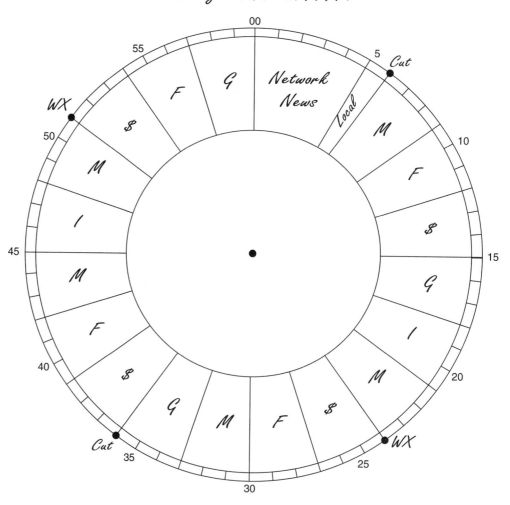

M = male, F = female, G = group,
$ = commercial break, I = instrumental.

Circle One: Men - Women - Total Persons

Fill In Stations Who Own The Demo	DEMOGRAPHIC						
	12-17	18-24	25-34	35-44	45-54	55-64	65+

Circle One: Men - Women - Total Persons

Fill In Stations Who Own The Demo	DEMOGRAPHIC						
	12–17	18–24	25–34	35–44	45–54	55–64	65+
WAAA			////	////	////		
WBBB	////	////					
WCCC							
KAAA				////	////		
KBBB			////	////			
KCCC						////	////
CFFF					////	////	

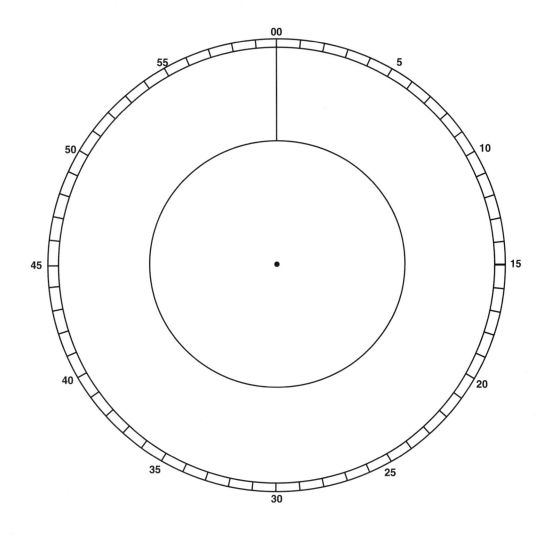

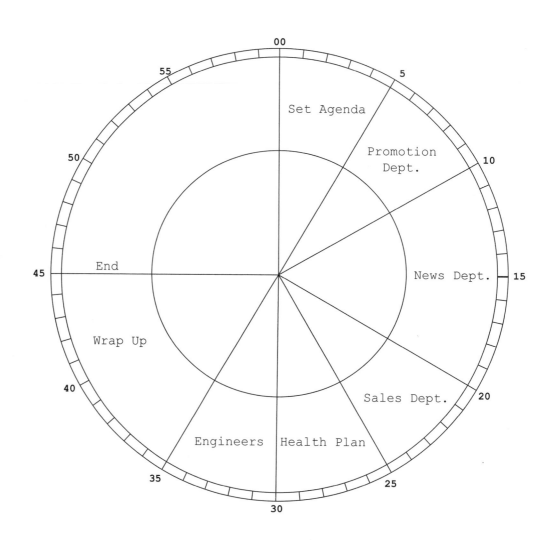

\# _____   Title: _____

Artist: _____

Intro: _____   Time: _____   End: _____   Tempo: _____

\# 342 Title: **I'm Fast, Really Fast**

Artist: **The Rocket**

Intro: ; 14 Time: 3: 14 End: Cold Tempo: 4

7/29 3pm	8/4 9am	10/11 4am	10/19 3am	11/0412N	11/23 6pm	12/9 5pm
12/27 3A	1/4 6A					

Sample music scheduling card. Duplicate the blank form provided (you can get 2 per page) and have printed on various colors of card stock (5X8).

Write-in times song is played (Date and/or Hour) either horizontally or vertically. Avoid playing song in same hour and allow # of days separation.

FOR THE WEEK OF: _____

TIME	MON	TUE	WED	THU	FRI	SAT	SUN
12:00 AM							
1:00 AM							
2:00 AM							
3:00 AM							
4:00 AM							
5:00 AM							
6:00 AM							
7:00 AM							
8:00 AM							
9:00 AM							
10:00 AM							
11:00 AM							
12:00 PM							
1:00 PM							
2:00 PM							
3:00 PM							
4:00 PM							
5:00 PM							
6:00 PM							
7:00 PM							
8:00 PM							
9:00 PM							
10:00 PM							
11:00 PM							

FOR THE WEEK OF: 7-20-92

TIME	MON	TUE	WED	THU	FRI	SAT	SUN
12:00 AM	AL	AL	AL	AL	AL		
1:00 AM							
2:00 AM							
3:00 AM						Sports	Eng. maint.
4:00 AM							
5:00 AM	Steve	Steve	Steve	Steve	Steve		
6:00 AM							
7:00 AM	Tom	Tom	Tom	Tom	Tom		
8:00 AM							Church
9:00 AM	BILL					Jim	Tapes
10:00 AM							
11:00 AM							
12:00 PM							
1:00 PM	News				Cooking		
2:00 PM	Watch				with		
3:00 PM					Sherry		
4:00 PM							
5:00 PM							
6:00 PM	Traffic					Request	Show
7:00 PM	News	News	News	News	News		
8:00 PM							
9:00 PM							
10:00 PM							
11:00 PM							

Initials or name of persons assigned

Long show tape

Department use

Blank spaces indicate open studio. Post this schedule several weeks in advance on Production Room Door. Fill-in in Pencil so changes or swaps can be noted

Use this form to document any/all activities, appearances, remotes, guest appearances, or contests conducted with the purpose of promoting the cause of a worthy public service organization. Fill in all applicable information completely and accurately, as this form will be submitted to our station's Public File with the FCC Thanks!

Submitted By: _____ Date(s)/Time(s) of event:_____

Sponsoring Organization:_____ Contact name/number:_____

Name of Event: _____

Check all that apply:

    [ ] I attended the event
        [ ] (So did other staff members:_____ **X** _____)

    [ ] We did a live broadcast. Date/Times:_____ _____

    [ ]   WBTR   promoted this event _____ times:
        [ ] Live reads (white card)
        [ ] Recorded promo

    [ ]   WBTR was a co-sponsor of the event
        [ ] Other media sponsors involved were _____

    [ ]   logo appeared on promotional material used by the sponsoring organization. Please attach.

    [ ] _____ from the sponsoring organization was invited to come on the

air on _____ (date/time) to talk about the event.

    [ ] The station received publicity or acknowledgement for the event. (Please attach copies.)

Please include any additional notes pertinent to the event here:

Signed: _____ Date: _____

Use this form to document any/all activities, appearances, remotes, guest appearances, or contests conducted with the purpose of promoting the cause of a worthy public service organization. Fill in all applicable information completely and accurately, as this form will be submitted to our station's Public File with the FCC Thanks!

Submitted By: _____Steve Warren_____   Date(s)/Time(s) of event: _2/12/24_

Sponsoring Organization: __HMCA__   Contact name/number: _____

Name of Event: _____Walk for Health_____

Check all that apply:

    [ ] I attended the event

        [ ] (So did other staff members: _____Bob X_____)

    [ ] We did a live broadcast. Date/Times: ____No_____

    [ ]   *WBTR* promoted this event _____ times: _____

        [ ] Live reads (white card)

        [ ] Recorded promo

    [ ]   *WBTR* was a co-sponsor of the event

        [ ] Other media sponsors involved were ____WDTR-TV____

    [ ]   logo appeared on promotional material used by the sponsoring organization. Please attach.

    [ ] ____Jertry Fleur____ from the sponsoring organization was invited to come on the

air on ____2-9-04____ (date/time) to talk about the event.

    [ ] The station received publicity or acknowledgement for the event. (Please attach copies.)

Please include any additional notes pertinent to the event here: *Newsletter attached*

Signed: _____   Date: ____2-14-04____

RADIO STATION (logo)

Date _____

During the time period from _____ to _____

Radio Station (call) _____ broadcast (number) _____

of Public Service Announcements for the benefit of:

(Agency Name and Address)

The total value of these announcements (had they been paid for at our present advertising rates) would be (Amount) _____ dollars.

DO NOT PAY! These announcements were donated in the Public Interest by (call)

Very sincerely,

Public Service Director

RADIO STATION (logo)

Date _March 4 2004_

During the time period from _Feb. 1_ to _Feb. 28_

Radio Station (call) CO _BTR_ broadcast (number) _20_

of Public Service Announcements for the benefit of:

(Agency Name and Address)

Firemans
P. P. Box 2718
Smithdale NT

The total value of these announcements (had they been paid for at our present advertising rates) would be (Amount) _400_ dollars.

DO NOT PAY! These announcements were donated in the Public Interest by (call)

Very sincerely,

Public Service Director

Account Executive: _____ Todays Date: ___/___/___

( ) Tape Provided   ( ) Tape Provided   ( ) Need____Spot(s)written

( ) Spec Copy Needed For Client Approval By: _____ ___/___/___

Copy Start Date: ___/___/___ Copy End Date: ___/___/___ Cart #: _____

client: _____

Location: _____

Contact: _____ Phone Number: _____

Spot Length: ( ):30%   ( ):60%   Needed By: AM PM   ___/___/___

Rotation Information: ( )100%   ( )**Even**   ( ) **Other** _____

Spot Tone: ( ) **Serious**   ( ) **Light**   ( ) **Hard**

Spot Tempo: ( ) **Fast**   ( ) **Medium**   ( ) **Slow**

Announcer: ( ) **Male**   ( ) **Female**   ( ) **Either**   (x) **Multi-voice**

===
                    COPY INFORMATION
===

Slogan/Catch Phrase: _____

Central Theme: _____

_____

_____

_____

Objective: _____

_____

_____

_____

_____

===
            ATTACH ANY ADDITIONAL COPY **FACTS**!
===
            BELOW IS FOR PRODUCTION USE ONLY!
===

Copy Received: _____ AM PM   ___/___/___

Copy Finished: _____ AM PM   ___/___/___

Comments: _____

_____

Account Executive: _____ Bill Meelater _____ Todays Date: _7_/_22_/_92_

(X) Tape Provided   ( ) Copy Provided   ( ) Need____Spot(s) written

( ) Spec Copy Needed For Client Approval By: _____ 8.00 X AM PM _____ _7_/_23_/_92_

Copy Start Date: _7_/_24_/_92_   Copy End Date: _7_/_31_/_92_   Cart #: _127_

client: _____ Al's House of Birthday Cakes

Location: _____ 411 Pigwallow Road

Contact: _____ Al _____ Phone Number: 555-2468

Spot Length: ( ):30   (X):60   Needed By: AM PM   ___/___/___

Rotation Information: ( )100%   ( )Even   ( ) Other   _6am-6pm_

Spot Tone: ( ) **Serious**   ( ) **Light**   ( ) **Hard**

Spot Tempo: ( ) **Fast**   (X) **Medium**   ( ) **Slow**

Announcer: ( ) **Male**   ( ) **Female**   ( ) **Either**   (x) **Multi voice**

COPY INFORMATION

Slogan/Catch Phrase: _____ Get lit for YOUR birthday

central Theme: _____ Bargain birth day cakes

Objective: _____ Product/service awareness

ATTACH ANY ADDITIONAL COPY FACTS!

BELOW IS FOR PRODUCTION USE ONLY!

Copy Received: _____ AM PM   ___/___/___

Copy Finished: _____ AM PM   ___/___/___

Comments: _____

NOTES: Important for all commercials to have some back-up paperwork
to track their airplay and description. Items like spot tone, tempo,
and general theme can be used by traffic systems in scheduling next
to other commercials for good sounding, non-compteing commercial
stopsets.

NAME: _____ DATE: _____

STATION: _____ DEPARTMENT: _____

REQUESTED **DAYS**: _____

_____

CHARGE TO: VACATION   PERSONAL   UNPAID LEAVE

VACATION DAYS ACCRUED: _____ VACATION **DAYS USED** TO DATE: _____

PERSONAL DAYS ALLOWED: _____ PERSONAL DAYS USED: _____

VACATION DAYS REQUESTED **IN ADVANCE**: _____

I AUTHORIZE THE COMPANY TO WITHHOLD COMPENSATION FOR ALL VACATION
DAYS USED IN ADVANCE AND NOT ACCRUED PRIOR TO MY LEAVING THE COMPANY
MY FINAL PAYCHECK.

EMPLOYEE SIGNATURE: _____ DATE: _____

MANAGER APPROVAL: _____ DATE: _____

TIME OFF REQUEST EXAMPLE

NAME: _Steve Warren_ DATE: _2 - 21 - 97_

STATION: _W p TR - FM_ DEPARTMENT: _Program_

REQUESTED DAYS: _May 1 - 7_

_____

CHARGE TO: ⟨ VACATION ⟩ PERSONAL UNPAID LEAVE

VACATION DAYS ACCRUED: _4_ VACATION DAYS USED TO DATE: _8_

PERSONAL DAYS ALLOWED: _3_ PERSONAL DAYS USED: _0_

VACATION DAYS REQUESTED IN ADVANCE: _6_

I AUTHORIZE THE COMPANY TO WITHHOLD COMPENSATION FOR ALL VACATION
DAYS USED IN ADVANCE AND NOT ACCRUED PRIOR TO MY LEAVING THE COMPANY
MY FINAL PAYCHECK.

EMPLOYEE SIGNATURE: _____ DATE: _2 - 21 - 97_

MANAGER APPROVAL: _____ DATE: _____

The author, Steve Warren, is available for programming seminars, lectures, speaking engagements, radio, press, and TV interviews, radio station consulting, announcer talent training, or corporate media planning through:

MOR Media International, Inc.
P.O. Box 683
New York, NY 10108
Phone 800-827-1722
Fax 212-868-5663

For additional information visit *www.radiothebook.com.*

INDEX

Index